MORAL REALITY

Moral Reality

PAUL BLOOMFIELD

UNIVERSITY PRESS

2001

OXFORD
UNIVERSITY PRESS

Oxford   New York
Athens   Auckland   Bangkok   Bogotá   Buenos Aires   Cape Town
Chennai   Dar es Salaam   Delhi   Florence   Hong Kong   Istanbul   Karachi
Kolkata   Kuala Lumpur   Madrid   Melbourne   Mexico City   Mumbai   Nairobi
Paris   São Paulo   Shanghai   Singapore   Taipei   Tokyo   Toronto   Warsaw

and associated companies in
Berlin   Ibadan

Published by Oxford University Press, Inc.
198 Madison Avenue, New York, New York 10016

Oxford is a registered trademark of Oxford University Press, Inc.

Library of Congress Cataloging-in-Publication Data
Bloomfield, Paul, 1962–
Moral reality / Paul Bloomfield.
p.   cm.
Includes bibliographical references and index.
ISBN 0-19-513713-2
1. Ethics.   2. Realism.   3. Health—Philosophy.   I. Title.
BJ1012 .B545   2001
171'.3—dc21   2001021916

1 3 5 7 9 8 6 4 2

Printed in the United States of America
on acid-free paper

For my father, Donald,
and my sister, Maryanne.

In memory of my mother,
Nerice Siegel Bloomfield.

Preface

He that can compose himself, is wiser than he that composes books.
Poor Richard's Almanack

This preface is not so much for the benefit of the few who might be interested in how or why I wrote this book, as much as it is for the sake of the many who are starting off at ground zero, with only passing or no familiarity with the subject and unsure of what someone might mean by the term "moral realism." Before setting out, it is always a good idea to get one's bearings straight and to make sure that everyone is facing in the right direction. With this in mind, my (straight-faced) cocktail party response to the question "What sort of thing do you do philosophically?" goes something like this: you've heard the expression "Beauty is in the eye of the beholder," right? Well, as an account of what it takes to be beautiful, most people seem to think that this is just fine; but consider the same sort of account of what it takes to be morally good. Hardly anyone will be happy with the idea that moral goodness is in the "eye of the beholder." Noting this difference between beauty and goodness pushes one in the general direction of moral reality, though our destination is still below the horizon. Being forthrightly clear about some assumptions concerning moral philosophy and metaphysical realism ought to bring us right into the proper neighborhood.

I see the domain of moral philosophy as ranging over certain relations. In particular, there are first-person, intrapersonal, or logically reflexive relations at stake, such as integrity and self-respect, as well as third-person or interpersonal relations, where the concern is how well one succeeds in interacting and getting along with others. Furthermore, there are relations that obtain between these relations: the intrapersonal affects the interpersonal and vice versa. If required to distinguish between morality and ethics, I would say that ethics concerns the subset of interpersonal moral relations, but I would hasten to add that one cannot study ethics properly without engaging questions of morality as a whole: how we view and treat others is directly informed by how we view and treat ourselves. I am second only to Mill in being the "last person to undervalue the self-regarding virtues; they are only second in importance, if even second, to the social." I *am* the last person to think the vaguely Hobbesian thought that morality is a necessary evil that arises solely for the purpose of providing a check on our "true nature." On the contrary, and perhaps most important, I take morality or moral philosophy as a whole to be a practical endeavor tautologically aimed at the fullest possible flourishing of the highest and best aspects of ourselves or our natures. Whereas I argue against Plato's thought that we necessarily pursue the good, I most wholeheartedly concur that we ought to pursue it. Being the best we can be morally is being the best we can be. Appearances notwithstanding, morality cannot lead us astray (assuming we are succeeding in following it). It is rarely easy and hardly ever fun to be good, though it is, of course, good to be good and better than fun.

Metaphysical realism is a bit harder to encapsulate. What I refer to by "realism" in these post-Dummettian days is a certain set of philosophical beliefs that one may have about the content of a particular subject or discourse, in this case, moral discourse. The focus on discourse is to forestall thinking in "global" terms and should not lead one to think that the issues are linguistic or even metalinguistic. Realists want to talk about the world, not words. Thus, one may be a realist about scientific or moral discourse and yet a nonrealist about aesthetic discourse or discourse about fictional characters. A realist's position regarding a particular discourse is to stake out the claim that the items that are the subject of the discourse are real (using the vernacular); that is, they exist "out there" (with a pointed finger), externally in the world. Realists about things that are x say that were we to make a list of the contents of reality or the world (an ontology), the things we call "X"s would have to be included, in the same way that sealing wax, sunshine, and succotash have to be included. These "real" items also have to exist in a fashion independent from our thinking and talking about them; for example, they cannot be "in the eye of the beholder." So, being a realist opens up the possibility that our judgments about which items exist and which do not may be mistaken, for what "really" does exist does not depend on us (our judgments) for existence. Realists will (most likely) want to acknowledge the things we call "the dreams of sleeping creatures" but will (most likely) want to deny thinking that the contents of those dreams, or other mirages or figments of the imagination, are real regardless of how real they may seem. Realists will be critical of what we ordinarily take to exist in our workaday thinking, for they recognize an appearance-reality distinction that is often blurred in workaday thought. Typically, what we take ourselves to experience, we thereby take as real, though on reflection we know that we cannot always infer from what we experience to the contents of reality. Still, despite this critical stance, realists think primarily that our experiences are as they are because they are the product of the world. (Assuming for the moment that we are animals and are realists about biological discourse, the preceding sentence is true, if only for evolutionary reasons: if our experiences were not primarily hooked up in a veridical manner to a preexisting reality, we would already be extinct.) We want to know which discourses are those in which the contents of our experiences are determined by what actually ("really, truly") exists in the world, and not the other way around. World precedes mind. Such thoughts are typical of metaphysical realism.

Given how the philosophical dialectic has run in the last 100 years, making sense of the claim that there is a portion of the world or reality that is peculiarly moral entails making sense of a number of interconnected theses. There is an ontological thesis that states, roughly, that moral goodness and badness and their ilk are (real) properties of people and their actions. They are not merely in the eye of the beholder, nor are they ontologically constituted by our consciousness of them. Rather, goodness and badness, rightness and wrongness, exist independently of our considerations of them; our judgments about when these properties are instantiated are (or ought to be) based on standards "more real" than any conventional, social, or personal decisions we may happen to make. In any particular case, even if everybody agrees that something is good, we are all only contingently correct: "us" thinking something good or consistently calling something "good" does not, indeed, cannot, make it so (whoever the "we" are). Morality is not up to us. Epistemically, the claim is that our knowledge of morality is, roughly, discovered and not invented; learning the way that some moral relationship ought to be, like parent to child, is more like learning about how the relationship of heart to lung ought to be than, say, flatware to china. We may (in our sharper moments) epistemically detect truths of a moral reality. From the point of view of language, moral realism implies that moral utterances, such as "Socrates was a good person" or "You ought to try to be kinder and gentler," are assertions capable of truth or falsity (even assuming a robustly realistic correspondence theory of truth), such that these utterances can succeed in referring to real properties of people and actions, toward which we may *also* adopt and express certain attitudes like commending and condemning. At least part of moral language intends to be representational, independent of any other expressive uses it may also have; in other words, there is more to moral language than praising and blaming and their ilk. Finally, when it comes to the practical import of morality in our lives, moral realism implies that we are only contingently good. We must become acclimated to the idea that what is normative or what ought to motivate us is something real; and since it is ontologically independent and external to us (in a way to be described), it can only contingently motivate us. (Thus, though a realist, I agree with Mackie that there are no such things as properties with "to-be-pursuedness" built into them.) Contra the hypothesis known as "moral internalism," moral reality implies that one is not necessarily motivated to do what one ought just because one knows what one ought to do. The goal of this book is to make and defend claims of this sort and to explicate their relations.

My linchpin thesis is that moral reality can be comprehended by ontologically modeling the quintessential moral property, *moral goodness*, on the biological property of *physical healthiness*. The claim has the following impressive force: the difference between the regular and irregular heartbeat is as real as the difference between life and death and nothing is more real than that; the difference between being morally good and bad, between being a wise person and a fool, is no more or less real. When we start here, the way smoothly unfolds. Without jumping the gun, but with an aim on what is to come, consider the fact that given our mortal nature, physical healthiness is a property about which we cannot be other than realists, though it is not a substance like water nor an object like the moon nor a sensation like pleasure or redness. It is not a product of our thinking. It is not up to us. It is an empirical property of some living things, and we can be stubbornly mistaken about which of these things instantiate it. We can be psychologically disposed to ignore it. We must theorize about health in order to comprehend it; we can accurately detect it via diagnosis and can truly promote it by following the correct prescriptions. Nevertheless, even if we have knowledge of what healthiness is and have heard the correct prescription, being motivated to act on this knowledge of how to be healthy, or healthier, is a different story altogether. Physical health is a property that confers on those who have it in a strongly developed fashion (athletes, dancers, yogis, and soldiers) a way of being that is unfathomable from the perspective of a merely normally healthy person. For all the same reasons, I think being deeply wise and good might be like something that is totally different from what we can imagine but very, very real nonetheless.

Storrs, Connecticut   P. H. S. B.
September 2000

Acknowledgments

I have no hypothesis to explain this rather odd coincidence, but with regard to the topics at hand I have been most inspired by four British, female philosophers. I am grateful to Philippa Foot, whom I read early in my studies of metaethics and who gave me the solace of finding kindred spirit. My debt to G. E. M. Anscombe's work is most especially evident in chapters 2 and 4. Iris Murdoch's inspired essay "On 'God' and 'Good' " demonstrated to me that metaethics could be both well grounded and profound. Finally, Julia Annas's writing and conversation have had a most salutary effect on my metaethical and moral thinking.

My family line has my deepest respect and gratitude. To all the other Bloomfields and Siegels, the Meyersons, the Backers and Barans, and the once-upon-a-time Ansylovichs, thanks from me, who was once the youngest of you. I thank the University of Connecticut for its kind welcome. The book itself has been a transcontinental effort, mostly researched while visiting at the University of Arizona in Tucson and wholly written in Montreal, while at McGill University. I am greatly indebted to the respective chairs there, J. Christopher Maloney and Philip J. Buckely, as well as to the rest of these departments. Special thanks go to Keith Lehrer for his intial encouragment and to David Norton for arranging an opportunity for me to write. I thank, as should the reader, Wendy Katz and xiv • *Acknowledgments*

Barbara Conner for their help with the writing. I am grateful to Peter Ohlin for being a patient and encouraging editor. I taught the book as a seminar at McGill, and I thank Sean Holland, Salim Lalani, Darlene Rigo, and David Turetsky for their help. To all my teachers and students, and to those at the various universities and conferences at which I have presented research on these topics, I hope the book justifies your kind consideration and indulgence, and I am much obliged. It would be wrong not to explicitly acknowledge Michael P. Lynch. A better philosophical brother no one could ask for: his keen wits (which he keeps about) and his steadfast support have been a boon to me for a decade. Thank you, Michael. As for all the errors contained within, the reader will soon see how well aware I am of unnoticed mistakes; I can only hasten to own them wholly and apologize at the outset.

I've some illocutionary force for those whom I am proud to call my friends, with great thanks for helping me to keep my work in touch with the world outside Academia. BOOM! to: Paul Beatty, Glendon Good, Bradly Jacobs, Matthew Lorin, David Moore, Nancy and Cooper, Devra and Uwe and Leora, Diane O'Leary and Sean too, Jon and Neomit and family, Eric and Sue-Ann, Donna Cooper, John and Lynn and Max and Zoe, Kurt M., Andre and Deborah and Hannah, David O. and daughter Laura, Terry B., Heather, Dan (where've you been?), Raul (where are you?), Virginia, Michael J. Weiss, Julia I., Ross and Merrik, Hal and Liz, Nancy D., Alan Patten, Steve and Dawn, all my "Aunts" and "Uncles" (especially Bobbie for all the flowers she brings) and the rest of the West Hartford gang, Mr. B. K. S. Iyengar, and finally, for Prakash Puriji, who I am sure is resting in peace.

Contents

Introduction: *Protrepticus*   3
    A Modest Transcendental Argument for
      Moral Realism   3
    Four Riddles   23

ONE   Moral Metaphysics: Reality Unobserved   25
    The Thesis   25
    A Primer on Being Healthy   29
    Healthiness, Conventions, and Relativism   33
    Healthiness and Goodness   38
    Supervenience and Reduction   43
    Blackburn's Challenge to Moral Realism via
      Supervenience   48

TWO   Moral Epistemology: The Skill of Virtue   56
    Outline for the Logos of Skillful Practice   60
    Medical, Navigational, and Moral Theories   74
    Stubborn Disagreement in Face of the Facts   88
    Aristotle's Rejection of Virtues as Skills   92

THREE   Moral Language: The "Good" Rules   103
             Following the Linguistic Turn   103
             Semantics   108
             Syntax   128

FOUR   Moral Practicality: Externalism sans Magnetism   153
             The Absurdity of Magnetic Tofu   153
             Intuitions behind Internalism   156
             Hume and Williams Meet Thrasymachus   159
             Kant, Nagel, and Korsgaard Meet Anscombe   164
             A Little Bit of Jimmy Carter in All of Us?   170

         Appendix: Entropy, Healthiness, and Goodness   179

         Bibliography   195

         Index   205

MORAL REALITY

Introduction

Protrepticus

A Modest Transcendental Argument for Moral Realism

How's that numb spot feel?

Not much of an answer to this question is possible, of course. Numb spots do not feel like anything; they are, after all, numb. Still, we can know that numb spots exist by comparing how they don't feel to how they normally feel when they are not numb, or perhaps by prodding a now-numb spot with another nonnumb body part (think of how the tongue and gums "feel" after an injection of Novocain by the dentist). If, however, a numb spot has always been numb, the case is different. People may not necessarily know by the introspection of their feelings or phenomenological experiences that there is a part of them that has always been numb. And were one asked how it would feel for such a perennially numb spot to cease to be numb, one would be quite at a loss for words.

Now, the idea of there being such a thing as this kind of invisible spot might be a bit suspect. After all, by definition, these are spots that cannot ever be experienced: as soon as they are sensed, they cease to qualify as examples. Add just a hint of verificationism, thinking that "if it can't be experienced, it doesn't exist," and the distinctly ontic conclusion might

3

be drawn that there are no such (suppositional) invisible numb spots. This, however, would be a mistake. The vast majority of us are hardly aware of ourselves at all. As perhaps the grossest example, most folks do not know the shape of their own spine nor the shape of a properly formed spine, and very few of us ever pay the slightest attention to our posture. It is no accident that people who are "cocky" walk around with chests and posteriors sticking out, nor is it mere coincidence that those who are sullen or tend toward depression also tend to have shoulders that are rounded forward, with withdrawn tailbones, tucked in and forward. (It is only very rarely that we find someone with a cocky posture who is really sullen and withdrawn. It is far more common to find those who are strutting around to be really quite insecure just under the surface and unconsciously using their posture as a defense; such possibly unconscious self-bluffing is only more fuel for the present argument's fire: evolutionarily, we are consummate compensators.)

Now, our postures are more or less static states that we have trouble sensing, but our lack of bodily awareness is true for dynamic physiological processes that require constant and regular motion. Walking is a symphony composed upon movements of muscles, and physiologists still speculate about the function of deep muscles, like the psoas. We are always breathing, and yet we hardly ever notice. Most do not even understand how they succeed in breathing, do not understand how it works. (When inhaling, the diaphragm ought to contract, creating negative pressure in the thoracic cavity and thereby a vacuum in the lungs, which is filled by air from outside.)[1] Each of us has a muscle that weighs approximately one kilogram in our breast (consider the mass and size of one kilo of meat), which physically convulses strongly enough to pump blood upward against the pull of gravity, from the thinnest capillaries in our feet, though we rarely feel a thing. Much of us is on autopilot most of the time, and this rarely ever *feels* like anything. This is normal. (The situation is quickly different when malfunction occurs, but plenty on ill health and malfunction follows.) More palpably, and bringing us back to numb spots, anyone who has received a massage from a trained professional knows what it is like to learn for the first time that one has old knots of muscle in the neck, shoulders, or back. Given such experiences, it would be right to

---

1. Quiz: To take the deepest breath possible, should the belly move in or out? More technically, to maximize the efficient use of the lung's capacity during inhalation, should the diaphragm draw back (toward the spine) and down (toward the pelvis) or should it move outward and upward?

infer that there are other places in our bodies that "we don't even know we have," even though no masseuse has pressed on them to reveal them to us. In fact, most of us probably have knots so deep and obscure that no masseuse could ever get to them. Our attention is drawn to what is not experienced but to what cannot be ignored. This is the central methodology of the present argument for moral realism (pure, unadulterated metaphysics).

To bridge the gap between the physiological and the psychological, we may consider the existence of psychological stress and how it physically manifests itself. The knots we all unknowingly walk around with are often the results or effects of psychological stress from some of the experiences in our lives. The same may be said of stress-related (or "psychosomatic") illness, such as some stomach ulcers. A rather different sort of effect, which is nevertheless of the same sort, is the placebo effect. (Here we find examples of so-called top-down or mental causation that should give pause to reductionistic skeptics of such causation, like Jaegwon Kim, 1993.) What is crucial for our purposes, however, is how blind we can all be to these very real phenomena, how psychophysical phenomena like the placebo effect can lack any sort of phenomenology. Crucially, almost paradoxically, conscious awareness of them detracts from their efficacy. And to bridge the gap from the psychological to the moral, it is easiest to begin by pilfering a thought from the minstrel Ian Anderson, who notes that wise people do not know how it feels to be "thick as a brick." A meditative and reflective person has no more inkling of what it is like to be unreflective than an unreflective person has of what it is like to be unreflective. Fools qua fools have no conception of their own foolishness, on pain of losing their foolish status.[2] It is difficult, if not impossible, to gain insight into confusion. Perhaps an even better psychomoral example found in the parent/child relationship: people who have had loving parents cannot imagine being abused as children, and vice versa. From the parental viewpoint, new parents often report anecdotally that they could not have imagined a love so strong preceding the birth of their child; those who have not had children cannot imagine such a love. If we use purely moral terms, someone who is good cannot comprehend what it is like to be evil,

---

2. "Only a fool proclaims his own wisdom," says *Poor Richard's Almanack*. We might add that fools never proclaim their own foolishness. As Plato puts it, "the trouble with ignorance is precisely that if a person lacks virtue and knowledge, he's perfectly satisfied with the way he is. If a person isn't aware of a lack, he can't desire the thing which he isn't aware of lacking" (*Symposium*, 204a).

and vice versa. By imagining what could happen to us, most of us learn as children that, say, the joys of torture (such as pulling wings off flies) are in some way fraudulent: most adults cannot bear the thought of what it would mean about them if they were the kind of person who relishs the pain of others.

Still, we often think we can imagine what it would be like to be a sadist; this might be part of how we learn not to be one. A lot of the moral work we do is in imagining what it would be like to be in places other than we are (Gibbard, 1990, chap. 4). We humans are often wont to view the experiences of others as if it were we who were having "those very experiences." Our interpretations of the experiences of others, however, are always from our nonobjective, partial points of view. It is important to empathize with others by trying to "stand in their shoes," but there is always at least a partial failure of imagination. The lives of others are, in fact, actually quite different from our own in ways that even the best of us cannot even imagine. (I'm pretty confident that no one else knows what it is like to be me, even though this is as real as can be; but to avoid the slippery slope to solipsism, I must recognize that everyone else may be just as justified in thinking the same.) Our phenomenological data, given to each of us by our first-person experience, fails to provide us with the data necessary to understand what it is like to be radically different than we are.[3] Taken by itself, this is certainly not meant to be an argument for moral realism. But it is a step toward one, a step that helps us to become accustomed to thinking humbly about how vast the possible range of moral experience is and our general inability to comprehend any but a small portion of it: it is normal to be missing most of what's going on, all the time.

A digression on arguments for moral realism based solely on phenomenological data will prove useful. Such arguments are fairly common, yet there are persuasive reasons for thinking they all fail (Hume, [1739] 1978, pp. 468–69; Harman, 1988). Consider the argument that points to the experience of making a moral judgment: I turn the corner, see the punks burning the cat, and *just know* it is wrong; I thereby conclude that there are moral properties that are eliciting this reaction. All such arguments fail for reasons discussed first by David Hume, and in our time (most famously) by Gilbert Harman: these experiences can be fully explained in terms of moral attitudes and judgments we may make, and (therefore) positing moral reality based on them is more than is needed to explain

---

3. My thanks go to Paul Beatty for helping me see this point.

the data. Everyone agrees that moral judgments are reactions to something, but it would be invalid to infer from this that what they are a reaction to is itself (somehow) intrinsically moral. There is no explanatory work for the putative moral reality to do, if all that needs explaining are our experiences. In conclusion, moral phenomenology does not provide a basis for an argument for moral reality. This brief argument can be explicated as follows.

There has been a long and distinguished tradition in moral philosophy, stretching back to Plato, in which it seems to be a working assumption that rationality is all that is required for seeing the moral truth. The tradition is carried through by Kant and is thought by some to be the key to his deontology, but it is shared as well by some consequentialists, especially those who think that game theory and related coordination efforts exhaust the structure of moral thought. Alongside of (but perhaps as a result of) this way of thinking, there has been a search for arguments designed to be able to make anyone rational see the moral truth. Thus, Plato has Socrates assume (or at least hope) that he can convince Gorgias, Polus, and Callicles in *Gorgias* of the superiority of philosophy over rhetoric, and in general of the sufficiency of virtue for happiness. More clearly, in *Republic*, Thrasymachus' views are the target of rational attack, in the hope of being able to persuade him of his rather staggering errors about morality. Unfortunately, although it seems as if Thrasymachus is capable of rational and even astute argumentation, he is nevertheless incapable of seeing his own moral errors. To put the matter more neutrally, he was incapable of sincerely addressing the (epistemic) possibility that his most central moral convictions are actually mistaken. No amount of rational argument will change Thrasymachus's, or anyone else's, moral convictions against his or her will. We should see this more clearly than Plato, here at the beginning of the twenty-first century, especially in light of one of the previous century's most rightly famous arguments: namely, Quine's ([1951] 1953) demonstration of the futility of trying to draw a sharp boundary between analytic and synthetic propositions. It should not surprise us to find that any given belief, but perhaps especially a moral belief, can be taken to be a central and indisputable element in a web of beliefs (taken as "analytic"); believing in such a way that any argument that shows the belief to be false is automatically taken to be a reductio ad absurdum of that argument. (Consider the certainty that accompanies many a strict belief in the word of the Bible, such that any argument for evolutionary theory *must* have a problem within it somewhere.) If Thrasymachus wishes to hold onto his belief that morality or justice is the interest of the stronger, "come what may," there will be no way to rationally demonstrate to him the errors of his ways. (See also Epictetus' *Discourses*, Book I, Chapter 5.) And it is noting that this "come what may" attitude often accompanies beliefs that one *just knows* to be true, based on the contents of one's phenomenological experience, which allows us to see the limits of arguments from phenomenology in supporting the existence of moral reality. For example, Thrasymachus might say that he *just knows*, "come what may," that morality is the interest of the stronger because of the content of his moral experience, and from there he may try to argue for moral realism. In this case, there would be no way to bridge the gap in a normative disagreement between him and someone else whose moral experience rationally yielded the contradictory "knowledge" of moral reality with equal certainty. Yet both parties to the disagreement might try to rationally argue for moral realism based on the content of their phenomenological experiences. Obviously, there is a problem in making an inference to moral reality from the contents of a data source that is so easily confounded. There is, in conclusion, no reason to implicitly trust the inferential process that moves from the character of moral phenomenology to the existence of moral reality.

Suppose, just for the moment, that moral reality does exist, despite the fact that we cannot know this by relying on phenomenology. If so, then there are first-person implications of the preceding argument for each of us. We all (Socrates included) may be similar to Thrasymachus insofar as we may be intransigent about our own most basic moral beliefs, especially if we limit our consideration to moral phenomenology: of course, things will appear to us to be just as they appear to us to be. It may be, and hopefully is, unquestionable that parents ought to love and not abuse their children. Most (though tragically not all) may be willing to hold to this, "come what may." The point would be that were one to come upon some human monster who *just knew* the opposite, "come what may," that parents ought to abuse and not love their children, one of the parties (presumably the monster) would have to be mistaken. Given the kinds of creatures we *Homo sapiens* are (more on this below), it simply cannot be, it is morally intolerable to think, that at the most fundamental, impartial, and objective moral level possible (whatever that may be) both these child-rearing practices are on a par. If the dispute proved irresolvable (as the dispute with Thrasymachus might well be), one of the parties would be making an error that he or she is incapable of recognizing. The moral realist best makes sense of this error by realizing that the process that moves a person from the content of phenomenological experience to the content of moral reality may be carried out in a perfectly rational manner and still present a false outcome (judgment). The error that presumably the monster is making is not necessarily a rational error (though it may be). Given the content of one's experience, one can be immoral without being irrational.

The first-person lesson mentioned above is that we may never be able to be absolutely *certain* of being error free, even when holding onto our most basic moral beliefs (and most especially when basing these beliefs on how things seem to us). At the very least, indeed, we must avoid being smug about it. Of course, in any case, actually claiming to possess such absolute certainty in morality is foolish hubris. And if it is the fool who proclaims his own wisdom, then the claim to certainty is often the error atop error. None of this is a problem for moral realism per se. Demanding that such a certainty must always be present for beliefs about moral reality to be justified puts an unfair burden on the moral realist: there is most probably no such certainty anywhere besides mathematics and logic, and clearly none in the physical sciences or in any other empirical inquiry. One can be a scientific realist without being certain of any scientific belief. The moral realist will believe that there are moral truths, and even believe that we may know some. But, as is familiar from general epistemology, though we may know some truths, this does not imply that we necessarily can know that we know them. Thus, the possibility remains for there being errors in our "moral knowledge" that transcend our fallible abilities to see them. If we suppose that moral reality exists, and given moral phenomenology and any other belief-forming practices we may engage in immoral thinking, the sum total of moral reality is only contingently within our epistemic ken. No one can say any more than that about any other empirical inquiry, biology and physics notwithstanding. No special metaphysical or epistemological pleading is allowed: qua realist, the moral realist is not making any sui generis claims.

So, returning from our digression about the limits of phenomenology and continuing the development of this modest transcendental argument, we noted that "wise men don't know how it feels to be thick as a brick." We confront now the conjunction of the two following thoughts: (1) there is always at least a partial failure in trying to stand in the shoes of another (we can't just change our minds like that): the phenomenological experiences of another person are in some way inconceivable for us; and (2) one cannot deny the existence of these other phenomenologies (on pain of solipsism). These two push us toward recognizing another first-person application of these general ideas: we are not as good at knowing others as we generally suppose, so we might well be equally skeptical of the extent of our self-knowledge. For the most part, we as humans are pretty mysterious to ourselves, and the phenomenological experiences we actually have and our thoughts about these do not exhaust who we are qua persons. This thought goes back such a long way that we in the West take as one of the first moral injunctions the inscription over the oracle at Delphi: *Know thyself*. And were this a trivial goal, it would not have been so inscribed, for morality would then be equally trivial. Such a basic insight was sadly (and a bit incredibly) lost at some point and had almost completely vanished by the seventeenth century. The "transparency thesis" of the early moderns is perhaps their most embarrassing presumption: the fact is that our minds are not transparent to ourselves in the least. (Leibniz was the exception to the early modern rule, as evidenced by his pointing out the fact that we cannot hear the sound of every drop in the crash of a wave.) Since the beginning of the twentieth century, however, we have disabused ourselves of this myth of transparency, in part because of the work of Freud, who showed us that our motives are often not consciously accessible (and that sometimes we do not want such access).

If one does not go in for analytic psychology, one may still be disabused by different work done in analytic philosophy. Whether or not there are solutions to Wittgenstein's skepticism about there being any facts at all about meaning, at the very least we must recognize that there are times that we do not understand what we mean by what we say. At least sometimes, we may say things we do not mean. This is most especially true if believers in "wide content" have the right picture about meaning (Burge, 1979). The problem about meaning is even murkier if Quine's (1960) claims about translation manuals are correct or Putnam's (1983) application of the Lowenheim-Skolem theorem to meaning works. Moving on from meaning, even if Anscombe's (1957) attempts to drive intentions completely out of our minds are not successful, we must nevertheless acknowledge that sometimes we are not doing what we think we are doing. Whether or not intentions are a type of motive, why we do what we do is something regularly obscure to us. For example, sometimes we have reputable motives mixed with irreputable motives: finding out one has such mixed motives is finding one has what Bernard Williams (1981) calls "one thought too many". Learning by experience that we ever have any of these "extra thoughts" should be sufficient for us to conclude that it is possible for us to have them without knowing it. As Iris Murdoch (1970) observes, "Moral choice is often a mysterious matter." Regarding modern philosophy of mind, two of the leading and diametrically opposed positions both contend that we are mysteries to ourselves. The Churchlands, in defending "eliminative materialism," think that much of our self-conceptions are based on old and fraudulent pictures of the mind (we don't even have beliefs as we think we do) (McCauley, 1996), whereas Colin McGinn (1990) has been arguing that it is impossible for us to know how our minds are related to our brains. Thus, we should know about ourselves that, at the very least, it is possible that we may not be fully aware of ourselves and what we do and why we do it. It is by paying attention to that to which we do not attend that we begin to see the existence of a to-*all*-appearances/reality distinction. And a part of this transcendent reality is moral.

This begins to become clear upon noticing that we, as humans, are most often ready, willing, and able to think well of ourselves. (Aren't we all "better than average" automobile drivers?) Of course, there are those who miserably loath themselves or are in general depressed or morose and reluctant to think well of anything. For the most part, however, we all tend to think that we are doing all right, and in fact most of us (it is hoped) are not too mistaken. But consider now the man who finds himself a part of an invading army during war and in battle and, half-crazed by the insanity surrounding him, takes part in the burning, pillaging, and raping of the land and people he is helping to conquer. Certainly and sadly, this has not been an infrequent occurrence in the course of human history. (As of this writing, the most recent examples can be found in East Timor and Kosovo and, before that, Rwanda.) Not all men involved in military action end up committing these acts of savagery, but very many have. The point of the example is to note that were these very same men born into a generation in which they were not called on to be soldiers, we would be hard pressed to predict whether they would be capable of such atrocities. Surely, there are brutes among us whom we might quickly suspect. But some men might lead perfectly normal lives, as husbands and fathers, without any inkling at all of what their own capabilities and dispositions actually are (or were). The full range of their moral characters lies beyond their experience, beyond their self-conception, and even beyond their ability to believe such things of themselves. It is the recognition of the ways in which people's moral characters can extend beyond their ability to have accurate beliefs about their own moral characters that brings us another step closer to the recognition of moral reality.

Philosophical arguments, even arguments in moral philosophy, rarely demand that we reflect on ourselves and our own lives, but the next step in the argument can only rightly be evaluated from the first-person perspective. We must move beyond fictional stories of would-be rapists we might never have met (though, chillingly, we probably have). Moral reality is best not to be discovered by thought experiment or imagination. Sticking to real life, the argument could be based on the idea of moral improvement, and perhaps this might be the most pleasant way to go about it. (Importantly, the argument does work both ways: it could turn instead on the existence of actual would-be heroes to the same effect.) But despite any pleasure we might find in pursuing this project, one ought not to engage a philosophical project guided merely by pleasure. A dose of realism may be most like a bitter pill, but if so, then so be it. Let us assume that most of us are already pretty good; optimistically, let's say it is normal to be pretty good. Well, in such cases, one ought to strengthen weaknesses before further fortifying strengths. What we need to focus on are our moral failings, especially since we are normally so apt to ignore them. It is here that this modest transcendental argument finds clearest purchase. We begin by looking at the moral failings that each of us can own in our most private consciences: our weaknesses of character and our own failings in our relations with others; and in the honesty of such an acknowledgment, we are forced to recognize the (epistemic) possibility of the actual existence of further failings that we have not seen, others we may yet see, and still others that are beyond our capacity to see. It is doubtful (but epistemically possible) that mortal humans are *necessarily* fallible, but as a contingent fact we certainly all are. From the fact that we can imagine lacking at least some of these moral failings (and how much is sheer laziness?), we may infer the fact that were we to lack these failings, our lives would have a quality that we cannot imagine from our current position. Whereas there are epistemic constraints on how much we can know about our moral selves (because we are locked into our actual first-person phenomenologies), we find there to be good reason to think that there is *some way it would be* for us to lack our actual moral failings, and that this way is better than what we've actually got. This demonstrates to us that there exist elements of our moral characters that are independent of how we are actually capable of conceiving them to be. Furthermore, if we could fashion our lives in these ways, which we acknowledge are better, then we ought to do so. Our moral self-conceptions are conceptions of something the existence of which is not dependent on being conceived.

This argument finds its best examples in the recognition that humans often employ a psychological defense mechanism that the experts call "denial." We begin by noting that *Homo sapiens* are generally insecure creatures. Life is hard, and at some level all but the lucky are working hard to merely keep up. Indeed, although insecurity may not be a universal truth about the human condition, the incidence of humans who completely lack it is infrequent at best. We find insecurity in the greatest of conquerors, the largest of egos, and it is often actually the driving motive in those we generally think of as being most successful. If we should learn, as a matter of empirical fact, that we have never had a single conspecific who was completely without insecurity, we should probably not be surprised. This is, of course, not to say that we are all cowering wrecks; it is just to say that each of us almost certainly has something about which to be insecure. Sometimes these failings are readily apparent, but they need not be, and we are better off here attending to more sublime problems. Consider the following: everybody plays the fool sometimes, but perhaps one plays it with an unfortunate frequency; or maybe one is just a bit of a social or intellectual coward, so that it makes it harder for one to achieve one's goals; maybe one thinks that small unjust liberties taken or lies told in one's favor, which no one else ever discovers, do one no harm (and maybe do nobody any harm); maybe one is apt to "lose one's temper" or get inappropriately angry, so that afterward remorse is felt because of a lack of self-control; or perhaps one tends to swallow anger, even in small doses, and so ends up bitter and frustrated and resentful. We do not like to look at our faults. Indeed, we find those who are clinically depressed to be the ones most conscious of their imperfections. It may even be somewhat adaptive to be able to ignore our problems, but this biological adaptation does result in having a moral propensity to ignore the areas of our lives that are often most in need of attention and help. Instead of paying proper but not obsessive attention to these areas, working on ourselves to improve, we often put up fronts and defenses. And after living with these fronts for any number of years, while simultaneously doing our best to ignore those original, unpleasant insecurities, we begin to convince ourselves that the fronts are our true nature. We try to minimize unpleasant cognitive dissonance. If we succeed in believing in our fronts, then we are in denial. We rationalize ourselves.

Now, most often, this is not too serious a problem; we have the sorts of defense mechanisms that we do because they generally work well and allow us to go about our business. Clinical depression is not the norm of even the modern world. The point is that these mechanisms can get out of control and can allow us to fool ourselves into thinking we are okay when, in fact, we may not be. And even if our lives are actually, truly good, we may still be in denial about ways in which we can improve our lives. To whatever degree each of us may actually be in denial, however, what we cannot deny is our ability to be in denial. As presumptuous as it sounds, (I think) the realist's bitter pill is that using the second person is here quite justified: if you think that there is nothing about which you are in denial, you can be quite confident that you are in denial about something. And it is a short step from this realization about our psychological complexities to the more powerful point of realizing that it might be psychologically impossible for some of us, in the most drastic cases, to recognize the truth about ourselves. Of course, happily, few of us are so badly off, but the fact that this is possible for *Homo sapiens* is what is crucial.

This is the lion's share of an argument for moral realism because it shows us that the facts that constitute who we are or what kinds of people we are, facts about the quality of our lives, are deeply independent of what we may happen to think about them. We might not be wrong about ourselves in the least, but we cannot be sure about this. Our powers of introspection, when turned to a reflection of the overall condition of our lives, are surely far from infallible. Crispin Wright (1987, intro.) has discussed the modesty that is one characteristic of realism, but when it comes to morality, we must, as humans, be downright humble. Natural selection has turned us into incredibly complex and often convoluted creatures, and knowing ourselves will only be possible after learning the most subtle lessons of which we are capable. (Some of the subtly is due to their tricky reflexive nature.) Even if we are perceptive enough to actually learn these lessons about ourselves, independent and objective confirmation that we are not mistaken is equally unlikely to come by. So, we must be humble and accept as a lesson learned that evolution has given us the ability to be wrong about ourselves and the quality of our lives. We must not fool ourselves about our continuing ability to fool ourselves. From a first-person point of view, it is often difficult to discern which aspects of our characters, which patterns of behavior, are helping and which are hindering the flourishing of our lives.

So far, this argument for moral realism does have precursors. Aristotle's (1985, 1101a1ff.) disagreement with Solon over whether a person's *eudaimonia* can be affected after one's death is also a consideration of the ways in which morality might transcend our awareness of it. The thought is latent in Thomas Nagle's (1979) comment about the nature of betrayal: "The natural view is that the discovery of betrayal makes us unhappy because it is bad to be betrayed—not that betrayal is bad because its discovery makes us unhappy." Finally, the same sort of thought is present in Peter Railton's (1986) argument for the reality of non–moral value, where he shows that drinking clear liquids might be "good for" and thereby popular with dehydrated travelers, even though these travelers may have no access to why they like clear liquids better than milk.

And now is the time to explain the sense in which this transcendental argument is modest. The more familiar variety of transcendental argument is contrastingly immodest: these are arguments based on (supposedly) indubitable premises from which a deduction concerning the nature of transcendent reality can be validly drawn. Such an argument is usually aimed at global epistemic skeptics of something more like Cartesian proportion (Stroud, 1968). A modest transcendental argument begins with a premise that is not (even supposedly) indubitable but one that it is merely very difficult to cogently deny.[4] Consider an argument for the reality of singular necessary causal connections based on a premise about the existence of memories. (See Martin and Deutscher, 1966 for a causal theory of memory.) It might be possible to doubt that we ever have genuine memory experiences, but granted that we do, one might be able to prove that the only way to explain their existence is through a recognition of the transcendental causation; and such an argument would make it difficult to maintain a Humean critique of this sort of causation, despite its unverifiability. In our present moral case, we begin with the difficult-to-deny premise that there may actually be aspects of our moral lives that we are incapable of recognizing, and we draw the conclusion that the scope of moral reality must transcend what falls contingently within our epistemic ken; moral judgments are more or less accurate judgments of a portion of reality that does not depend on being judged for its existence.

Saying exactly how strong a conclusion this is, just how strong a form of realism the argument establishes a presumption for, is tricky. We can get a handle on the answer by figuring out just how contingent it is that we gain insight into our lives, just how contingent wisdom is. Our modest argument shows that there are limits to our ability to understand morality, but what exactly are these limits? One might say, yes, perhaps we are fallible, but if we could somehow have all the time in the world, and this allowed us to eliminate our errors, then moral reality would be fully open to us. A stronger form of realism, which is what the argument actually supports, would say that even if, *per impossible*, we could eliminate mistakes in our cogitating about morality, moral reality might still be too subtle and complex in how it ramifies for mortal humans to actually work it all out. There might be actual problems whose actual solutions forever

---

4. I am particularly indebted at this point to the tutelage of José Benardete.

elude or only remain obscure to the actual human mind. Even if we assume, as we must, that there cannot be any single aspect of moral reality that, in principle, makes no noticeable difference to anyone's life, still, there is no reason to think that it is necessarily the case that we are actually capable of discovering every aspect of moral reality. It might actually be too big or complicated or diachronic to comprehend it all at once with minds like ours. And even small portions, single moral problems, might be too difficult for the vast majority of us to grasp their complexity. In general, we operate under conditions of incomplete data, and this is particularly so for morality.

We may imagine the degree to which moral reality transcends our ability to know about it by imagining different levels of epistemic access we can gain to moral reality. Begin by imagining a better sort of access to moral reality than we are actually capable of attaining. Imagine that a god can whisper the truth about us into our ears. If we could hear a god like this, then there is no reason to think that moral reality could transcend our ability to know about it: if there is a god who is omniscient and willing to share information, we could know everything there is to know. Given that we cannot actually count on a god in this way, the question then concerns what we are actually capable of learning and how much of moral reality may actually be beyond our ken. The best epistemic conditions that we fallible, mortal, often not too bright humans are capable of are often described in these term: thinking in a cool moment, given all opportunities to be fully reflective, not under the influence of mind-altering drugs or brainwashing techniques, and so on (Rosati, 1996). These are ideal or optimal epistemic conditions for actual humans, and given them, we can try to get a clearer handle on how much of moral reality might forever elude our searches or, in other terms, how incomplete our moral understanding is doomed to be.

We best improve our prospects of finding the limits of actual human access to moral reality by attending to the capabilities of those who are wise, for they seem most likely to be capable of plumbing the depths of morality and incorporating these insights into the broadest of possible understandings. Let's also note again that the presence of wisdom is contingent; there are few real prodigies in this sphere. Since we are engaged in Western philosophy, let's allow Socrates to set a reasonable standard for wisdom and then ask how many wise humans there have actually been throughout the actual world's history. Probably not many. (It is estimated that there have been 85 billion humans since the first [Dillard, 1998].) Have there been 1 million wise people? 10 million? How many are alive today out of the 7 billion living humans? No matter how wise, of course, humans are humans and no one is perfect. Given the actual record of humans as far as one can tell, there is no reason to conclude that it is possible for any single human to be able to see to the bottom of every possible moral conundrum. Let's even make the large assumption that for any given actual moral conundrum, there has been at some point in history an actual human capable of understanding it. If this were true, no actual problem would be in principle unsolvable. Still, what stands clear is the contingency involved here. Were some given actual individuals the only ones capable of solving some actual moral problem, then our epistemic access to those solutions are just as contingent as those individuals themselves. There is no guaranteed actual success in morality, such that if those individuals had not existed then there would necessarily have been others to take their places. It is the same with any other field of inquiry.[5]

In the very beginning of the *Nicomachean Ethics* (1094b3ff.), Aristotle (1985) notes that moral theorizing is an inexact science, and the conclusion here is in complete agreement. The inexactitude does not, however, stem from the "fact" that morality is not fit for realism nor from the existence of some, in principle, unverifiable or unknowable elements of morality; instead, it comes from the cognitive limits of the actual human condition. Moral theorizing will be incomplete and inexact for exactly the same reasons that meteorology is incomplete and inexact: even if we are actually clever enough to learn all the general laws about the weather (Why is there a Gulf Stream? Whence Indian summers, January thaws, and El Nino?), we still simply cannot learn everything about ever-changing, actual meteorological conditions quickly enough. And even if we could gather so much information so fast, we would not be able to compute it all quickly enough for it to be of practical use. The complexity of all the interaction effects is too large to calculate. (Every heat-generating source must be considered.) Analogously, even if we are clever enough to figure out all the actually true general principles about morality and human flourishing, this moral reality is too differentiated and particularized in actual fact for us to be cognitively capable of knowing everything about it. And to top it all off, it is entirely possible that were we told the actual moral truth about ourselves, we might not believe it.

---

5. Take the thousand greatest physicists our world has ever seen and imagine the possible world at which they all died at birth. It is not the case that given enough time, *Homo sapiens* necessarily learn about quantum reality.

The argument for moral realism needs one further boundary tested to be completed.[6] One skeptical of moral reality may have been anxious to say long ago, "Yes, yes, perhaps, you are right and there is more to our moral selves than we may be capable of acknowledging. But this does not yield moral realism. Take, for example, your would-be wartime rapist and pillager who is actually a loving husband and father. You are making a moral judgment of this man's character as being morally defective in ways that he cannot appreciate. But this judgment you are making (with which any decent person must sympathize) is based on a particular moral point of view that ultimately has no deeper foundations in reality than any other moral point of view, for the fact is that morality does not have its foundations in reality at all. These aspects of this man's character are themselves neither bad nor good independent of our judgments about them, and although we all may disapprove of the latent disposition to be a rapist in the strongest terms possible, even this strongest of disapprovals cannot buy anyone moral reality."

Such an objection is quite to the point. And perhaps, then, at this point, a bit of specification is required to say something more about what moral reality might be like (though of course this is the project of the book as a whole). The subject matter of morality concerns the difference between acting and living well and badly, though not all aspects of our lives are relevant. From the moral point of view (as opposed to, say, the purely physiological point of view), living well or poorly will be determined by an individual's relations to himself or herself and to others. The subject matter of moral discourse is constituted by intrapersonal relations (integrity, self-respect, etc.) and interpersonal relationships (family, friend, citizen, etc.) and the relationships of these relationships. If these relations are as they ought to be or are good, then a person is living well, and if not, not. And whereas it is a step toward realism to acknowledge that these relationships are not constituted by our impressions of them, the clever moral nonrealist can acknowledge this and still go on to make the further denial—that even if these relationships are not determined by what we think of them, whenever we are *morally evaluating* them we are not doing so based on standards of goodness or badness that exist independent of how we judge them. Fair enough. What the moral realist must show is that the standards by which we morally judge these relationships as good or bad are standards that are not merely personal or

6. I am grateful to conversations with Terry Horgan and Roderick Long for helping me see the place of this objection at this point.

conventional or somehow "constructed" by us; that they are standards that we are not free to invent but which we must discover; that they are grounded in a reality that is sufficiently independent of any judgments that we actually happen to make.

And it is here that the moral realist must turn to the kinds of creatures we are: our natures as *Homo sapiens*. We must return, once again, to the actual human condition. Moral inquiry is practical, is salient to our lives, insofar as it informs us about what it is for a member of *Homo sapiens* to live well. And we are beasts with certain talents, capacities, and needs. Given the kinds of creatures we are, at the very least, there are some environments in which we flourish and others in which we flounder. (Here we are no different from the lion or the tomato.) Some practices engender the full development of human potential; other practices stifle it. The aspects of our lives that are moral are also aspects of our lives qua living creatures. We are no more free to make up the rules for morality than we are to make up the rules for nutrition, for denying this is asserting that human morality is somehow alienated from how we live, from human nature or from the human condition. We may not take the biology out of the human condition, and we may therefore not take the biology out of morality, either. One might try to justify this point by taking a normative position on some issue, such as a stand against child abuse on the grounds that abuse stunts children morally because of the contingent kind of creatures they are. This may suffice for some, though for others it would be improperly deriving an "ought" from an "is." In any case, one need not engage normative stances to see the force of the point. All sides of these normative debates think that many moral issues are intimately tied up with our being the sorts of mortal, biological creatures we are; abortion and euthanasia are two obvious examples. We could also point to issues surrounding temperance or capital punishment. How would our morality be different if we were all by our biological nature self-sufficient loners instead of social animals? Having any answer at all to that question or thinking that morality would differ in any way due to this change in circumstance is thinking that what our biology actually is is a cause of (determines, fixes) how we ought to be or which goals we ought to pursue. This is the sense in which biology is foundational to morality. (This is not to derive a conclusion with a normative "ought" statement from premises that are descriptive "is" statements, but rather to present an argument which concludes that what is the case fixes standards according to which we ought to make our judgments: "ought" statements are not of an altogether different kind than "is" statements; rather, "ought" statements are a subset of "is" statements. These topics are pursued in chapters 3 and 4.)

There will be skeptics who will get off the boat; this is, of course, to be expected. (For any belief X, there is a philosopher Y such that Y is skeptical of X.) There are skeptics about the external world, and that there are such skeptics presumably does not make a belief in the external world unjustified. A moral skeptic at this point may simply insist that the question is still being begged. Saying that biology fixes a moral standard against which we can make judgments regarding moral issues is itself the reflection of a particular moral point of view: in the cloak of metaethical argument, a normative moral point of view is being pushed which says that our morality, or the way our morality ought to be, is a contingent manifestation of the way natural selection has fashioned us, as opposed to it being discernible a priori or determined by pure rationality alone, independent of the sorts of biological creatures we are. Furthermore, the critic might add, there has been no *proof* that this point of view is capturing anything beyond itself that is deserving of being called "moral reality."

The realist first answers that this "normative" position is not being used as an argument for moral realism, but rather comes at the end of such an argument, the premises of which concern the content of ongoing issues in normative ethics. Take the question: At what point of development does something that was once a zygote become a conscious (rational?) human being? In the right context, the asker of that question is committed by the content of the question to thinking that any satisfactory moral position on abortion will not swing free of the biological facts. (This is what Wright, 1992, calls having "wide cosmological role.") This cannot be rightly construed as an argument from some normative point of view to a metaethical conclusion; rather, it is a response to the fact that human morality is embedded within actual human nature. We are animals through and through, morality notwithstanding. The realist must agree that no certain proof of a transcendent, external moral reality has been presented, nor has there been any proof that we may capture it (when, say, learning good child-rearing practices). Our transcendental argument has a more modest conclusion. In any case, this skepticism is not a special problem for moral realists, because there is no certain proof of *any* portion of transcendent, external reality. The one who doubts that the answer to the abortion debate (whatever it may be) will depend on the sorts of biological creatures we are is epistemically on par with the one who doubts the facts of life or that we are biological creatures set in a natural world, with trees and birds and rocks and things external to ourselves. Such a skeptic is not, then, presenting any problems for moral realism per se, nor does the skeptic's worries about this modest transcendental argument keep it from establishing a presumption in favor of moral realism.

There will be more about this presumption in a few pages, but some worry may still linger for those who do not see themselves as such radical skeptics but who are also not yet convinced. One possibility is that this worry may be due to the use of the word "moral" to indicate a particular point of view, or portion of reality, and if this is so, then let it be said that we can do without the word, a là Anscombe (1958). This is moral reality demystified; calling this point of view "moral" confers no status on it by which it may be metaphysically or epistemologically differentiated from the other empirical sciences. We are concerned with living well or poorly, with getting along with or killing our neighbors: we can leave the word "moral" out of it. What is pragmatically central from this point of view (however we label it) is that child-rearing practices can be judged as either good or bad and that at least some of the standards by which these practices ought to be judged are given to us by nature and are not projections or stainings of sentiment on reality, nor are they constructions on reality like the standards of convention. We cannot simply decide what we like concerning the sexual abuse of children, as we can with regard to which side of the road we drive on. Saying that the practices are either "morally good" or "morally bad" adds nothing at all to the content of the judgments we make; what the word "moral" signifies is the fact that we are engaging in a particular discourse, a moral one, whose subject matter (child, spousal, or racial abuse; cowardice or infidelity; capital punishment; etc.) is agreed on by all parties to the metaethical debate. The metaethical debate is over the nature of the standards by which judgments are made in normative moral discourse, and the argument shows that there is at least a presumption for thinking that some of these standards are best understood in realistic terms. (There may be types of praising and blaming that are our reactions to moral reality, and these may be special "moral evaluations." They may carry a certain kind of weight for us and society; but we must not conflate the reaction with what it is a reaction to: a moral reality just as mundane as biology.)

In general, this is an argument for moral realism based on the existence of moral error, and as such it is, again, familiar metaethical territory (Less familiar, but related, is the discussion of global moral error on pages 122–8.) What makes this argument different is that it forces us to acknowledge the (epistemic) possibility of the actual existence of moral errors that are impossible for us to discover, and which we may be unwilling to accept, even were they to be revealed to us. We cannot wholly account for these errors in moral judgments by appeal to any set of further judgments we might make at some other point, for the errors we are considering are errors that we may be incapable of recognizing as such; we cannot, therefore, account for them as errors solely by appeal to hypothetical "rectifying" judgments we might make about them later. One must be capable of recognizing errors in order to be capable of rectifying them, and we have found our recognitional capacities to be limited. In any case, the only way those future judgments could be rectifying is if they do a better job at getting the moral facts right. Mere change is not sufficient to ground a notion of improvement, and we have also seen that pure rationality also lacks those resources. It is sheerest hubris to accept an error theory about our ability to be in deep and persistent error about morality; nor does it do to say that we project moral reality onto the world or that we construct it or that we stain the world with our moral sentiments, for none of these leaves us enough ontic depth wherein we may harbor illusions about ourselves.[7]

The conclusion of the argument is inconclusive, but to expect any more would itself be foolishness. The naive idea that one could prove moral realism true based on a single sound argument could only be regarded nowadays with amusement. If we have learned anything at all about meta-ethics in the past hundred years it is that it is subtle and multifaceted, intertwining issues of metaphysics, epistemology, language, and motivation. What moral reality needs is a worked-out position, a theory. At best, all a single argument could hope to establish would be a presumption in favor of moral realism, and in this limited endeavor the modest transcendental argument succeeds. Couple our limited access to moral matters with what must exist in order to explain the moral mistakes that may forever be beyond our epistemic ken, and we get the conclusion that moral reality must exist independently of our very fallible access to it.

---

7. I'd like to thank Mark Timmons for discussion on this matter. Long before this discussion, I recognized that Timmons (1993) is the nonrealist who most forthrightly faces the difficulties of explaining moral error. Despite his best efforts, he acknowledges that the nonrealist cannot account for error in a way that preserves the intuition that it is something external to our judgments and practices that sets the standard determining what is an error and what is not. Simon Blackburn (1993, p. 4) also acknowledges that if expressivism cannot adequately account for moral error, it will "lack a becoming modesty." This, I take it, is understatement.

What the argument gives us by itself is a reason to pursue moral realism, such that if a position were established that was able to provide answers to the important problems that moral realists have traditionally faced, then we would have a theory of moral realism that deserved our utmost attention.

Four Riddles

It is easy to toss around words like "quality of life," *eudaimonia*, and "goodness," but if these are to be predicates that name some properties, we still need to know what kind of properties these may be. We need a model for moral properties that answers to our philosophical needs while respecting the presumptions for realism the preceding argument engendered.

Perhaps a concrete example of heinous moral failure will prove helpful in motivating our thoughts on the issue. Consider the case of three Ku Klux Klan members, who on June 7, 1998, in Jasper, Texas, dragged from the back of their pickup truck a kidnapped and innocent black man by the name of James Byrd, Jr., who was dismembered and decapitated as a result of their actions. We may all agree that what occurred is morally wrong or bad,[8] but we may ask further to what this wrongness or badness amounts. Were we to have been in Jasper, Texas, at the time, and perhaps even been witness to the horror, we might have made an empirical, forensic inspection of the scene: we would find the murderers, with their drunken brains, false beliefs, and twisted psychologies (to beg the question just a bit); Byrd, with his battered body and brain, his physical pain, but nowhere do we directly observe or discover any wrongness or badness per se. Indeed, it is senseless to say that one directly observes wrongness (even the intuitionists denied direct empirical observations of moral properties). We can seemingly explain the entire event (capturing, chaining, dragging, dismemberment) without finding a necessary causal role for the property of wrongness to play. If these moral properties are unobservable, perhaps

8. It is true that the Klan staged a rally in support of the murderers. It also may be true that Thrasymachus could not have been persuaded to give up his theory of justice. The point of the preceding argument is that there are some people who will never be able to see their mistakes: upon being sentenced to death, the only regret one of Byrd's murderers expressed was that his crime did not serve to inspire further violence against blacks.

the best explanation for our condemnation of what happened to Byrd resides not in any wrongness or badness, which is somehow inherent in his murder, but in our own psychologies and in the attitudes that we take toward the murderers and what they did.

The problem just laid out for the moral realist has four important interpretations, one ontic, one epistemic, one linguistic, and one that concerns practical motivation. Each can be posed as a riddle. The ontic riddle might go something like this: what kind of property is there that cannot empirically be observed and may lack observable causal efficacy? The epistemic riddle assumes that the ontic one can be solved, and it goes on to ask this: assuming these properties do exist but cannot be observed, how do we learn about them? Moral realists of this century have also faced the linguistic riddle that addresses moral discourse per se, and they ask this: if moral language is used for more than commending and condemning, what sorts of linguistic rules regulate these varied ascriptions of goodness and badness? For instance, what do we mean by calling both Boyd's murders and their actions "bad," or how can things as different as people and acts fall under the range of a single predicate? What rules could govern usage as disparate as this? The riddle regarding the practical aspects of morality asks us to explain the sorts of connections that may exist between moral properties and our motivational structures. How do we become motivated to live well? What relations obtain between what is normative and what motivates us? In particular, does recognizing what is good automatically lead one to be motivated by it (as many since Plato have thought), or if not, then what is the relation between our moral knowledge and our motives? The answer to the epistemic riddle will constitute chapter 2, and chapter 3 will answer the linguistic riddle. The final chapter deals with practicality and motivation. Now, we begin in chapter 1 with a focus on metaphysics and ontology.[9]

---

9. It was only unfortunately late in the production of this book that I read Timmons's pellucid and scholarly treatment of the problem of moral error that comprises the third chapter of his *Morality Without Foundations* (New York: Oxford University Press) 1999. I am sure my presentation of the problem would have been clearer had I had the benefit of his work before me earlier.

. . .

ONE

Moral Metaphysics
Reality Unobserved

The Thesis

Whereas few of us are truly bad in what we do, most of us are not actually as good as we could be. Sometimes we do not do what we ought to do, so we might not even be as good as we ought to be. Sometimes when we do what we ought not to do, we do so knowingly and "on purpose" (which is very bad), and in some of these instances we may later care and express regret (which mitigates) and in others we may not (which aggravates). At other times, when we do as we ought not to, we do so by mistake. Some of these mistakes pass by unnoticed, but the introduction has already contained talk of unnoticed mistakes and what they say about moral reality. Here, we begin by focusing on other mistakes we make, namely, those about which we learn. Before thinking about moral mistakes, begin by thinking prosaically: consider the work of auto mechanics, doctors, or naval navigators. Whenever someone makes a mistake, we may watch it, but we can only sometimes spot the mistake being made. Sometimes we find out about the mistake later, or sometimes one can be in the middle of a mistake being made and become cognizant of it but not be able to stop or undo what is already being done.

The ontological riddle, concerned with the nature of unobservable properties, is already just below the surface. It seems hard to deny the thought that we make mistakes. One may ask, however, if one has ever observed a mistake. Yes, we can watch someone make a mistake; but consider, for a moment, what a mistake looks like.

Foolish, a nonphilosopher might impatiently say, trying to talk about what "a mistake looks like." Mistakes do not look like anything, our friend might insist—which is, of course, the point exactly. We know we make mistakes, but they do not look like anything; people simply do what they do. The riddle rises. And in considering mistakes, we consider only half the problem. For if saying how mistakes are observable is tricky, there is no reason to think that the opposite of making a mistake, or getting it right, is any easier to observe. What's that look like? One can describe what one does, but how does one describe getting it right qua (or when considered as) getting it right, as opposed to merely describing the behavior in which one engages and what follows. Considering mistakes qua mistakes, there does not seem to be anything that a mistake looks like, despite the fact that we can, wittingly or otherwise, watch them occur. One can say the same of a job well done, or a good job, versus a job poorly done, or a bad job. Rightness and wrongness, goodness and badness—it is hard to say what makes them differ.

Sometimes we do as we ought, and sometimes we make mistakes. But it is hard to observe or describe what we are talking about. Things may be as they ought to be, and thus good, or they may be otherwise mediocre or worse, downright bad; things are these ways, somehow, "on top" of being everything else that seems unproblematically observable. One might conclude that because we cannot observe and describe what makes the cases differ, then there is really no difference among them. Perhaps all there is is the job or our behavior. Getting it right, making a mistake, being good or bad, these may all be just in the head or decided on by convention or perhaps are merely figures of speech. To make a difficult situation even worse, it is hard to see if any causal results arise because of, say, making a mistake. Do things one way and something will follow after that. Do them another way and something different will follow. He clamps, then tightens, or he tightens, then clamps. The properties of getting it right or making a mistake are not really needed at all to describe everything that happens and all the differences between all those things that may follow. So, not only can we not observe these properties, but also it is even hard to see how one could ever need to avail oneself of these properties in a causal explanation.

Let's assume for the moment that we can neither observe how doing a good job differs from a bad one nor see how the difference makes a causal difference. Let's also assume that we cannot even describe it. Still, just because we cannot describe something does not imply that it does not exist. Certainly, as a first reaction, this would be hasty. We do, after all, have words like "ineffable" so that we may say something when we get stuck in this way. Ineffability is hardly succor for a philosopher who is seeking insight, however. And in any case, one might remain puzzled. We would prefer to be on firmer ground here, and ideally we would find a way to say what seems obscure at best, ineffable at worst.

If, however, what we are after is really ineffable or unsayable, then perhaps the conclusion should be that our approach has been wrong. We can, as an alternative, reassure ourselves in our belief in the difference between making mistakes and getting it right by finding other types of situations in which we cannot observe how two things differ and where we simply cannot deny the existence of that difference. The problem is not one of how we may justify a belief in the existence of something that seems to fail according to a standard of observability; it is a problem with the standard. We wish, therefore, to avoid having an overweening sense of empiricism. (It was this that led Hume, at one point, to deny the self; and this may have been the Hume most true to his principles.) In a manner reminiscent of a reductio ad absurdum, if denying that two things differ implies something that we simply do not think is the case, then we seemingly have good reason to think that there exist these differences, despite any unobservability or perhaps even our inability to describe them. For example, if denying the existence of an unobservable difference between ϕ and ψ entails that we are not mortal, living creatures of the species *Homo sapiens*, then we would have sufficient reason not to deny this difference. This shall be our strategy for discerning an ontology for moral realism.

Moral realism will be most cogent if moral properties are no more ontologically suspect than other properties that we are all convinced exist. So, at least for the moral realist, the ontic riddle has again arisen: what kind of property cannot be observed and thereby cannot be seen to do any causal work? The answer is actually rather obvious, as is the case with many riddles. Consider the property of being alive, as contrasted with the property of being dead. If we make an empirical inspection of a living organism, we find tissue, fluid, and movement, but we do not directly observe life, nor does that particular property seem to be needed in explaining any particular, observed biological event. But being a nonrealist about life does not seem to be an option for a human being. Even if life "reduces" to chemistry and physics, we will still want to insist on a real distinction between being alive and being dead. The metabolism of a living organism is also not observable, and any particular event that happens in a body can be explained without mentioning it, but again nonrealism is not an option. Similarly, as an easy case, mammals have immune systems that are not directly observable, and although we can observe white blood cells fighting an infection (or any other particular action of the immune system), we do not need to posit the system per se, in order to explain anything we observe. Finally, we come at last to what is best suited to be our unobservable model for goodness: healthiness. Healthiness is a property of living systems that cannot be directly detected; when observing a marathon runner run, all our observations can be explained in terms of muscle, bone, and sinew. Healthiness does not seem to play a necessary role in explaining how the marathon got run. Specifically, we all are quite confident that we are in various states of health and ill health, though saying what this amounts to is at best no mean feat. In general, many properties that humans have in virtue of being living, biological creatures are not directly observable yet are not candidates for nonrealism.[1]

So, the moral realist faces the ontological riddle. It asks us what kind of thing moral properties could be such that they are invisible to observation and may not be required for causal explanations. The answer is that moral properties have the same ontological status as healthiness or other biological properties. If being invisible to observation and not playing a role in causal explanations are not problems for realism when concerned with being alive and healthy, then these cannot be problems for being good or bad or getting it right or making a mistake. If we are committed to realism about other properties with these attributes (these properties of properties), then moral properties having these attributes cannot be a problem for realism with regard to them. So, we arrive at a form of moral realism that takes its lead from the metaphysics of physical health.

The central thesis of this book is that moral goodness has the same ontological status as physical healthiness, so that if we are realists about the latter, then we ought to be also about the former. With a few words

1. Consider also concepts from evolutionary biology like "fitness" and "environment"; the latter is a case in which reductionism may quite literally ignore the forest for the trees.

here about the strength of this claim, we can avoid a way of easily and naturally misunderstanding it. Claiming that being good and being healthy have the same "ontological status" is not, thereby, to claim that goodness is a kind of, sort of, subset of, or type of healthiness. Goodness is not healthiness. Morally good people need not be physically healthy, nor need physically healthy people be morally good. Still, one might have concerns about the viability of this thesis upon noting how the normative theory of morality differs from the normative theory of health. For instance, one might suggest that there is no correlate in the theory of health for an idea of altruism that has an obvious place in moral theory. As a result, one might think that healthiness was not a suitable model for moral goodness: our physical health is something that only directly affects us as individuals, whereas morality implies interacting in relationships with others. Such a worry could lead one astray when evaluating the thesis being defended. The metaphysical status that being morally good and physically healthy are said to share is purely ontological. So, as another example of two properties that have the same ontological status, we may consider sweetness and redness, both of which are traditionally said to be "secondary qualities." Tastes and colors belong to the very same ontic category, though they are dissimilar in many ways and in no way could one be said to be a kind or type of the other. The present claim about goodness and healthiness is no stronger than this.

A Primer on Being Healthy

First, some background about the property of healthiness. Note that whereas we may talk metaphorically of a "healthy economy," healthiness itself is a property of living things; it makes no sense to say of something that is dead or inanimate that it is healthy. Healthiness is a property primarily instantiated by tissues, organs, and organisms. ("Healthy food" and "healthy blood pressure" are addressed in chapter 3.) Being alive can be placed at one end of a spectrum with being inanimate at the other end, and in the middle of the spectrum we find coral and viruses that are neither clearly alive nor clearly inanimate. But being alive can also be contrasted to being dead and in between these we find various levels of healthiness. As Christopher Boorse (1977, p. 547) says, "The most extreme disability, death itself, one judges to be some sort of analytical opposite of health." The modern analysis of health most often proceeds in terms of proper function (Boorse, 1977; Macklin, 1972).[2] There is some in-house debate about how to fix the standard of "properness" in regard to functioning in specifying how well a function must perform in order to be healthy. Some have thought that the absence of disease should determine what counts as healthy, though it seems that one's heath might fail because of an unhealthy condition that preceded the failure. Others have placed the bar higher and said health is fixed by what is statistically normal. The problem here is twofold. First, there are some health problems, like tooth decay, which has a higher frequency than "normal" but is nonetheless not healthy. Second, there is no room for a positive conception of health. We

2. The literature on the theoretical standing and nature of proper function divides basically into four areas: cybernetic, etiological, propensity, and learning theories. For cybernetic views, see, A. Rosenblueth et. al. "Behavior, Purpose, and Teleology", *Philosophy of Science* vol. 10, no. 1, pp. 18–24; E. Nagel, *The Structure of Science* (New York: Harcourt, Brace, and World) 1961; R. Braithwaite, *Scientific Explanation* (Cambridge: Cambridge University Press) 1953; G. Sommerhoff, *Analytic Biology* (London: Oxford University Press) 1950; W. Ashby, *Design for a Brain* (2nd. edition, New York: Chapman & Hall) 1960; M. Beckner *The Biological Way of Thought* (New York: Columbia University Press) 1959, pp. 132–58; R. Taylor, *The Explanation of Behavior* (London: Routledge and Kegan Paul) 1964; and the early work on this topic by J. Bennett, *Linguistic Behavior* (Cambridge: Cambridge University Press) 1976. The best exposition of the view is Bennett's.

Etiology and propensity theories are most common today. See L. Wright's, "Functions", *The Philosophical Review*, 1973, 82: 139–168, and *Teleological Explanations* (Berkeley: University of California Press) 1976; C. Boorse, "Wright on Functions" *Philosophical Review*, 1976, 85: 70–86; R. Millikan, *Language, Thought, and Other Biological Categories* (Cambridge: MIT Press) 1984; K. Neander, "The Teleological Notion of 'Function'," *Australasian Journal of Philosophy* 1991, vol. 69 no. 4: 454–468; P. Godfrey-Smith, "A Modern History Theory of Functions", *Nous*, 1984, vol. 28, no. 3: 344–362. J. Bigelow and R. Pargetter, "Functions", *The Journal of Philosophy* 1987, vol. 84 no. 4: 181–196.

For learning theories, which I personally find most promising, though they remain the least explored, see C. A. Mace, "Mechanical and Teleological Causation", reprinted in H. Fiegl and W. Sellers (eds.) *Readings in Philosophical Analysis* 1949 (New York: Appleton, Century, and Crofts) 1949, pp. 534–539. I. Scheffler's thoughts on learning models of function are guarded, but see his "Thoughts on Teleology", *The British Journal of the Philosophy of Science* 1959; vol. 9, no. 59, pp. 265–284. B. Enç and F. Adams, "Functions and Goal Directedness" *Philosophy of Science*, 59 (1992), pp. 635–54. See also Wimsatt, (1972).

For an analysis of the taxonomy, see D. Walsh and A. Ariew, "A Taxonomy of Functions", *Canadian Journal of Philosophy* vol. 26 no. 4 (Dec. 1996) 493–514.

think that Olympic athletes are healthier than the statistical norm, and our account of health should reflect this fact. The standard for what counts as "healthy" is not fixed by the norm but by some notion of the best possible or most efficient level of functioning. Thus, the norm's relationship to the ideal is contingent. We understand how healthy we are by reference to how healthy we could be.

Understanding this thought implies some use of the notion of a final end or purpose, though presumably there is no need to think that this entails a theistic or supernatural influence (see Ariew, forthcoming). A heart has design specifications set for it by the size of a creature and the principles of hydrodynamics that govern flow rates, turbulence, and so on. Hearts also are *for* something; they have purposes.[3] For example, hearts pump blood for the sake of exchanging oxygen for carbon dioxide. Given that hearts must accomplish this task within those specifications, they will only be able to work within a certain degree of efficiency. (There are no perfectly efficient or perpetual motion machines; see the appendix.) Given what a heart has got to do and the circumstances in which it must do it, it can only do so well. There is an upper limit to how healthy a heart can be. There is also a lower limit, presumably attached to survival. Biological functions are understood as contributions to fitness, where fitness is understood as success at surviving. So, for the minimal standard of health, we can say that if a function is operating in a manner that endangers survival, then it is not healthy. Regardless of whether or not "survival of the fittest" is a tautology (as some suspect), survival (or the difference between life and death) establishes a constraint or a standard fit for realism that is crucial to the empirical science of biology.[4]

3. Although, of course, open to debate, I believe that none of the above-mentioned theories of function has succeeded in analyzing function fully without recourse to purposes. Wimsatt (1972) provides an ingenious example to show why the cybernetic view requires purposes (pp. 21–22). If one holds an etiological view, Enç and Adams (1992) have persuasively argued that purposes must be included here as well. If one holds a propensity view, then the purposes will be understood, eventually, in terms of an increased probability of survival and procreation. Learning theories come with purposes obviously packed in. There are also reasons, which will come up in chapter 3, to think that without including purposes in the analysis of function statements, one will not have the resources to fully explain ascriptions of malfunction.

4. For a denial of this, or something close to it, see Hare's (1952, sect. 6.2) discussion of what counts as a "good cactus," where he thinks that at some level we can simply decide what we like.

Though much of our understanding of health is tied to proper function, there is no reason to think that healthiness is a functional property, at least insofar as we would want to say that a heart's pumping is a functional property of hearts. We would no more want to say that healthiness is a functional property than we would say that unhealthiness or sickness is a functional property. Healthiness is a property of a functional property: biological functions can be more or less healthy. At the bottom, at the least healthy end of healthiness, they cannot endanger survival; at the high end, we are concerned with peak performance. Perhaps more details about the nature of health per se are not required now, especially since much more will come out as the dialectic develops. For now, we can say that health is understood in terms of proper function, where "proper" is understood to be a certain level or capacity of possible functioning as measured against biological standards.[5]

From this perspective, what needs to be stressed is that no properties are more deserving of realism than those of being alive and being dead, and since the difference between them is one of healthiness, we cannot be other than realists about health without also denying that life differs from death. Health gives us as much realism as anyone could ever ask for. Even the most hard-boiled empiricist could not point to anything that would be a clearer case of something about which we ought to be realists, on pain of denying death and our mortality. Certainly, to demand more

---

5. There are, of course, many senses of the term "function." Here I use what I take to be the colloquial usage. So, this is not, for example, the same sort of "proper function" primarily discussed in the work of Millikan (1984). There is another sense of "functional property" in which healthiness is a functional property, and that is the sense in which it can be specified by the Ramsey-Carnap-Lewis method: "healthiness" plays a role in a (biological) theory. This is a role that can be said to (i) be engaged in the presence of some specific conditions, (ii) has (internal) causal-theoretic relations to other (biological) properties, and (iii) is part of why certain outcomes are predicted by the theory. We should not conflate, however, the mathematical sense of "function" at play in Ramsey-Carnap-Lewis with the biological sense of "function" at play in everyday talk about what a heart or a carburetor is for. If functionalists in the philosophy of mind are troubled by the theory's lack of a role for phenomenology, it might be because they are thinking of functions mathematically, or in a "black-boxed" sense, as opposed to thinking of them as biological functions, which require purposes or intensions. See Wimsatt (1972) for the distinction between these senses of "function"; see also L. Wright (1973) for more on the explanandum involved in discussions of biological function.

than this from moral realism is to hold it to a higher standard than that for other empirical inquiries like biology.[6]

Healthiness, Conventions, and Relativism

If physical healthiness is going to be a suitable model for moral goodness, then we should find that what we are willing to say about the metaphysics of health is something we would be willing to say about goodness. And the place to start this process is by investigating the aspects of the meta-physics of health that are said to be involved in problems arising for realists regarding goodness. In this way, we can see how problems that moral realists have struggled with in the past can be resolved by attending to what we say about health. Two such problems concern the relations between healthiness and conventionalism and healthiness and relativism.

Beginning with the former, one might think, contrary to what has been said above, that healthiness is not fit for a realist's treatment because humans at different times (or even today, cross-culturally) have had different conceptions of what it is to be healthy. For example, some cultures might think it is healthy to be fat, whereas in the West today we see this as unhealthy. And it does seem most likely that, to some limited degree, what counts as "healthy" may be conventionally driven. "Convention" means here what David Lewis (1969) means by it: that is, (roughly) behavior determined by a coordinated effort between people, such as etiquette. Lewis himself refers back to Hume. Insofar as this is true, these aspects of health are not fit for realism. To draw general conclusions about the nature of health from this is, however (coining a Strawsonianism), a

6. In discussion, I have found some philosophers to be rather obstreperous in their denials of the reality of healthiness. If, failing the discussions above and below, you still think that we should be nonrealists about health, then I ask you, in explicitly ad hominem fashion, to consider the last time you were sick and to ask yourself if the fever or the nausea you were experiencing was not fit for a realist's treatment (barring the possibility that you are a hypochondriac). Failing even reflection on past illness, learn the lesson by going to an intensive care unit at a local hospital and observe those who are truly and direfully sick; watch the news for pictures of children with bellies bloated from malnutrition, or remember a loved one who has died of an illness. Read Camus's *The Plague*, which although fiction, paints a picture of disease that is horrifyingly realistic. Though, as will be noted, there are surely some conventional elements to our concept of *health*, it is absurd to say that we should be non-, anti-, quasi-, or irrealists about health.

non sequitur of numbing grossness. For there are certainly some constraints on what counts as healthy that are not conventional at all. Whereas other cultures may think that it is healthy to be fatter than we think is healthy in the West, certainly being so fat that one's heart cannot sustain the needs of the body and thereby fails must be thought of as being unhealthy, regardless of the culture. Metastatic cancer is unhealthy for a human, *tout court*. If one's lungs are 90% destroyed by smoking cigarettes, so that one is out of breath at the top of one flight of stairs, we may conclude that one's cardiovascular system is unhealthy. In general, it must be acknowledged that a healthy body is as it is so that we may do things (like survive and procreate), and if, because of maltreatment or disease, our bodies cannot function well enough to accomplish these purposes, then we must conclude that some ill health is present. Note that this leaves plenty of room for conventional difference, but it does not entail that health is something to be understood in a completely conventional manner.

To put this point in a slightly different way, health (as mentioned) is commonly understood in terms of functions, where a function is (very roughly) a behavior that gets a particular job done. Note, however, that there are many ways to skin a cat; for any particular goal, there are many ways to accomplish it, and there may not be anything to make one option preferable to another, both may be equally efficient. These are cases in which we speak of "functional equivalence." Concepts of *health* may vary from one culture to another and be functionally equivalent. If they are not functionally equivalent, what differentiates them is not merely conventional: these would be differences that express themselves as variations in fitness and mortality rates in those cultures. Merely conventional differences in health have no functional effect; if there are functional differences, then we do not want to say that what causes them is merely conventional.

To put the point in a third way, we may say that concepts of health that differ only conventionally are ones that establish the same standard of health. "Standard" means here what John Mackie (1977) means by a "standard of evaluation." Some standards of evaluation are purely conventional, such as the standards of "good table manners" or those involved in the judging of a dog show. On the other hand (contra Brandom), validity is a standard of evaluating arguments that is not conventional in the least: if the logical form of an argument necessarily preserves truth from premises to conclusion, then the argument meets the standard of validity. The standards of evaluating health are nonconventional insofar as they measure real differences in fitness, and they are conventional insofar as they are functionally equivalent. The realistic standards of health determine what may be called "border constraints" on what can count as healthiness, but these constraints allow for cultural variability.

So, the reality of health is consistent with there being some conventional (nonrealistic) differences in what is considered a healthy person. Underlying these differences are standards of health that can only be accounted for by realism. But we must not assume that these standards are some sort of absolute standard. And here we find health's compossiblity with relativism. It is of the first importance to realize this, as ignoring the consistency of realism and relativism has often been the cause of confusion in the metaphysics of morality (Mackie, 1977; Harman, 1985; Horgan and Timmons, 1996a) and in normative moral theory, too, insofar as relativism is often taken to imply "cultural relativism," which always implies nonrealism. Of course, some forms of relativism may be nonrealistic; the most famous of these is captured by Protagoras's formula: man is the measure of all things. Mistakenly, however, relativism is often taken, perhaps even conceptually, to be contrary to objectivity or even realism in general. In fact, relativism is strictly contrary only to absolutism, and absolutism is a moral dead end. (Kant's absolutism will be treated a number of times in what is to come, but not here.) There are no absolute moral rules; all prescriptions have a delimited scope of application, even though in a formal sense they are "universalizable" (more on universalizability later in this chapter and also in chapter 3). It is, however, ludicrous to think that moral realism dies along with moral absolutism. In morality, as in general, *realism does not entail absolutism*. Relativism, as it is being understood here, obtains when there is no single fixed standard, no absolute against which all cases (in a particular discourse) are (or ought to be) judged. Relativism obtains when the appropriate standard by which one is to judge a specific case is one that is relative (relational) to a specific set of cases (in a discourse) that are all importantly similar, such that if another case is importantly dissimilar, then a different standard is needed. This does not imply that the standards that are needed to discriminate between such cases need to be conventional or are up to us or are a matter of invention or anything smacking of subjectivity. It becomes quite obvious why realism (about a subject matter) does not entail absolutism as soon as we take the blinders off metaethical debate and look beyond metaethics. We find that, in general, realism neither excludes relativity nor entails it, and vice versa. Realism is consistent with relativism, and in the case of health, we find them both.

This may perhaps be best seen by first considering the status of relativity as it is found outside of health, beginning with the "hard" sciences—physics, particularly length and time—in light of special relativity. If we assume that Einstein ([1947] 1961) is correct, there is no absolute frame of reference against which length or time can be measured or understood; instead, these are always relativized to particular inertial frames of reference. We do not conclude from this, however, that length or time are unreal: relativity theory is consistent with the facts that we diachronically grow physically into adults, during which our length, or height, changes. We grow older through time; our memories are of times gone by. According to Einstein, time goes; it just does not go at a fixed rate. And there is nothing more real. Examples from other sciences abound. Another example from physics concerns entropy, which also displays this sort of relativity to a chosen "level of description." Take "Gibbs's paradox": if we treat both ortho- and parahydrogen as simply hydrogen, then mixing these gases yields an entropy of zero. If, on the other hand, we discriminate between them, based on the different alignments of their nuclear spins, mixing the same two volumes yields an entropy that is nonzero. We are not tempted by this, however, to conclude that there is something non-objective or subjective about entropy. To quote Lawrence Sklar (1993, p. 346) on entropy and Gibbs's paradox: "For a property to be relational [or relative] is one thing, for it to be 'subjective' (in any of the multitude of meanings of that notoriously ambiguous word) is quite another matter." William Wimsatt (1972) has shown that biological functions are relativized in a variety of ways: the behavior of swallowing in humans has one function in the digestive system and another in the system that regulates air pressure in the aural canals (relativity to system); but swallowing in another species may not have both these functions (relativity to species). The air bladder in a lungfish functions as a rate-of-climb indicator when the fish is in an environment of water, but it functions as a lung, exchanging O_2 for CO_2 when the fish is trapped in mud during a drought (relativity to environment). In engineering, the standard of "structural integrity" is relative to different levels of analysis, so that a house of cards may lack it but each card individually may have it. In none of these cases does the relativity cited interfere with the appropriateness of realism.[7]

7. For general metaphysical relations between realism and relativism, see Lynch (1998).

The relativized character of health works at the species-wide level and at the level of sex and of age, as well as at the individual level. (Boorse, 1977, recognizes many of these.) At the level of species, what counts as a healthy plant will be very different from what counts as a healthy *Homo sapiens*. It will be impossible to set out necessary and sufficient conditions for what counts as health that must be met by every healthy organ or organism. There is no single standard against which to measure how well all organs or organisms are functioning. Absolutism about health is a non-starter. At the level of sex, within any single species, what counts in being a healthy female will be different from what counts in being a healthy male. And the standards for being a healthy 10-year-old girl will be different from those for a healthy 60-year-old woman. On the individual level, having low blood pressure is healthy for most athletes but is not healthy for people who are quite small (who weigh, say, less than 100 pounds) or for those with a tendency toward anemia. On average, the normal temperature of a healthy adult human is 98.6 degrees Fahrenheit, but in reality it varies from person to person. The same may be said of blood pressure and pulse rate. Being in "good shape" will amount to very different things for people of different sizes, weights, and proportions. Moreover, each of us can be in better or worse health than we presently are, but there is no reason to assume that being at the pinnacle of health will give each of us some absolute set of identical morphophysiological characteristics. Each living organism is unique in its physical makeup, and thus perfect health will amount to something different for each individual organism. Health is relative in myriad ways, but this does not interfere in the least with the reality of its nature.

Given how deeply pervasive the mistake is regarding the consistency of realism and relativism, it is worth driving the thought home by making it clear in one subfield of "the health sciences," namely, nutrition. Good nutrition for a living creature is highly relativized but as "factual" as can be. Proper nutrition for a plant is vastly different than for an animal. Of course, the same is said for different species. But it is important to note that good nutrition is relativized all the way down to the individual, and even to a particular time in that individual's life or development. The healthiest diet for me need not be the healthiest diet for you, and what was healthy for me to eat as a babe would be a poor diet for me as an adult. None of this inveighs against realism about proper nutrition in the least. As a general statement about metaphysics, it must be emphasized once again: *realism is perfectly consistent with relativity*. In particular, a proper account of the ontology of health will require adverting to both relativity and conventionalism.

In the end, despite any possible conventional or necessarily relative aspects in the standards of health, there are realistic constraints on which standards apply to which cases, realistic constraints on what can count as a healthy tissue, organ, or organism. It is these constraints or standards that form the foundation of the realist's treatment of healthiness, so that no one can be a nonrealist about health in any way that matters. To think otherwise is to be committed to denying that being healthy differs from being sick, that life differs from death. And if one can be as much a realist about morality as about health, this is as much realism as anyone could need, want, or ask for.

Healthiness and Goodness

Remember our first riddle: what sort of property is unobservable and may not be needed for causal explanations? The riddle is solved by conceptually locating a property, physical healthiness, whose realism is beyond reproach yet is not directly observable or a necessary part of what is needed to explain what is directly observable. It is important that the details of the ontology of this type of property are not of the last consequence because of our preexisting commitments to the reality of life, health, death, and entropy; what is important, at the moment, is that goodness is similar to healthiness in these respects (though more will be said about the details of the ontology throughout this chapter and more again in the appendix). Another similarity between goodness and health, which perhaps needs no further discussion than that in the introduction, is that we can be in denial or can be incapable of being made to see (or just plain in deluded error) about how unhealthy we are, just as we can be in denial about our moral problems. We no more like to look at our physical weaknesses than we do at our moral weaknesses.

Beyond these claims, however, let us see how health can serve as a model for understanding how the reality of moral goodness is related to conventions and relativism. The irony is not to be missed: the very reasons that others have given for rejecting moral realism, namely, by pointing to either conventionalized or relativized aspects of morality, turn out to be reasons or arguments for accepting moral realism: these are the very clues by which we can spot how similar goodness is to our very model of realism, namely healthiness.

Starting with relativism, we noted that healthiness is a property that is relativized to both species and individuals. Moral goodness shares this same relativization. Holding off on Kant for one more paragraph, we see that there is no substantial absolutism in morality either at the universal level (that may apply to all possible species) or at the level of our own species (that may apply to all individual *Homo sapiens*). At the level of species, we cannot assume that moral practices that are good for *Homo sapiens* will be good for every sentient form of life. A quick flight of imagination ought to allow anyone to envisage another possible species for whom a good life is radically different from our own. For example, in most cases we think it bad for parents to encourage or even allow sibling rivalry; competition between family members is (again, in most cases) a bad thing. But in another possible sentient species (jumping to a thought experiment), in which birth occurs to a large number of offspring at once, all of whom cannot survive, competition among siblings will be unavoidable, and the selection process from among them may be morally understandable and acceptable. Thus, keeping proper nutrition in mind, we must relativize goodness to species. At the level of individuals, we should not assume that what one individual ought to do in a particular situation is what every individual ought to do in that situation. People are different from one another, and what is good for me in some set of Φ conditions may not be good for you in similarly describable Φ conditions; people have different talents, capabilities, responsibilities, and characters. In a situation in which dangerous action is called for, it is not necessarily the case that everyone present is equally obligated to do what needs to be done: it might be the particular responsibility of one person to engage the danger, or one might be particularly skilled in some similar sort of situation and would be more obligated to become involved just by dint of having an increased chance of success. If I observe a crime, what I ought to do (what my obligations are) will depend both on my relations with the victim (presumably I may be obliged to risk my life to save a close family relation, whereas it is supererogatory to risk my life for the sake of a stranger) and on any possible relations I may have with the perpetrators (whether I am one of their parents, another of their friends, a police officer, etc.).

Noting this sort of relativization might be seen as noting the relational character of being good. But there is also a second way in which morality is relativized that is contrary to what has commonly been called "moral absolutism." We can define this way as thinking that there are substantive moral rules that apply universally; the formalization of such rules includes a quantifier that ranges over all moral creatures. Contra Kant, absolutism about morality is bankrupt. For any given moral rule, we can cook up some sort of situation in which the rule ought to be broken. What ought to be done in any given situation depends crucially on who is involved and exactly what the relevant nonmoral facts of the case are. This can be seen most clearly when working within applied ethics, for example, medical ethics, where the smallest difference in a case history or family situation might radically alter the proper program of treatment. The Kantian instinct will be to disagree, at least insofar as the categorical imperative is categorical or applicable to all moral creatures, perhaps in virtue of their shared, bare rationality. The appropriate reply comes from within Kantian doctrine itself: the categorical imperative, insofar as it is of practical use, is itself only a standard or test for the moral adequacy of particular maxims, which are themselves relativized to the agent's particular circumstances. And if this point still leaves Kantians dissatisfied, they must admit that determining the scope of a prescription, saying to which situations it applies and to which it does not (based on universalizability) has been perhaps the largest of traditional problems for Kantian deontology. (There will be much more on this problem chapter 3.)

So, goodness is relativized, as we find in healthiness, insofar as (1) what either a good life or a healthy life for an individual will be like will depend on both the species to which the individual belongs and the facts about that individual, and (2) there is no universal prescription for being good or healthy. (Just as there are no universal or absolute rules for nutrition.) Far from goodness's relativity being an argument in favor of moral nonrealism, we instead find that goodness's relativity makes it amenable to being modeled on the realistic ontology of healthiness.

Moreover, goodness, like health, also allows for some flexibility in conventional or cultural differences. It is important that a moral realist need not hold that all of morality is deserving of realism, only that some (presumably nontrivial) aspects of morality must be understood in that way. Some examples of this flexibility in the face of conventional differences should suffice. Demonstrating respect properly is surely a matter of moral import, and it is an anthropological fact (if there are any of these at all) that different cultures show respect differently. In some cultures, apologizing to someone for an unintentionally insulting comment demonstrates respect for that person. In other cultures, such an apology, or any other further acknowledgment of the insult, only makes the insult worse. But this is consistent with there being "border constraints" on how respect can be shown: killing someone for the fun of it, or on a whim, will not show respect for that person in any culture, and the same can be said for any instance of rape. Without engaging the daunting literature on "thick and thin" concepts, sexually violating someone against the victim's will is always disrespectful to the victim.[8] In an example concerning the virtues, the existence of some variability in the standards by which different cultures judge acts as courageous is consistent with there being some acts that are obviously either courageous or cowardly: in the modern West, we might well disagree with the ancient Greeks or the Japanese samurai when discussing the courageousness of ritual suicide after being disgraced, as we find in the case of the elder Ajax or in any example of hara-kiri. Nevertheless, it will still be agreed all around that deserting friends and comrades in the midst of battle because of fear is cowardly. Just as there are constraints that serve as the foundations for a realist's understanding of health, there will be moral constraints that serve as the foundation for moral realism, and again these "border constraints" are consistent with the existence of some conventional differences or cultural variability. Once again, the compossibility of these conventional differences, in structurally isomorphic ways, with both healthiness and goodness are reasons to accept the proposed moral ontology. (If health did contain cultural variability and a relativistic character, whereas goodness lacked them, we would have reason to doubt the ontology.) All of morality need not be fit for realism for moral realism to carry the day.

So moral realism well accommodates both aspects of a limited cultural variability, as well as properly understood aspects of relativism. And indeed, if moral realism were not capable of respecting at least some of the reasons that people have given for being nonrealists about morality, one would have to think twice about it. Thinking about health pilots us through these metaphysical shoals. And the success here warrants further

---

8. Perhaps I cannot completely avoid the question of thick and thin moral concepts, especially since in the preceding paragraph I argue that there are no absolute moral rules, whereas in this paragraph I say something that seems to entail the moral rule "never rape anyone." But we can, in the extreme, doctor up a situation in which a rape ought to occur to keep some hugely more widespread disaster from occurring. The status of this kind of consequentialist thinking in such extreme situations is itself a complicated issue. For the moment, it is enough to say that even in that improbable situation, in which one person ought to rape another, the rapist does not escape without dirty hands or without damaging the quality of life of everyone who is directly involved. For more on the moral phenomenon of "dirty hands," see Stocker (1990).

exploration. If the ontology of goodness can be understood by looking at healthiness, then we should expect certain results to obtain. The first, and perhaps most important, is that the epistemology of goodness could be modeled on the epistemology of healthiness. We can look at the empirical ways in which we learn about health and use them to help us understand how we learn about goodness. Establishing the framework of this rather large task is the subject of chapter 2, but here we may note that following this program places the subject matter of normative ethics in the same empirical category as the subject matter of medicine, physical training, and nutrition. These are all normative enterprises, insofar as each entails that there are behaviors that one ought to engage in and others that one ought to avoid in order to obtain a certain goal given by nature. Since, given the proposed ontology, morality can be grouped with these other empirical discourses, this affords us the same level of confidence in the reality of goodness that we have in the reality of these other respectable, empirical discourses; this is to say that we can be as confident in the reality of morality as we are in the reality of other empirical sciences. There is one further related and important point of similarity between goodness and healthiness that deserves emphasis now, though further discussion is put off until chapters 3 and 4: they are both normative. Both entail purposes that are given to us in virtue of being the kinds of creatures we are and establish standards by which we may evaluate what we ought to do. Knowledge of both goodness and healthiness is practical knowledge insofar as we ought to do what will make us good and healthy.

We are about to embark on an exploration of whether or not healthiness and goodness, as properties, are reducible to some set of lower level properties. This is philosophically interesting, though technical, work. It may be skipped by those readers not concerned with ontological detail without damaging the flow of the general argument. And it may be skipped because moral realism, as defended here, is importantly neutral about these specific questions of reduction. If moral goodness and physical healthiness are ontologically of the same type, then questions of reduction become moot in the debate about moral realism. The reality of our being living creatures is safely assumed. If biology reduces to physics, and thermodynamics reduces to statistical mechanics, we cannot thereby conclude that it is proper to forego realism with regard to life. Reduction or no reduction, we cannot deny the reality of the difference between life and death or the reality of our own mortal, biological existence. Placing goodness in this company gives it the same status. Whether or not moral realism will be vindicated by this proposed ontology will not be determined by figuring out if it reduces or not but by how well all of the theoretical pieces fit together, fulfills our expectations, and resolves traditional problems. The proof will be in the pudding.

Supervenience and Reduction

Since the proposed moral ontology is neutral on the question of reduction, as mentioned above, the exact status of moral realism per se now takes a back seat to a more technical discussion of the exact status of healthiness and goodness. Those not interested in metaphysical detail might want to proceed to chapter 2, but leaving these issues completely unaddressed would be unsatisfactory to an analytic temperament. In particular, there is the question of the relation of these properties to ontologically more fundamental, or lower level, properties. It is generally said that if higher level properties, such as healthiness, do exist, then they supervene on these lower level, or more fundamental, properties. In particular, we are concerned with the thought that there is "nothing more to" healthiness (or goodness) than these lower level properties, in which case the higher level properties ontologically reduce to the lower level ones. To get an intuitive grasp of the issue at hand, consider the relation between a mind and a brain. Are they identical to each other, or are mental and neurophysiological properties distinct? Perhaps when we know more about how the brain works, we will see that there is nothing more to the mind than the brain. Perhaps we will find that there is something about the mind that cannot be explained by a description of the events in the brain, perhaps not. Is the whole greater than the sum of its parts (in which case the mind does not reduce to the brain) or is it equal to the sum of its parts (in which case it does reduce)? We may ask the same sorts of questions about healthiness (and goodness): perhaps health is something that can be fully explained by a description of events in the body, perhaps not. For instance, perhaps they require history or purposes to be explained, perhaps not. Healthiness and (thereby) goodness may or may not reduce. It is not supposed that these concerns about moral properties will be settled with finality here, though some progress will be made. I hope, however, that it will become apparent that even at these more abstruse levels of ontological inquiry, goodness zigs where healthiness zigs, and zags where it zags. This should lend further support to the idea that this is no accident: moral goodness merits the same ontic status as physical health.

A metaphysician cannot go far today without encountering the topic of supervenience, especially as it relates to questions of reduction. If there is a problem with any of this discussion, it is that "supervenience" has become understood in so many different ways that it lately seems as if the word is used at least a little idiosyncratically every time it is uttered by a different philosopher. There are strong forms and weak forms and global forms, and the modalities become swiftly complex. "Supervenience," as a term of art, was first used by G. E. Moore in 1902 (1988), to help make sense of his nonnatural realism, though Richard Hare (1952, sec. 5.3; 1963) picked up on it fairly early on and ran with it as a naturalistic nonrealist in the middle of the century. More modern Cornell realists appeal to it as a part of their variety of realism, as do their cousins, the "moral functionalists," like Frank Jackson (1998). Quasi realists or projectivists, like Simon Blackburn (1993), see it as posing a strong threat to forms of realism stronger than their own (and this supposed threat is the subject of the final section of this chapter). It is worth pointing out that the same sort of situation has occurred with the use of supervenience in the philosophy of mind: it plays on many different teams.

As roughly and quickly as is practical, one can understand supervenience as a relation between two levels of properties, a lower "subvenient" level of property and an upper supervenient level. The crux of the issue is the nature of this relation. The relation can be either stronger or weaker. At its weakest, the relation seems to have a bottom-up structure: the subvenient level determines the supervenient level insofar as changes at the supervenient level require changes at the subvenient level. Even given this weak strength, it can be seen that supervenience allows the upper-level properties to be "multiply realizable": the very same upper-level property can supervene on a variety of kinds (or sets) of lower level properties. Given this weak supervenience, changing a lower level property does not necessarily change a higher level property; but (as noted) one cannot change a higher level property without changing something at the lower level. This shows an asymmetry within this weak relation. We can strengthen the relation by eliminating the asymmetry: not only does changing a supervenient property require changing a subvenient property, but we may add that changing a subvenient property requires changing a supervenient property. Given this increase of strength, so that changing something at either level requires changing something at the other, one can begin so see that if we strengthen the relationship enough, it becomes doubtful whether or not these really are two levels of properties or, in fact, just one. Perhaps we have two different sets of terms for a single property. If we do, then we have "reduced" the contents of our ontology from two sets of properties to one. The strongest form of supervenience relation is a reductive one. Most likely, we will all agree that the health of a person will supervene somehow on how well that person's body is functioning; what we want to know is whether healthiness (and thereby goodness) reduces or if it is a genuine property in its own right.

Now, healthiness is a biological property, as is the property of being alive. Ideally, at this point, we could advert to the clearly shared opinion of philosophers of biology about whether or not biological properties reduce to chemical and more fundamental physical properties. Unfortunately, there is no consensus. And there has been a long and large debate about whether or not biological properties, such as being alive, are properties that reduce. At least one very austere ontologist, Peter Van Inwagen (1990), does not countenance the existence of normally accepted physical objects like rivers and mountains because he thinks they reduce to their components (they lack a "principle of compositionality"), but he thinks living objects do not similarly reduce. Some philosophers of biology are happy with the "autonomy" of biology (Ayla, 1976), but they are in the minority. (For an excellent discussion, see Grene, 1976.) It seems that most biologists (not themselves philosophers) are anxious for the reduction to go through, on pain of having to admit some scientifically non-respectable solution to what makes biology resist reduction—some substance like élan vitale or even nonmaterial souls. There is, however, some reason for the biologist to relax here because biological systems, living things, are a subset of physical systems, which are a subject of physics proper. The subfield of physics called "thermodynamics" describes the behavior of all physical systems, biological systems included. And "entropy" is the name of a property of all physical systems, where entropy is a measure of disorganization or disintegration or lack of structure.

Healthiness and entropy are at least ontological peas in a pod, if they are not even more closely related. Both concern structure or organization (required for proper function) and lack of structure or disorganization (resulting in illness and death). A full argument here would be out of place, but if we interpret entropy as it is found in information theory, then entropy is the level of noise in the signal-to-noise ratio and the signal is the level of information. When considering biological systems as a subset of physical systems, we can interpret the certainty of our mortality as the eventual breakdown of the physical systems that keep us alive: entropy increases. For the sake of brevity, let us work quickly through the analogy: the degree to which one is healthy is the amount of signal, while the degree of unhealthiness is the amount of noise. With regards to biological systems, healthiness and entropy are related as signal to noise. The status of entropy and its relations with health are the subject of the appendix, wherein an argument is given to the effect that thermodynamics does not reduce to statistical mechanics; the asymmetry of thermodynamics's second law cannot be reduced to the symmetrical laws of mechanics plus statistics (even including initial conditions). If the argument of the appendix works, then there is reason to think that entropy is a nonreducible but fully physical property. And if the reasons for thinking that health and entropy have the same ontological status are good reasons, then it would follow that health does not reduce either. The same conclusion, therefore, would hold for goodness.

The ontological worries that have plagued moral realists are not unrelated to ontological worries of biologists and physicists. If we accept the existence of moral properties, like goodness, that are not directly observable (a feature, by the way, that goodness shares with entropy), then we want to have some account of the ontology. This has proved a difficult task for moral realists. The difficulty, however, is not special to metaethics. The problems of how to explain the ontology of properties that are fundamental to a discourse but resistant to a reduction to the mere movements of particles are problems that are found in both biology and physics (thermodynamics). We do not infer from the existence of these problems, however, that there is some reason to be doubtful of those biological or physical properties. So, again, it would be wrong to hold moral realists to a higher standard. Entropy, healthiness, and goodness, properties invisible, one and all, stand or fall together.

So, returning now to the topic of supervenience, we have seen that the supervenience relation, which holds between healthiness and some lower level biochemical properties, may well not be strong enough to provide a reduction of one to the other. And the same may be said for goodness. The question remains of how strong a supervenience relationship holds here. We wish to say that the biochemical properties determine or necessitate how healthy something is, but this leaves open the nature of this necessitation. Perhaps it is causal; perhaps it is something stronger than this, such as the way in which causes necessarily precede their effects.

The nature of the modality here is no more, but certainly no less, mysterious than the modality involved in the relationship between a living plant's doing well or thriving and its getting enough sunshine or energy. One might say that this is merely a causal necessity, insofar as sunshine plays a causal role in photosynthesis, and indeed this may be so. But the relationship between energy and being alive might be "tighter" than a mere causal necessity. There might be justification to say that there is a sense in which energy is essential to a plant, in a way deeper than it might be said that sunlight causes plant life. Energy is converted into life; there might even be a sense in which one may say that energy (at least partly) constitutes life or is essential to life (in the same way that Kripke, 1972, argues that an object's origins are essential to it). If so, then there is reason to think that the modality involved in the way health supervenes is metaphysical. This would be the case if the necessity involved between energy and life had the same force or modality that comes when we say that origins are essential to identity or that causes necessarily precede their effects. Admittedly, the intuitions here are sublime, if not downright obscure. Deciding if this is a causal or a metaphysical necessity is going to be difficult.[9]

It seems easy to say something about the supervenience of health, for we know that at least a weak form of suprvenience obtains here: changing the healthiness of an organ or organism would require changing something at a lower level of organization, but not every change at the lower level (the displacement of a molecule or two) produces a change in health. Health is multiply realizable. In the end, however, there is no literature on the status of the supervenience relationship in health as there is in the supervenience of moral properties, so perhaps a shift of gears is in order. To get a handle on the nature of the supervenience relationship that obtains when moral properties are instantiated, it will probably be most

9. Jackson (1998) has suggested that the modality here is logical or conceptual. To see why this is not the case, using the lingo of the Chalmers-Jackson view of "two-dimensional modality," we may note that the primary or A intensions of "life" are not going to be necessarily linked to what constitutes life at the actual world. (See also Chalmers, 1996.) Yes, there is an overlap between the properties that map the primary-A intensions ("watery stuff") onto the secondary-C intensions ("H_2O") at the actual world; but primary-A intensions can map onto a different set of secondary-C intensions ("XYZ") at other possible worlds. Such would be the case were we to say that "there is a sense in which it may be possible for there to be life without energy." This is the same as saying that "there is a sense in which it may be possible for there to be water without H_2O," and neither of these is a logical contradiction. (They both may be contrasted with "there is a sense in which it may be possible for there to be a square circle.") The possibilities of life without energy or water without H_2O exist, but they give us no insight whatsoever into the actual nature of life or water; they give us no insight into the nature of our actual reality and are therefore of no use to (serious) metaphysicians.

helpful to turn to some of the extant and (for some) familiar literature on the topic. This is especially so since there is a well-known challenge to moral realists by Simon Blackburn (1993, chap. 7), which comes within a discussion of supervenience. Responding to this challenge will help further support the thesis at hand, as well as help to situate the present position among competitors.

Blackburn's Challenge to Moral Realism via Supervenience

Supervenience is most often taken to be a useful tool for the realist. For example, in the philosophy of mind, it allows one to be both a good scientifically minded materialist and a believer in the reality of mental properties, in a manner that is somewhat neutral with respect to exactly how the brain and the mind are actually related. Supervenience is taken to be compatible with both reductivist and nonreductivist programs and incompatible with eliminativism or other forms of nonrealism about the mind. The situation is somewhat different in moral philosophy: as mentioned, Hare (1956, 1963) picked up on the usefulness of the notion of supervenience early on (no realist he) as a way of framing the commitments to which (some) nonrealists ascribe. As we'll see, supervenience is also consistent with projectivism, or "quasi realism," though such a position about the mind seems less attractive, as is noted by Blackburn (1993), our leading quasi realist. In his hands, supervenience is taken to place constraints on morality that are inconsistent with realism.

Blackburn establishes the following machinery. In saying that F properties supervene on G properties, we are first saying that a particular F will supervene on some particular set of G properties called "G^*", and in such a case we will say that G^* "underlies" that particular F. The "underlying" relation is represented in (S) as "U." The fact that different sets of G are all capable of underlying F is what makes supervenience consistent with "multiple realizability." Supervenience is formulated thus:

(S) Necessarily $((\exists x)\ (Fx\ \&\ G^*x\ \&\ (G^*xUFx)) \supset (y)\ (G^*y \supset Fy))$

Given the above, (S) reads as follows: "As a matter of necessity, if something x is F and G^* underlies this, then anything else in the physical or natural (or whatever) state G^* is F as well" (Blackburn, 1993, p. 131). If (S) is true, then there are no worlds that are, as Blackburn calls them, "mixed": no single world can be such that some objects in it have G^* and are F while other objects in it that also have G^* are not F. The truth of (S), all by itself, establishes a ban on these "mixed worlds."

(S) does not, however, entail the stronger claim:

(N) Necessarily $(x)(G^*x \supset Fx)$

for the same reason that one cannot infer "Necessarily q" from "Necessarily $(p \supset q)$." This implies that the following formula is consistent with (S):

(P) Possibly $(\exists x)$ $(G^*x$ & $\sim Fx)$

where (P) says that it is possible for something to be G^* and not be F as well; or, there exists a possible world at which things are G^* but fail to be F. In the vernacular: it could have been the case that things were G^* and these very same things may not have been F. Blackburn then suggests that moral nonrealists (in this case projectivists or quasi-realists) can give a better explanation than the realist of two different facts (hence, the challenge mentioned above). The first fact is the ban on mixed worlds. The second is that holding both (S) and (P) together seem to be morally unproblematic, whereas, for reasons we will see, the realist (supposedly) may not ascribe to both.

First, let's look at what Blackburn's projectivist will say, and then we will treat the realist's responses. Blackburn (1993) first argues that the ban on mixed worlds is guaranteed by (S) because subscribing to (S) is part of what is constitutive of moral thinking and moral practice.

> It seems to be a conceptual matter that moral claims supervene upon natural ones. Anyone failing to realise this, or to obey the constraint would indeed lack something constitutive of competence in the moral practice. And there is good reason for this: it would betray the whole purpose for which we moralise, which is to choose, commend, rank, approve, forbid, things on the basis of their natural properties. (p. 137)

That is, it is not the purpose of moral practice to be describing moral properties in the world but merely to chose, commend, rank, and so on some natural but nonmoral properties. When seen in this way, we can note why the (S)/(P) combination is not worrisome to Blackburn. Although there can be no mixed worlds, for this would imply inconsistent moral thought, there is no problem in thinking that our moral practices could have been different than they are. Thus, whereas G^* implies F at our world, there is another possible world at which something is G^* but fails to be F, for at that world they have different moral practices. This seems fairly unproblematic as it stands, but if the realist cannot make proper sense of this sort of moral thinking, the supervenience of the moral on the nonmoral stands as an argument against moral realism.

The realist's response begins by noting how the discussion has been ambiguously cast so far. The realist and nonrealist agree on what counts as the subvenient base of morality, that is, some set of nonmoral properties. (Here, I am lumping quasi-realism in with other form of nonrealism, like Hare's.) But the realist holds that what supervenes are moral properties, like moral goodness, whereas the nonrealist holds that, not properties, but moral commendations, rankings, approvals, and so on are what supervene on nonmoral properties. It is these judgments that must be consistent, that must incorporate (S), in order to even count as being "moral." Thus, the nonrealist takes supervenience to be a constraint on moral thinking, insofar as not thinking in that way removes one from the moral game altogether. So, as a regulative principle of moral thought, supervenience, from the nonrealist's point of view, is closely related, if not identical, to a traditional Kantian understanding of universalizability. According to Hare (1991), universalizability is based on the following fact:

> One cannot with logical consistency, where *a* and *b* are two individuals, say that *a* ought, in a certain situation specified in universal terms without reference to individuals, to act in a certain way, also specified in universal terms, but that *b* ought not to act in a similarly specified way in a similarly specified situation. This is because in any "ought"-statement there is implicitly a principle which says that the statement applies to all precisely similar situations. (p. 456)

Thus, moral judgments or claims, like prescriptions or "ought" statements, supervene on the situations to which they apply: if a situation is *G* and this implies that one ought to *F*, then anytime something is *G* one ought to *F*. There is nothing problematic about this in the least. There is a problem, however, with construing this as some sort of conceptual test for moral competence.

Contra Blackburn (1993), believing that moral practices must incorporate (S) is a substantive lesson learned within normative ethics; the same could be said for universalizability or even the Golden Rule. But not subscribing to (S) does not entail that one does not have a moral theory or is not even in the game. Psychological egoists and many hedonists, out to seek their own pleasure, do not subscribe to (S); presumably, such people would be happy if everyone in the world catered to their whims, but obviously they cannot think everyone else should also think the same with regard to themselves. In general, if one wished to take a eudaimonistic approach to moral theorizing, where it is understood that the point of the theorizing is to lead one to live a good life, then learning that one cannot live a good life without subscribing to (S) is a substantial lesson, even if it is a lesson we often learn as children, that is, as entry-level "beginners." Not everyone learns the lesson, however, and this does not take them out of the game. Think of it this way (though this is a blatant argument by authority), if people who do not subscribe to (S) are not even in the moral game, then why would Plato have taken so much trouble to argue against the likes of Polus, Gorgias, Callicles, and Thrasymachus, where none of them seemed to put much stock in (S) at all. According to them, (S) is for the dupes. In fact, they could assert that they were taught (S) as children and only later "learned" by empirical experience that it is false. (Of course, they would be in error here.) Thrasymachus has a theory of the good and the right, cast in terms of the interest of the stronger, and he then claims that living by what is good and right does not lead to a well-lived life. This is a moral theory, a false moral theory to be sure, but a moral theory all the same. Rejecting (S) does not remove one from the moral game.

There is one historical conception of morality, perhaps first articulated by Hobbes and more recently by those who attempt to build morality out of decision or game theory, in which it may make sense to say that one is "out of the game" by rejecting (S). If one sees morality as something that is imposed on us externally, so that we may be able to get along with one another for the sake of our own "self-interest," then it is easy to see how someone who did not subscribe to (S) is out of the game: thinking in accordance with (S) is what allows us to get along. Thus, (S) is instrumentally necessary to make the game work. It is also easy to see why the (S)/(P) combination is unproblematic, for we could have come up with different (perhaps equally effective) ways of getting along, and thus different sets of "nonmoral properties" would have been either commended or condemned [in accordance with (S)].

But one need not look at morality in this way. If morality, or what is good for us, is something that "arises" out of human nature or is determined by who we are, what kind of creatures we are, then we will look to the nonmoral properties that we have, in virtue of being the kinds of creatures we are, to provide the subvenient base for moral properties. Being good, or what our morality is (or ought to be) sensitive to, in ways characteristic of supervenience, indicates certain aspects of the human condition. (Exactly which aspects these are is the final topic of this chapter.) What supervenes, in this conception of morality, are not moral claims, judgments, evaluations, condemnations, and so on but moral properties. And if our normative moral theory says that living well, for creatures like *Homo sapiens*, means behaving in ways that are characteristic of courage and not cowardice, wisdom and not foolishness, temperance and not gluttony (*pleonexia*), then this is true because we are the kinds of creatures we are and not some other. Thus, we cannot go to some other possible world that has creatures *just like us in all the relevant nonmoral respects* and find them living well there as cowardly, gluttonish fools.[10]

If this is a reasonable story, then the realist also has reasonable stories to tell about how and why (S) holds, as well as why the (S)/(P) combination is unacceptable. First, note that (S) holds twice over for the moral realist. It holds for moral properties on the nonmoral, as being a good or bad person will supervene on the kind of character a person has, in the way just described; call this (S1). But (S) will also hold for the way in which true moral judgments will supervene on moral properties; call this (S2). In the moral case, (S2) is just a special case of all true predication; truth (at least for a variety of discourses, if not all) can be understood in terms of supervenience between propositions and the world. We note, therefore, that (S2) strongly supervenes on (S1): were moral properties to supervene on the nonmoral in a different manner than they actually do [changing (S1)], this would require a change in (S2); for (S2) to be different but still obtain, changes must occur in how moral properties supervene on nonmoral properties (S1). Moral judgments will be true if and only if they represent the moral facts or states of affairs accurately, and they can only do so if they covary with how moral properties are instantiated. Since these instantiations are in accordance with (S1), mak-

---

10. Any relevant nonmoral differences between us and those other possible creatures is what Blackburn (1993) calls a "releasing condition." Concerning Jackson's (1998) position, as mentioned in the preceding note, it may be logically possible for humans to flourish as foolish cowards, for nothing about the laws of logic prevent this. A foolish human coward who is flourishing has the same status as life without energy or water that is not H_2O: although logic permits such possibilities, they are of no use to metaphysicians concerned with the nature of actual reality. To use Chalmers's lingo, once God fixed our human nature, he didn't have to do anything more to determine what it is for creatures like us to morally flourish.

ing true and consistent moral judgments (S2) will be possible only if these judging practices are responsive to (S1). Learning to think in accord with (S2) may come from learning the metaethical lesson (S1), or more likely it is learned as a substantive lesson in normative ethics learned while we are children being taught the Golden Rule. Either way, the moral realist has more than enough of an explanation for why (S) obtains.

We can also see why the (S)/(P) combination is unacceptable for the realist. If it is the case that being morally bad supervenes on having some set of nonmoral traits, then it would be impossible to go to another possible world where a creature was just like us, behaves like a cowardly fool, and yet is morally good. True, we could go to another possible world with creatures just like us who have settled on different moral conventions. They could establish different Hobbesian "traffic rules for self-assertors" (to use a phrase of Baier, 1994), but either those traffic rules are, as a matter of empirical fact, no better or worse, no more effective, than ours for promoting well-lived lives (in which case, we could not say they are behaving in some way they ought not to behave even though they don't do it like us) or one set of traffic rules is in fact better than another one, in which case one world is in moral error but the other isn't. (Or both worlds are not doing it as well as they could and everyone's in moral error.)[11] In any of these cases, however, it is our nature as *Homo sapiens* that fixes the constraints on what counts as good, not our moral practices, which can be only more or less efficacious at helping us to live well. Regardless of our moral practices, living well will supervene on the kind of person one is. And this explains the problem with the (S)/(P) combination, which allows for the possibility of creatures just like us in all the relevant, nonmoral respects to live well or flourish while being very different kinds of people than we need to be in order to flourish (here in the actual world).

This statement does imply that the realist is committed to the proposition Blackburn (1993) lays out as

$$(?) \ N \ ((\exists x) \ (Fx \ \& \ G^*x \ \& \ (G^*xUFx)) \supset N \ (y) \ (G^*y \supset Fy))$$

11. We will be returning to similar issues, disagreement among experts, in chapter 2 and to a problem similar (though different) to the one Blackburn (1993) poses in chapter 3's discussion of Horgan and Timmmons's Moral Twin Earth problem.

which differs from (S) in that the consequent of the conditional has a necessity operator in front of its quantifier.[12] Thus (P), which expresses the possibility that would falsify (?) is itself taken to be false. Assume that being F is here the property of being a morally good person, and G^* is a set of nonmoral properties. To understand how being F supervenes on being G^*, the supervenience relationship (as applied to morality) must be strengthened to disallow the possibility that someone could behave in ways that would make a human good here in the actual world and yet would fail to make a human good in another possible world. The supervenience relationship needed for morality is one in which the subvenient base necessarily determines the supervenient property. Given the kind of people we are, morality could not possibly be different (within the limits of functional equivalence, as discussed above in regard to conventionalism).

One final issue has not been addressed: what kind of nonmoral property is it that moral properties supervene on? This is actually a very complicated issue, for the answers come from many different perspectives. Normative ethical theory should give us some description of these properties, whether they are properties of an agent's behavior or properties of one's character. (Moral properties are predicated of both agents and acts; how this works, at least from a semantic level, is taken up in some detail in chapter 3.) It is an open question of whether these are to include so-called "thick" moral concepts, like *courage* and *bravery*; these are concepts the analysis of which seem to involve both pure descriptions of observable behavior (say, fighting until the very end) and some element that already seems to have positive or negative moral connotations, like *virtue* and *vice*. Whether "character" itself is a thick concept is a matter for debate: it is possible that being morally good is a property that supervenes on the psychology of the agent. (Again, which elements of psychology are relevant will depend on the normative ethical theory: deontologists typically think that motives are important in a way that consequentialists do not.) There

---

12. The equation reads as follows: "Necessarily, if something x is F and G^* underlies this, then necessarily anything else in the physical or natural or whatever state G^* is F as well." There is room here for argument about the formal aspects of these propositions, to the effect that (S) and (?), understood as expressing the supervenience of moral properties (and not primarily moral practices) on nonmoral properties, should be recast as *de re* modalities and not *de dicto*, as Blackburn (1993) has them. Given the comments in the rest of the paragraph, it should be clear how such arguments would proceed.

is also, however, the possibility that nonpsychological traits contribute to whether one is a morally good person or not. Consider that a person's temperament, say, having an addictive temperament, might be a purely biological (nonpsychological) element in that person's being an immoral alcoholic. These are only some of the parameters involved.

What does seem agreed on by all parties involved is that moral properties, if they exist, are important to us, insofar as they inform who we are as individuals. One might even attempt to argue that moral properties, such as being a good or a bad person, are essential properties of a person's identity, insofar as a radical change in a person's moral standing requires such a wholesale difference in the nonmoral properties of that person that they must give us, quite literally, a different person to consider. In this thought, Gandhi could not have been downright perniciously evil and still have been Gandhi. This would make moral properties essential to a person in the way origins are essential to a person, or in the way that energy may be essential to life, as suggested above, and would be a very strong claim, indeed. But everyone thinks that moral properties are in some way very important to a person's identity. Indeed, if this is the case, then moral properties might be said to supervene on a person's nonmoral personal identity. Of course, issues that involve personal identity are the topic of ongoing research in metaphysics: what is constitutive of personal identity is a difficult and vexed issue. Presumably, however, it is rather difficult to be a committed nonrealist about personal identity (though, at one point, Hume did try). If we can assume the reality of personal identity, then moral realists can appeal to metaphysicians who are working specifically on these issues, saying that whatever it is that constitutes our personal identity is that on which our moral standing as good or bad or mediocre people supervenes.

. . .

Moral Epistemology
The Skill of Virtue

We hear from both Xenophon and Diogenes Laertius that Socrates spent quite a bit of time talking with artisans. Xenophon, in his *Memoribilia* and dialogues, has Socrates speaking with saddlemakers and makers of armor, respectively. Diogenes Laertius tells us that Socrates would go to the shop of a cobbler named Simon to talk with him and the workers there. Perhaps the first Socratic dialogues written took place between Socrates and Simon, though these have not survived, if they ever existed at all.[1] From Plato (1993a) we have Socrates discussing cobblers in the *Apol-*

My thanks go to Randy Gallistel for piloting me through the complicated literature on animal navigation and to William Alston for driving home the importance of Aristotle's final argument against the idea of virtues as skills. Observing and talking with artist-builder-mechanics Glendon Good and Steven Foster has helped me understand a great deal about practical rationality (*phronesis*) and how things work; in the realm of pure aesthetics, Piet Mondrian and Philip Glass similarly construct their works. Ontologically, the lesson is learned from Quine's "penchant for desert landscapes."

1. We do have some evidence of a cobbler's shop in the Agora, as well as some pottery found there with the name "Simon" on it. Its dating does not comport well with the years of Socrates' life, however.

ogy (22a–e) and in *Gorgias* (1994a). It is in *Gorgias* that Callicles exclaims, "You simply never stop going on and on about cobblers and fullers and cooks and doctors, as if they had the slightest relevance to our discussion" (491a). This is hyperbole, at best, for earlier in that dialogue (464a–c), Socrates discourses at length about the similarities between what might be called the sciences of the body and the science of "statesmanship," or the "political sciences." The sciences of exercise, proper nutrition, and medicine, on the one hand, and legislation (i.e., the just making of laws) and execution (i.e., the just pursuit of laws broken), on the other hand, are all intended to be empirical sciences (sustained by metaphysics, of course) aimed at practical goals. Thinking of ruling morally as a skill that can be learned is, of course, assumed throughout *Republic*, wherein even at Socrates' first salvo with Thrasymachus, it is the latter who, without argument, lumps (errors made by) rulers in with (errors made by) doctors, mathematicians, and teachers (340e). Exercise, nutrition, and legislation all concern maintenance and proper development and functioning, whereas medicine and execution come into play when something has gone wrong. Even if the analogy breaks down eventually, it has certainly been of use.

The badly named "craft analogy" has received some attention among modern philosophers who study ancient Greece (e.g., see Irwin, 1985, 1995; Annas, 1993, 1995). As Annas notes, "craft" nowadays rings of "arts and crafts," connoting finger-painting, macramé, and other summer camp pastimes. What is really at issue is the idea of a skill, in particular whether or not learning to be moral is learning a skill. Everyone even Aristotle, agrees that the virtues are like skills in many ways, but is being just, virtuous, or morally good simply the possession of one or more kind of expertise? The beginnings of an answer to this question are found in our earlier claim about the shared ontic standing of moral goodness and physical healthiness. If this is so, then one might think that learning how to take care of oneself morally is epistemically of a piece with learning how to take care of one's body; if the two properties have the same ontology, then presumably our epistemic access to them will be of the same kind as well. At least two pieces of prima facie support for this idea are that both morality and medicine typically yield prescriptions (as a syntactic type of utterance or proposition) and often yield actions that follow prescriptions. And if we are led to pursue the idea that a good life is a virtuous life, we are then presented with the thesis that just as one might learn a skill like medicine, one might also learn to be good.[2] Being a doctor, athletic trainer, navigator, or chess player will be of the same epistemic sort as being courageous, just, temperate, and wise: the knowledge of each is justified by the same methods. If this is so, we have a moral epistemology that quickly becomes rather powerful. Let us not go quite so fast, however.

Let us first answer the second riddle in the introduction (remember James Byrd, Jr.). The first riddle was to ask how moral properties could be unobservable yet real, and this was answered by noting that physical healthiness (as well as other biological properties) is unobservable yet real. The second riddle asks us how we could come to know anything about these unobservable properties. Moral realists have traditionally had difficulties in answering this riddle: their best comprehensive response came to be called "intuitionism." According to this epistemology (if it really merits that approbation), we come to be acquainted with moral properties via a priori intuitions, where these themselves are primitive and unanalyzable perceptions of a given moral reality. Such a sui generis, ad hoc, last-ditch answer was sure to be problematic, and Strawson's ([1949] 1952) critique was rightly the end of it (though see Audi, 1996, for an attempted reincarnation). More recent, and impressive, Sturgeon's (1988) crack at an answer to the riddle was in terms of abduction, or inference to the best explanation. This is on the right track, for abduction is surely used in other discourses and so cannot pose any special problems for moral knowledge; it is widely recognized as a valuable knowledge-gathering tool (though see van Fraassen, 1980, for a dissenting view). The only apt criticism is that Sturgeon's answer to the riddle is merely the beginning of a theory of moral epistemology; presumably no complicated discourse's epistemology could be founded solely on inference to the best explanation, morality included.

The idea is that if goodness can be ontologically modeled on healthiness, then moral epistemology can be understood by looking at medical

---

2. I assume that virtue theory has something positive to contribute to normative ethical theory; indeed, given the proposed ontology, it is natural to assume that it will be the centerpiece of such theorizing. This does not commit moral realism to the primacy of virtue theory in normative ethical thought, however. Normative ethical thought is supposed to help us be moral, live well, and do what is right; and if it turns out that either deontology or consequentialism are more effective than virtue theory in these endeavors, there is thereby no reason to think that this is incompatible with moral realism. As will become clear below, however, such choosing among normative theories is not necessary.

epistemology. If being a doctor, a nurse, a midwife, an athletic trainer, or a nutritionist is being an expert in a skill (an hypothesis with prima facie plausibility), then medical epistemology is one example of the epistemology of skills generally. If we accept the idea that moral knowledge is merely the kind of knowledge that one obtains when learning any skill, then the basis for a more complete answer than "abduction" is delivered to us: we can learn about morality as we learn about nutrition and athletic training and medicine. The sorts of epistemic processes involved in the latter skills will be the same sorts of processes engaged in moral thought.

Moreover, the idea that the virtues are skills is one with a respectable pedigree. Among the Greek philosophers, only Aristotle and those of his school, the Peripatetics, resisted identifying the virtues as a subset of skills. All the others accepted the thesis. Such a wide concurrence on what amounts to a fairly substantial epistemological and ethical thesis is quite remarkable, and though really only an "argument by authority," it should at least add some more prima facie weight to the thesis (though given modern psychology, we may disagree with the Greeks somewhat over the analysis of "skill"). But despite the recent flourishing of virtue theory in the fields of epistemology and ethics, the idea that virtues are skills has received little attention.[3] Undoubtedly, this is due to a combination of Aristotle's dominance over modern thinking about virtue and his rejection of the idea. Any defense of it with a hope of acceptability must attend to Aristotle's rejection of it, and the present chapter will conclude with the required detailed attention. We will begin, however, with a tripartite analysis of skillful practice. We will then proceed to a discussion of three normative inquiries: medical, navigational, and moral. From there, we go to a discussion of a traditional argument against moral realism that is based on the existence of seemingly unresolvable moral disagreements among those who know "all the facts of the matter"; this is taken up with reference to both morality and medicine. But first, we start with the nature of a skill.

3. A noted exception is Linda Zagzebski's (1996) *Virtues of the Mind*. Zagzebski is an Aristotelian about these matters, and she rejects the thesis that the virtues are skills. I take it that disarming Aristotle's arguments below would satisfy her own reservations. A more typical treatment of the thesis is in the otherwise very helpful review article on virtue epistemology by Guy Axtell (1997), who dismisses skills in a single sentence.

Outline for the Logos of Skillful Practice

In what follows, a rough tripartite analysis of skillful practice is laid out. These three parts, to be addressed in turn, are the presence of a logos for a practice, the experience needed to learn the practice, and the presence of practical rationality.

In the following passage from *Gorgias* (Plato, 1994a), in which Socrates is building up an argument for the idea that knowing good from bad is a skill (*techné*), he sums up an earlier discussion in the same dialogue (461b–466a), which concerned how skills differ from what he calls "knacks":

> To my mind cookery was a knack rather than a branch of expertise as medicine is, and I went on to say that one of these processes—medicine, in fact—had considered both the nature of the object it looks after and the reasons for its actions, and could therefore explain its results. Pleasure, however, is the sole point of the other's [i.e., cookery's] actions. There's absolutely no expertise in the way it pursues pleasure; it hasn't considered either the nature of pleasure or the reason why it occurs. It's a completely irrational process—it hasn't itemized things at all, so to speak. All it can do is remember a routine which has become ingrained by habituation and past experience, and that's also what it relies on to provide us with pleasant experiences. (500e–501b)

On its surface, the distinction that Socrates is making here looks plain enough: practitioners of skills have an understanding of their subject matter, so reasons can be given for why what is done is done, and the effects of the actions undertaken can be explained. Practitioners of knacks simply continue to do what has in the past produced the result they sought; no explanations for success can be given, as there is no understanding of the goal or why some routines achieve it and others do not.

As a piece of analysis, this is quite satisfactory for giving us some of what it takes for a practice to be a skill; the difficulty of the distinction between skills and knacks comes in trying to apply it.[4] Consider medicine, which is supposed to be our paradigm of a skill. Doctors certainly know a lot about the human body, but there is certainly a lot that they do not

---

4. What follows is an emendation to what I have written elsewhere about skills and knacks (Bloomfield, 2000). I would like to thank the members of the Philosophy Department at the University of Mississippi, especially Bill Lawhead, for graciously making me see the problems with my original account.

know as well. If you have a headache, a doctor might tell you to take aspirin. If you ask the doctor how aspirin relieves the pain, the doctor may not be able to say (for it is still unclear if today's science understands the matter fully). Aspirin does work, however, and undoubtedly there are chemical reasons to explain why. Even in medical processes that are understood best, there is a limit to our current medical knowledge; that is, there is still more to know about many of the procedures we already know to be effective. Sometimes, if doctors are asked why they go on as they do, at some point they end up by giving the same answer that practitioners of cookery give, the same one that Socrates finds distinctive of knacks: "Because it works." (This point seems strangely missing in *Gorgias*.) Consider now, on the other hand, something that might be thought to be a paradigm of a knack, riding a bicycle. (Once you get the hang of it, you don't forget.) There are most certainly reasons for why certain methods of bike riding work and others do not; these have to do with balance, inertial forces, and angular momentum, as well as a combination of principles of biology and chemistry. [Biology and chemistry are involved because of the mechanisms that allow us to know the position of our limbs in space (proprioception) and those that help us keep our balance.] And we know that these sciences are based on laws and principles, as are skills; all of a sudden, bike riding seems more rationally grounded than a knack ought to be.

Luckily, understanding the nature of skill does not entail contrasting it to knacks. There might, in fact, be no such thing as a "knack" in the sense that Plato has Socrates describe. Knacks may simply be skills wherein we may be experts in attaining a desired result yet do not explicitly understand "the nature of the object it looks after and the reasons for its actions."[5] Philosophy is literally understood as the love of wisdom (*philosophia*), though presumably one gains some expertise in the skill of

---

5. There still may be some mileage to be had from the skill-knack distinction. If we stick with cooking as a knack, there might be some reasons, based on nutrition, why certain foods taste good to us and others do not (some amount of salt is healthy for us; rotten food is not), but these reasons do not extend far enough to explain all of our taste preferences. Much of this preference might have to do with memory, upbringing, convention, and so on. The degree to which someone is proficient at pleasing others where there are *no underlying principles* that determine what works and what does not is the degree to which that person may be said to have a knack for pleasing others.

philosophy without "explicitly understanding" love, much less wisdom (one hopes). What does seem to be necessary for a practice to be a skill is for there to be reasons underlying the successes of the practitioner, of which the practitioner has either an explicit or an implicit grasp. For example, one might learn the skill of speaking a language at "mother's knee" or as an adult in a classroom; here, we find a difference between knowing the rules of the language implicitly or explicitly, but either way there is knowledge of the language. Neither the mode of epistemic access in using a language nor the method of learning a grammar is relevant to the judgment that speaking a language is a skill.

To revert to a helpful term of the Greeks, what is essential is that a *logos*—a set of basic principles, laws, or rules that governs the "objects the skills look after"—must underlie any practice that is a skill. For speaking a language, the logos will include semantic, syntactic, and pragmatic rules (such as conversational implicature) that are themselves learned in areas of the brain designed for such work (assuming Chomsky's work in linguistics is on the right track). So, for the skills of medicine, nutrition, and athletic training, the logoi will contain respective subsets of the laws of physiology, biology, chemistry, and so on, along with empirical facts about the species and individuals under consideration. We learn these logoi empirically, through the "scientific method." We become masters of them by gaining experience in dealing with "the objects the skills look after."

If the virtues are skills, then they will have logoi. Just as a particular skill will have a "set of objects" to look after, a particular virtue will have a range of application. There will be certain types of situations, describable in very broad and most likely vague terms, in which a person must make a decision and act on it, where these situations, decisions, and actions are the provenance of a particular skill. Very roughly, justice concerns situations in which the distribution of resources is required; temperance concerns situations in which temptation is present; courage concerns situations in which one must interact with what is (at least normally considered) fearful. The range of situations in which wisdom is required will be quite broad and may only be specifiable by saying that all situations in which moral thinking and action are required in some way involve wisdom. It is likely that a member of *Homo sapiens* will have to confront these sorts of situations at some time or another, and one may comport oneself at those moments well or otherwise. Perhaps it is better to say that how one comports oneself at those moments is how well one is living, how good a job one is doing with life.

So, the logos of a virtue will have to include principles by which these situations are recognized as such, as well as principles that are capable of guiding decision making. We will shortly be talking about the thought processes of diagnosis and problem solving that are involved in all skills, virtues included. For now, we can think of the logoi of the virtues, on the model of the logoi of particular biological systems within a body, such as the immune, endocrine, and circulatory systems: each of these systems has a provenance, in the same way as the virtues, and one may see how, by engaging the various virtues, they may overlap or affect one another, just as the systems in the body overlap and affect one another. Perhaps a discussion of the logos of a particular virtue may prove helpful, and courage (naturally) volunteers itself. For simplicity's sake, the discussion to follow is simplified to the extent to which courage is disengaged from the other virtues.

Courage involves situations in which we must interact with what is fearful. Exactly what this interaction amounts to is not completely clear, and there are at least three different hypotheses at play. One hypothesis is that courageous people know how to endure fear; that is, brave people feel fear just like everyone else, but what makes them brave is their ability to keep their fears from interfering with their behavior. Then there is Aristotle's hypothesis. He thought that courageous people feared appropriately; that is, brave people feel fear only when there is good reason to not proceed, and they check their behavior as a result. Discretion may be the better part of valor, as the saying goes, and courageous people, according to Aristotle, are those who use their fear properly as a sign that discretion is in order. The last hypothesis (that we shall canvas) is an interesting point of agreement between the Stoics and Epicureans, who both thought that brave people feel no fear, for a proper understanding of our lives and "fearful objects" reveals that there is no good reason to fear anything (death included). Discretion, in this theory, would be the result of a purely cognitive judgment based on the necessity of engaging what is normally thought of as "fearful," measured against the probability of success, and so on. Now, whatever the truth is about courage and fear, it is part of the logos of courage, and the debate over this interaction is one that moral psychologists may pursue. Settling it may aid in moral education. The point here is merely to have given some shape to the notion of the logos of a virtue. Recalling *Laches*, we note that there have been plenty of brave people throughout history, without anyone having settled every question about the logos of courage (and, *mutatis mutandis*, for the other virtues as well), so more support is found for the thought that skills can be mastered without the expert fully and explicitly knowing the logos of the skill; this may be too much to expect. (Compare this with being able to speak a language as a native, while lacking an explicit understanding of the language's grammar.)

Of course, there is more to the logos of courage than just how fear is appropriately dealt with. Recalling a discussion in chapter 1 (concerning suicide because of disgrace, or hara-kiri), we may even note that there can be some cultural variability in how courage gets played out in action. But there will also be some underlying principles, such as "Don't abandon your comrades in arms, in the midst of melee, due to fear" and "The need for courageous protection increases proportionally to the love of what is protected" and so on. There may even be nonsupererogatory demands made on courageous people for deep self-sacrifice. And so, the logos of courage will be built up out of facts about creatures with psychologies like ours, along with principles or standards for courageous behavior, which we strive to attain for the sake of our well-lived lives. Learning such a logos will be an empirical endeavor, as one learned, to take an extreme example, how to be a samurai and this will not be different from learning the logos of any other skill. But this grasp of the logos of a skill, required to master the skill, may not be achieved only through books; true expertise requires experience.

The psychology of having experience and garnering expertise from it is obviously a large topic, and for the most part investigating it is not a philosophical endeavor. But there are some metaethically relevant points to note about the role of experience and the gaining of mastery in a skill, especially insofar as the ability, as well as the phenomenology, involved in expertise is different from the ability and phenomenology of beginners. For example, one difference is the ability of experts to recognize exceptions to rules. The notion of an exception is itself a bit tricky; one can mean by "exception" either that a rule is broken in a particular case or that a particular case, which prima facie looks as if it falls under the scope of a rule actually does not because of extenuating circumstances. I mean the latter usage. Whereas beginners approach a skill by habitually applying rules to all the situations to which they seem to apply, an expert may see why a rule does not apply, even though it prima facie seems as if it ought to. So, doctors will know that there are certain times when a particular drug is not to be prescribed because of some preexisting condition of the patient, that general dietary rules do not lead to proper nutrition for those with diabetes or anemia, and so on. Famously, Plato has Socrates recognize exceptions by noting that whereas justice demands that we return what we borrow, we ought not to return a sword to a distraught or angry friend (more on universalizability later).

Beginners also need props or supports for which experts have no need. These may include books or devices (training wheels) or, most likely and often, teachers or supervisors. In some cases, the support is there to make the task easier, in other cases the support is for guidance, and in still others its presence is to ensure that mistakes are not made. If the props are actually helpful and do not end up being crutches, leaned on to make up for lessons unlearned, then they should help beginners to become experts; they should help beginners to gain the ability to practice the skill without the use of the props. Thus, good students will learn from using the props, learning lessons that would otherwise be beyond them. And once this experience is gained, not only do the props become unnecessary, but also the student begins to think about the skill in a different manner and actually practices the skill differently.

To see the moral import of the epistemological and phenomenological differences between beginners and experts, the briefest of glances into the psychological data will be helpful. Psychologists and computer scientists who are working on artificial intelligence have developed an account of five different stages of learning a skill: novice, advanced beginner, competence, proficiency, and expertise.[6] (The details need not be exact here, only that an account approximately like the one described be correct.) Each stage is distinguished by successively difficult feats of learning. Rules cease to be referred to; then information begins to get "chunked" together; then experimental risks are taken; then "intuitions" are proved trustworthy. (We return to intuitions below.) Finally, when the skill becomes so ingrained that practitioners begin to be able to express their individuality, or their own style, through their practice while working within the logos of the skill, expertise has most likely been achieved.

From the epistemic point of view, what is perhaps most interesting about experts is that they lose insight into their own thought processes. (This is consistent with some experts, like native language speakers, never

6. The research began in the 1960s with de Groot and was carried on by Chase, Chi, Glaser, Larkin, Simon, and others. The five-stage account presented above is that of the brothers Dreyfus (1986); although I accept their account of the differences between experts and beginners, I do not follow them through to their conclusions about computers and the mind.

having insight into how they speak.) Typically, beginners in skills such as playing-chess know explicitly how they reach conclusions; very often they must think step by step and can, in retrospect, accurately redescribe their actual decision procedure. But there is quite a bit of empirical evidence to suggest that the same is not so for experts (Chase and Simon, 1973; Larkin et al. 1980; Chi et al., 1981). Experts, it seems, quite often do not know how they make their decisions; they just "see" what is going on without having to go through the options serially. Expert chess players and doctors can immediately know what to do. (This is especially true in easy cases.) But research shows that, for example, doctors in experimental settings, when asked how their diagnoses are made, sometimes give retrospective accounts that cannot have been their actual decision procedure. Expert physicists and mathematicians work in the same way. Those who know best often know least how they know. An example recognizable to most adults is our ability to solve, with practical immediacy, "traveling salesman problems" that can stump the mightiest of supercomputers for minutes at a time. We do not know how we "see" what the shortest route is, once all the cities are plotted on a map, but in many cases it is obvious to us nonetheless. We need not serially consider every possibility. Such questions of navigating are as intuitive to some as a "sense of direction" that allows one to know where one is: navigation is surely a skill, but often those who are best at it "just know" their way home.

There are ethical payoffs immediately at hand, for expert decision making has the phenomenological quality of an "intuition." Obviously, these will not be the sorts of intuitions championed by the "intuitionists" (e.g., Moore, [1902] 1988). Those were supposed to be a priori intuitions, or knowledge that is the result of something like pure rational thought and is, in any case, not based on empirical experience or learning. Where modern psychology can help is in explaining why our moral "intuitions" "just come to us," unbidden, as it were. We might call these empirically based intuitions "a posteriori intuitions." One does not solve chess or navigational problems in an a priori fashion, nor do doctors treat their patients with this kind of epistemological tool. We have to *learn* how to perform these tasks, which require skill. And so, when people, in some (easy) moral situations say they "just know," morally, that something right or wrong has occurred and this seems like a "moral intuition" to them, what is going on is not quite as mysterious as it may seem—at least no more mysterious than how experts in medicine, chess, and navigation have intuitions. We have to empirically learn what is right, presumably in childhood, and then as adults, at least in easy cases, we can just immediately or intuitively know.[7]

For example, we may encounter someone whom we "instantaneously" do not trust. If queried on our mistrust, we might very well respond, "It's hard to say why I don't trust this person; it's just a gut reaction, just an intuition." We do not have to be able to use introspection into our reasons for mistrust in order to be able to trust judgments of this sort; however, our inability to do so need not affect our confidence in these judgments. Surely, though, such "intuitions" could not be considered a priori; we must empirically learn how to trust well. Thus, we may be able to (defeasibly) detect whether or not someone is trustworthy, even though we may not be able to say which signs we are detecting that tell us what is correct.

So, regarding the status of "moral intuitions," we may now return to James Byrd, Jr., and our second riddle. We inspect the scene of the crime, Byrd's murder, and the chains and the blood but find no empirical observations of the property of wrongness. Nevertheless, we know that what happened to Byrd is wrong. The moral realist is then asked, how we can know this? What are the epistemic links between the wrongness and our belief in the wrongness? The answer is that we know this through an a posteriori intuition that phenomenologically "just comes to us." Upon seeing the brutal dismemberment and decapitation of an innocent, we immediately come to the conclusion that something wrong has occurred, just as a doctor immediately concludes, without conscious inference, that a patient has liver trouble upon seeing jaundiced eyes. We may be able to say something about how we learned that it is wrong to cause needless suffering, but we may not be able to give a full account (as yet) of how those learning processes led us to know that what Byrd's killers did is

---

7. Prichard (1912) agrees that morals must be learned: "Any one who, *stimulated by education*, has come to feel the force of the various obligations in life." (p. 149; emphasis added), and later, in a footnote discussion about disagreement between people's intuitions, he refers to a "developed moral being." Presumably, Prichard would say that mathematics is learned as well, and mathematical intuitions are neither empirical nor a posteriori. I suppose the thought would be that the validity of moral intuitions is in some way immediately apprehended. A full discussion of problems concerning a priori intuitions is not possible here. The important point for the present concerns how well a posteriori intuitions answer to the needs of moral epistemology.

"intuition" is not mysterious...it is a product of repetition.

Moral "intuition" is a priori.

Bloomfield is wrong.

doctors

wrong. In the same way, the doctor may recite the lesson learned about jaundice and livers but may not be capable of telling the story about how this lesson was internalized and then applied in context. The only conclusion to draw is that there does not seem to be present in the moral case an epistemological mystery greater than the one present when doctors look at a patient and "just know" what the diagnosis is. Obviously, in both ethics and medicine, there are going to be easy cases and hard cases, and even wise people and doctors will have trouble with the latter. In such cases, even the thinking of these experts might need to be made explicit, possibilities may have to be considered serially, and diagnoses may lack the practical certainty present in the obvious cases. In difficult cases, experts may be reduced to acting like beginners. Importantly, however, it seems we have solved our second riddle: our epistemic access, to at least easy moral cases, is through a posteriori intuitions. So far, we have not uncovered any sui generis problems for moral epistemology.

At this point in our outline of the logos of skillful practice, we have noted that skills possess a logos, that in order to master a skill experience is necessary, and that experts can spot exceptions and in easy cases can confidently rely on a posteriori intuitions. But there is another important component of skillful practice, especially relevant to intuitions. It is what philosophers today call "practical rationality" and what the Greeks called *phronesis*. Giving a general characterization of *phronesis* is not easy, but it involves having knowledge of how things work, where the scope of "things" is suitably broad and vague. (Here the classical notion of practical rationality will be treated; obviously modern decision or game theory is an attempt to codify such thought. At least, however, insofar as this is driven by prisoner's dilemmas, the modern account of practical rationality is very narrow indeed.) If you have ever met someone who is just plain good at tending to things and fixing them when they're sickly or broken, be they animals or crops, sockets or faucets, or clocks, you have come across a *phronimos*. As a beginning, we can look to an understanding of mechanics as a means to understanding *phronesis*.

Anticipating the material in the appendix, we may begin with the pioneering work of Carnot on thermodynamics as applied to the mechanics of engines; his deep insight into the nature of how machines must work is (defeasible) evidence of his being a master of practical rationality. We find that we want our machines to be efficient, that is, that they do as much work as possible while expending as little energy as possible. Thus, we recognize simplicity as at least one virtue of machines, for simplicity increases efficiency. It is a result of this fact that we espouse the expression "build a better mousetrap" and avoid Rube Goldberg contraptions (when we are *phronimos* enough to be able to recognize them as such). But *phronesis* is not only at play in the designing of machines; it also seems to be at work in nature. For example, the tendency toward efficiency and simplicity also informs the principles of least action and time, and we see it in nature whenever we see water running downhill and taking "the path of least resistance." (Even a physicist as antimetaphysical and hyper-empirically minded as Feynman, 1964, vol. II, 19–3, twice in one published lecture refers to the facts described by the principle of least action as "miraculous.") The drive toward simplicity is also of epistemic import, insofar as parsimony influences our explanatory practices: Ockham's razor famously tells us to favor the simplest explanation. Appreciating these sorts of facts and their effects on how systems develop, work, and fall apart leads one to an understanding of *phronesis*.

Now one might think that being a *phronimos* is, in and of itself, being an expert in a skill, but there is some reason to debate this point. The best understanding of *phronesis* is one in which we find it to be a component of every skill, as actually embodied by the structure of the logos of each skill itself: the logoi themselves are pared down by Ockham's razor. And it is by being a *phronimos*, to whatever degree, that allows one to learn these *logoi*. Our understanding of *phronesis* need not be limited to these vague generalities, however, and pursuing the matter further will take us farther down the road to understanding moral epistemology. *Phronesis* has two components of its own, though these are not recognized as such within the large body of literature on practical rationality. These two components are diagnosis and problem solving. Let's address them in turn.

Diagnosis can be casually characterized as the reading of signs or symptoms. It is not clear what this means, however, for we are at once limited by our incomplete empirical understanding of what was above called "a posteriori intuition." When we begin to be familiar with the logos of a skill, we begin to have these intuitions, by "automatically" detecting certain features of situations (e.g., yellow eyes) that stand out as relevant in understanding the nature of that situation. These features are signs or symptoms of the underlying nature of whatever is at hand. Exactly how these features "stand out" (as solutions to traveling salesman problems "stand out") is the nexus of the mystery. In everyday experience, nothing could be more natural and commonplace than animals attending to some feature of their environment that stands out: for example, deer in a field catch a scent of another animal that is approaching and react to it. It is hard to imagine how evolution could proceed without such abilities. But these abilities imply, at the very least, differentiation of what is "normal" from what is not, what is background from what is salient, or what is signal from what is noise. How this differentiation is accomplished in such an automatic, intuitive way is still a baseline mystery for epistemologists, philosophers of mind, and in the end, most probably, cognitive psychologists and physiologists.

But if, in our understanding of diagnosis, we can help ourselves to the notion of "standing out," we can get some grip on how diagnosis proceeds. When an expert diagnoses or evaluates a situation, some features of it (symptoms) stand out as being able to provide information by which the underlying nature of the situation may be known. Part of learning the logos of a skill will involve learning about the causal relations between the surface features of a situation and its underlying nature. In this way, the practitioner learns to identify what is occurring within a system merely by looking at it (or making some superficial tests, e.g., taking a pulse). To complicate matters, in most skills there is a variety of different kinds of causal relations that may obtain between a symptom and its cause. Some of these relations are direct, but very often the relationship between sign and cause can be quite obscure. To see how crucial it is to understand the intricacies of these causal relations in order to be able to make correct diagnoses, consider an alternative theory of diagnosis, holding that all that is needed is an ability to correlate symptoms with causes and that understanding the precise nature of the causal mechanism, the reason for the correlation, is not necessary for making a diagnosis. For example, let us consider a fever. One may get a fever for a variety of reasons, but one does not (normally) get a fever without there being some other physical malady. Fevers and illness are closely correlated: the former is a symptom of the latter. For years, until quite recently in fact, it was so clear that fevers indicated the presence of illness that fevers were often attacked by doctors as part of the illness. If one was sick and had a fever, it was thought that one way to alleviate the sickness was to rid the body of the fever. We have, however, finally learned better. Fevers are, in fact, the body's *response* to illness. A fever is the speeding up of the body's metabolism to help it combat sicknesses, and as such it is a part of the immune system's bag of tricks for fighting illness. Of course, a fever high enough can kill, so at some points fevers must be controlled; but for many years our attempts to fight all but the most severe fevers in order to rid the body of sickness were actually counterproductive (at least insofar as removing symptoms without taking care of the underlying problem may fail to help in solving the problem). This sort of thinking is not available to a theory of diagnosis that limits itself to understanding how symptoms and underlying causes are correlated. Good diagnosis is a subtle affair of causal detective etiology.

Thus, diagnosis entails appreciating the causal relations between symptom and cause. It is an etiological study that deals with causal chains between underlying conditions and superficial symptoms. There are times when these causal chains can be obscure, as in the case of fever. They may also be more straightforward, as in the case of the diagnosis of hepatitis from jaundiced eyes, where the latter are caused by an increase of bilirubin in the blood, itself caused by an overactive liver. There are even times when the symptom of a problem is identical to the problem itself; as in the case of an obviously broken bone. Causal chains come in a variety of lengths and configurations, but understanding them constitutes diagnosis.

We will be returning to diagnosis soon, but we'll begin the discussion of problem solving by noting a difference between it and diagnosis. In the latter, a determinate causal connection is already involved (between symptom and cause), whereas in the former such determination very often does not exist; this nonexistence is due to the fact that not only does the future not exist in the present but also in most problem-solving situations there are "many ways to skin a cat." This indelicate phrase now reappears after having been used to refer to functional equivalence, conventional difference, and the number of ways in which one may "get the job done." Very often there are many ways in which to solve a problem. Some solutions may indeed be better than others: (to use an example of Anscombe, [1974] 1995) one may light the house afire to roast the pig, but one may also use an oven. Considerations of simplicity and Ockham's razor are at play in problem solving, as well as in diagnosis and explanation, for we typically do not want to cause new problems while solving preexisting ones; rather, we seek to solve problems while disturbing as little else as possible. We have learned that one ought not to throw out the baby with the bathwater.

It is in addressing problem solving that we find traditional characterizations of practical inference. Going back to Aristotle, who formalized the notion, a practical inference is one that has an action as its conclusion. Or at least, this is typically how these inferences were conceived. We will explore the nature of the connection between the premises of this sort of inference and their conclusion in chapter 4, wherein we engage the "internalist-externalist" debate about motivation. What will be instructive here concerns the logical structure of diagnosis and problem solving, as these provide insight into the differences and similarities in the epistemology of their methodologies. The easiest and best route to take here would be just to insert the entirety of G. E. M. Anscombe's ([1974] 1995) magnificent "Practical Inference."[8] Since this is not quite practical, some of her conclusions will be cribbed and some terminology changed to suit our present purposes. The difference between diagnosis and problem solving concerns, so to speak, what we take to be the starting points and what we take to be the end or goal. In diagnosis, our starting points are our symptoms, and where we want to end up is at an understanding of the causes of, or an explanation for, these symptoms. In solving problems, our starting point is our diagnosis of the problem, and our end is to have the problem solved. As different as these starting and stopping points are, Anscombe elegantly shows how the inferences involved in both diagnosis and problem solving are of the same logical form. The following schemas are quite simplified, though (it is hoped) not to the detriment of their usefulness.

> *For diagnosis:*
> Given: p (the symptoms).
> If q, then p.
> If r, then q.
> To investigate as cause: r. (Is "r" true?)

> *For problem solving:*
> Wanted: that p (p is our problem solved).
> If q, then p.
> If r, then q.
> To solve the problem: do r.

Anscombe gives us, as a concrete example, one case in which we have spectacular plant growth and want to diagnose or explain its cause, and another in which we want to grow spectacular plants where we now have none.

---

8. This article has scarcely received any attention in discussions of practical rationality; in the internalist-externalist debate about motivation; and broadly speaking, in questions of action theory. These discussions have suffered as a result, as Anscombe, in this case, is many steps beyond perhaps everyone else. The article originally appeared in *The Philosophy of Georg Henrik von Wright* in 1974 but was reprinted in 1995 in the *festschrift* for Philippa Foot at Foot's "especial request."

To diagnose:	Problem to solve:
Spectacular plant growth.	Grow spectacular plants.

If plants are fed with certain substances,
there will be spectacular plant growth.

If these substances are in the soil,
the plants will be fed with them.

Conclusion:	Conclusion:
To examine the soil so as to check whether those substances are present	To put those substances in the soil

So, as we see, the logical form of inference is identical in these "two" forms of practical reasoning, even though problem solving is forward looking and diagnosis is backward looking. To switch to another terminology, diagnosis concerns explanations: it is the use of reason to cite causes. Problem solving is concerned with what is often known as instrumental reasoning: the use of reason to affect certain results. Despite these differences, the logic remains the same. What distinguishes them might be called "purely practical": diagnosis is distinguished from solving problems by determining what our goals or purposes are as we are engaged in the situation. Given the differences of their goals, they have different empirical methodologies by which those goals are achieved: determining that *r* is the case will be quite different from bringing it about that *r*, but figuring out what *r* is, in both cases, is achieved by the same sort of inference.

Thus, our outline of the logos of skillful practice involves three parts. The first is that skills have a logos. The second concerns the role that experience plays in the gaining of the skill. The third involves the ability to think like a *phronimos*. At the very least, we can say that being virtuous will bear great similarities to skillful practice. We have discussed the notion of the logos of a virtue as involving a range of situations, decisions, and behaviors. The centrality of practical rationality to virtuous behavior is news to no one, though exactly how diagnosis and problem solving fit in are only just becoming clear (and there will be more on this below). In any case, we find that the three components, distinctive of skills in general, are present within the virtues. From here, we may continue with the investigation. Those with further doubts about the thesis that the virtues are skills are asked to hold these worries in abeyance, at least until the final section of the chapter.

Medical, Navigational, and Moral Theories

If we are going to build a moral epistemology on an ontology that takes goodness and healthiness to be of the same ontic sort, then we should expect that the ways in which we learn about what it is to be healthy will be epistemically on a par with how we learn about what it is to be good. Working along the lines of the modest transcendental argument of the introduction, the place to start our epistemology might be with the thought that we learn, from a first-hand point of view, about the existence of the property of being healthy by becoming sick. The idea goes something like this. There is nothing that it is like to feel normally healthy; phenomenologically, this is something we are so habituated to that it is neutral, unobservable, and invisible. We are generally quite unaware of the workings of our bodies when we are feeling well. Our heart beats within our breast, and we normally do not feel it beat. We are unaware of our breath, our posture, and the movement of the muscles in our legs when we walk. Most likely, we know first that there is a property of being healthy because we have been sick (or have seen others be sick). The result is that we infer the existence of a property that is invisible and unobservable to us, namely, healthiness, from the existence of another property of which we cannot deny the existence, namely, sickness. But given the existence of health and ill health, how do we learn about them? So far, the suggestion is that we learn about these properties by the epistemic means of diagnosis and problem solving, as elements of practical rationality.

Here the goal is to gain some further insight into the structure of normative ethics, as it stands today, by investigating further the ways of other normative empirical practices, like medicine and navigation. It turns out that given the complex four-way relationship among illnesses, their symptoms, diagnosis, and problem solving, two basic medical strategies naturally present themselves. Roughly, one is to seek the causes and try to affect change from there; another is to work toward the causes by alleviating the symptoms. One can work from root to tip or from tip to root, so to speak. It turns out that these two strategies are similar in some gross respects to the two dominant strategies of normative ethics today, namely, deontology and consequentialism. We can learn about different ways in which moral problems are approached by looking at the ways in which medical problems are approached. The claim here is (again) intended to be modest: when virtuous people are involved in moral thought, sometimes they think like deontologists and at other times they think like consequentialists [perhaps they also sometimes think like neither or act (naturally) without thinking at all]; typically a virtuous person is thinking like a deontologist when focusing on the diagnosis of a situation in order to see what the "deep structure" of moral reasons is (what reasons for action or obligations are present, which have priority, what rule applies, etc.) and thinking like a consequentialist when the reasons for the situation or problem existing are not as important as resolving the extant problem as best as possible. As approaches to the methodology of moral thought, deontology and consequentialism are as compatible as medical practices that emphasize either diagnosis or problem solving. This is not to say that the Theory of Deontology is compatible with the Theory of Consequentialism, whatever theories these may turn out to be, but that the ways of approaching moral problems used by proponents of these theories can be understood as epistemological and moral methodologies and that, understood in these terms, thinking like a deontologist is apt for some sorts of situations and thinking like a consequentialist is apt for others. The virtuous person is expert at both sorts of thinking, as the best doctor will be expert at both diagnosis and problem solving.

The following discussion about differing medical cultures is merely illustrative and not meant to depict any particular, actual cultures. The idea, however, is to simplify such a possible cross-cultural debate to high-light epistemic issues. Nevertheless, and anticipating a bit what is to come, the debate that rages in normative ethics between deontologists and consequentialists can appear to be as futile as a debate between a Western style doctor and an Eastern style doctor over whose medical theory is "the best." Obviously, one need not choose between the two; as patients, we would prefer to pick and choose, depending on the case, and we would prefer doctors who were schooled as thoroughly as possible. (It is interesting that Western and Eastern medicine even have distinct ontologies insofar as the latter accepts the existence of *chi*, which the former denies. Obviously, from a metaphysical point of view, either chi exists or it does not. If it does not, Eastern medicine is thereby not deemed ineffective or no good but rather effective for reasons its practitioners do not fully comprehend.)

Medical Theories

As indicated above, with any medical problem some distinction will be made between the symptoms of the problem and the causes of the symptoms. Sometimes the distinction will be merely logical, as in the case of a broken leg, and at other times quite a long causal chain may be involved.

In cases of the latter sort, one can imagine a medical practitioner addressing the problem in one of two ways. Either the symptoms themselves or the ultimate causes of the symptoms can be attacked: there is a top-down approach and a bottom-up approach. Either way, presumably, an illness can be cured, and there need be no difference in the healthy end state: with either strategy, if it is successful, the problem (from root to tip) will be taken care of. But the causal chain can be approached from either end: the top-down methodology is to focus on alleviating the immediately observable symptoms, or solving the most obvious problems and working "down" toward causes until no symptoms are apparent, at which point it can be assumed that the problem is gone; the bottom-up methodology focuses on the etiology or diagnosis and attends directly to the causes of the symptoms themselves, working "up" through the causal chain and alleviating the symptoms of the illness by eradicating their causes.

We can imagine two different medical cultures arising, which emphasize these different methodologies. Perhaps the cultures within which these medical practices are situated are themselves different enough to promote one way of thinking over the other; the top-down culture might define health as the absence of disease (no symptom, no problem), whereas the bottom-up culture may have a more positive conception of health. This is not to say that the top-down approach can do without diagnostic procedures nor that the bottom-up approach can do without problem-solving techniques; the difference is one of method, strategy, or approach. The two cultures may find themselves with medical practices in which one strategy becomes more sophisticated than the other. It is important that both methodologies have their strengths and weaknesses. To see how this is going, it will help to take actual examples of medical practice as manifesting these two ways of thinking. If one has a headache, a broken leg, gangrene, or an appendicitis, it seems that a top-down approach is best. Wondering why or how these problems have arisen, speculating on the deep reasons for these maladies, may not be the best way to bring about health in the case at hand. What is needed is a more direct approach: we have an obvious problem, the etiology of which is not terribly relevant to effecting a cure. On the other hand, this top-down approach will not be as effective in curing problems that involve, for example, the body's own immune system: given a top-down approach, we should not be surprised to find fevers being treated as a part of the problem. Disentangling the actions of the immune system from those of the problem can be difficult, especially since the immune system itself can malfunction, as in, for example, asthma or lupus.

Consider two cases. First, it has actually just been found that those with a common form of stomach ulcer have a larger number of a certain bacterium in the stomach, which we all normally have in smaller quantities. A top-down approach would be to prescribe an antibiotic that kills this sort of bacterium, thereby removing the ulcers. A bottom-up approach would be to find out why the patient is not able to control this bacterium like a healthy person; whatever system is responsible for maintaining normal levels of this bacterium in healthy humans is malfunctioning. Fix the system, bringing the bacterium under control, and the ulcers will go away. Consider a second case: two patients each with excema, one in each culture. The patient in the top-down culture is prescribed a steroid cream, which is itself an immunosuppressant. The excema recedes and eventually disappears, the medication is stopped, and the patient is considered cured if the excema does not reappear. In a bottom-up culture, excema might not be seen as a problem to be cured but as a symptom itself of a deeper problem. The goal then is not to treat the skin per se but to determine what caused the skin to develop a rash in the first place. Diagnose the problem to its root and treat it from there.

In these cases, especially if the problem is not too severe, the results of either methodology might be functionally equivalent (back to cat skinning). But such methodological parity need not be the case.[9] In the case of a broken leg or an appendicitis, it seems preferable to take a strictly top-down approach. With problems involving the immune system, a bottom-up approach promises results that may be more thoroughly successful; consider how much better a bottom-up approach will be in the treatment of illness that involves a fever. In the case of the ulcers, it is not clear if one approach has any merits over the other. In other cases, the patient may be in such bad shape that neither approach can help very much. Quite often, we would find it far from clear which methodology will be more effective; and the epidemiology needed to judge methodological efficacy would be very complex and may perhaps even be biased or otherwise suspect. Moreover, medicine is casework, and especially in serious cases, doctors ought to treat each patient as an individual with a distinctive history and in need of tailor-made treatment. Even if we know what normally works in cases of *this kind*, it may be far from clear what will work *here*. (Recall the discussion about recognizing exceptions.) We can very easily imagine doctors within one school agreeing on all empir-

---

9. Confucius (1998) says, "To attack a task from the wrong end can do nothing but harm," *Analects* II, 16.

ically observable facts of a case yet disagreeing on both diagnosis and how to proceed. A fortiori, such disagreement between practitioners of the top-down and bottom-up schools would be even more widespread.

Leaving aside these disagreements between experts for the moment (we will return to them shortly), let us note now that most likely no doctor is either purely of the top-down or the bottom-up school. As mentioned, we would, as patients, want a doctor well versed in both approaches. The best doctors will be able to think in both fashions, and these methodologies, these epistemic strategies, will not "compete" against each other for prominence. The moral payoff of all this will come when inspecting normative ethical theory. What we find is that sometimes virtuous people think like deontologists and at other times they think like consequentialists. These ways of thinking should not be seen as competitors, but they need to be articulated as different ways of thinking about moral problems, as different approaches to moral situations, or as different moral strategies within one coherent, normative framework. To see how this is to be developed, consider the example of navigation.

Navigational Theories

Although not too much has been said so far about navigation as a skill, there is much of interest here, as well as application; in particular, there is some insight to be had into the strategy suggested below about normative ethics. Research on a variety of insects and animals has provided a rich source of information about how creatures solve the practical problems of moving through the world and arriving at an intended end. Human navigation, of course, has become quite sophisticated, especially since the invention of the compass and the clock. (The clock is necessary for calculating one's longitude.) But there are stories of prodigious feats of unaided human navigation. For example, in Gallistel's (1990) discussion of navigation, he tells the story of Joshua Slocum's solo sail in the sloop *Spray* around the world in the 1890s. Slocum sailed without a clock and was capable of sleeping in his ship, which was remarkably able to hold a constant course unattended. On a 1,500-mile sail from Chile, he made the small island of Juan Fernandez "right ahead" on the fifteenth day. On his next leg, he sailed for 43 days and 4,500 miles, headed toward the Marquesas. At this point, he made difficult astronomical sightings to confirm his "dead reckoning," which had left him around 20 miles offshore. After passing by these islands (without stopping) he sailed approximately 4,000 more miles to Samoa. Truly, this is a remarkable feat of human navigation by intuition. (Of course, this is a posteriori intuition and not "pure, rational thought.")[10]

As mentioned, Slocum used a very informal but very accurate form of what is known as dead reckoning, "the process of determining the change in one's position by integrating one's velocity (direct speed) with respect to time" (Gallistel, 1990, p. 35). This is the method of navigating long voyages through open waters. "It remains a fundamental aspect of modern navigation in its explicit, formalized aspect. In its implicit, unformalized aspect, it probably accompanies virtually every change of position a sailor or an animal makes" (p. 35). There is, however, another method of navigation, called "piloting," which is used in very different circumstances.

10. Slocum's journey has a clear moral component, as well as the epistemic one mentioned here. Alongside knowledge of stars, tides, and winds, it required courage and other virtues. This extended quotation demonstrates an interesting weave of moral psychology and navigational epistemology ([1899] 1997):

> On the morning of May 5, 1896, I sailed from Juan Fernandez, having feasted on many things, but on nothing sweeter than the adventure itself of a visit to the home and to the very cave of Robinson Crusoe. From the island the *Spray* bore away to the north passing the island of St. Felix before she gained the trade winds, which seemed slow in reaching their limits.
>
> If the trades were tardy, however, when they did come they came with a bang, and made up for lost time; and the *Spray*, under reefs, sometimes one, sometimes two, flew before a gale for a great many days, with a bone in her mouth toward the Marquesas, in the west, which she made on the forty third day out, and still kept on sailing. My time was all taken up those days—not by standing at the helm; no man, I think, could stand or sit and steer a vessel round the world: I did better than that; for I sat and read my books, mended my clothes, or cooked my meals and ate them in peace. I had already found that it was not good to be alone, and so I made companionship with what there was around me, sometimes with the universe and sometimes with my own insignificant self; but my books were always my friends, let fail all else. Nothing could be easier or more restful than my voyage in the trade-winds.
>
> I sailed with a free wind day after day, marking the position of my ship on the chart with considerable precision; but this was done by intuition, I think, more than by slavish calculations. For one whole month my vessel held her course true; I had not, the while, so much as a light in the binnacle. The Southern Cross I saw every night abeam. The sun every morning came up astern; every evening it went down ahead. I wished for no other compass to guide me, for these were true. (pp. 116–17)

Piloting uses recognized landmarks to determine one's present position. Gallistel quotes Bowditch, "the Moses of American navigators," as saying that "piloting is used to mean the art of safely conducting a vessel on waters the hazards of which make necessary frequent or continuous positioning with respect to charted features." Around our homes, in recognizable or charted neighborhoods, we rely on piloting to know where we are. If, however, we are traveling afar (without guidebooks to name landmarks) we are forced to reckon our position.

Importantly, it is not just sailors who use these two methods of navigating. Of course, other humans may do the same, but so do other species. Dogs, homing pigeons, wasps rodents, and others have been shown to use both methods, dead reckoning and piloting (Etienne, Maurer, and Seguinot, 1996). Particularly well documented, though still not completely understood, are the navigational techniques of the various species of honey bee (Dyer and Gould, 1983). Honey bees have more than one way of doing their dead reckoning: they use the sun (as a kind of compass), or when the sun is not visible in the blue sky, they use the polarization of light. But on cloudy days, when the bees have no sun or blue sky by which to reckon their position, they can pilot by relying on large, featured landmarks (such as flying along a line of trees).

Note, however, that these two navigational techniques are similar in important ways to the medical techniques previously discussed. There is a bottom-up, or etiological, approach, which is dead reckoning. Here, to find our current standing, we look back over our shoulder, calculating from where we've come to where we must presently be. There is also a top-down, or symptom-based, approach that is similar to piloting. Here we look to readily available signs that will indicate to us what our current situation is. We have no need, when piloting, to concern ourselves with how we have gotten to the place we are; just as in treating an appendicitis, we are not concerned with what caused the inflammation of the appendix. When there are no readily available signs, however, or when these seem contradictory or ambiguous or unclear, and when there is no land in sight, we must look back to our origin and figure our position from there.

Some comments on the epistemological aspects of navigating are apropos, especially since the issue of introspective access and our ability to give accounts of what we know has already arisen. There are some navigational tasks that we can perform without being able to say how we do them; for instance, blindfolded and earphoned humans are reliably able to dead-reckon their way back to a starting place after being led in an L-shaped path, where each leg is six meters long (Etienne, Maurer, and

Seguinot, 1996). (Hamsters and dogs are capable of performing similar tasks under similar conditions.) Presumably, we cannot use introspection into our methods of reckoning under these conditions. Of course, dead reckoning over long sea voyages may be something we do quite explicitly, recording speeds and headings with great care and diligence. Most interesting, however, is that expert dead-reckoners, like Slocum, navigate by what seems proper to call a posteriori intuitions, in which their dead reckoning is as immediate as the diagnosis of easy cases by doctors. Similar observations may be made about piloting. Navigation is a skill that we perform both with and without introspective access to our methods, and experts under difficult conditions may not be capable of nonexplicit navigation but may operate intuitively in easy cases.

Given even this briefest of outlines of medical and navigational epistemologies, or problem-solving strategies, we are now prepared to look at normative ethics.

Normative Ethical Theory

Two prominent normative ethical theories have dominated the field for the past 200 years: deontology and consequentialism. These have often been placed dialectically as competitors, each assuming a mutual exclusivity as a theory of ethical truth. Indeed, the very form such theories take builds in the exclusivity: the right act is defined (roughly) as "the one performed for the right reasons" or as "the one productive of the best consequences." But "rightness" cannot be defined as both, so one has to go. Such an attitude, which has become a norm of professional ethics, should strike one (especially by this point) as hopeless. It is preposterous to think that there is either nothing to be learned about morality from thinking like a consequentialist, assuming deontology to be the "truth," or nothing to be learned from thinking like a deontologist, assuming consequentialism gets it right. This would be throwing out the ethical baby with the theoretical bathwater. Even if we do not buy into one of these theories, hook, line, and sinker, surely we have things to learn about ethics from the genius of both Sidgwick and Kant, as well as from other proponents of these two schools of moral thought.

If we could find a way to structure these "ways of moral thinking" that could show how each could contribute in proper measure, we would have found a structure of normative ethical thought (oddly placed on the line between metaethics and normative ethics) worth considering. Thinking of virtues as skills provides us with such a structure, for understanding *phro-*

nesis in the terms laid out above gives us a way of articulating what is worthwhile about both deontological and consequentialist thought, particularly when viewed in the light of how diagnosis and problem solving are related and complementary.

We can begin with moral theories that are concerned broadly with living well and work from there toward deontology and consequentialism. To live well, people must become clear about what goals they should set for themselves. In medical theory, the goal is a healthy life, and in navigation, the goal is a geographical location. For morality, we are trying to live or act well, and for rough and ready purposes, we can say that this is achieved by pursuing virtue and avoiding vice. We can learn to live well, as we can learn to be healthy, but as in medicine, solving particular ethical problems is casework, and different cases call for different strategies. Sometimes thinking like a virtuous person means acting for the proper reasons (letting consequences be damned), whereas at other times thinking virtuously means getting the job done or obtaining the proper results (where the ends justify the means). Sometimes one ought to think and behave like a deontologist, and at other times one ought to think and behave like a consequentialist. Perhaps at other times, neither of these strategies is of much help, whereas in still others, both may be equally satisfactory (functionally equivalent) from the point of view of a good life or right action. Giving a full account of how and when these different strategies are to be employed ethically is the business, of course, of a normative ethical theory per se; thankfully, this difficult task is not ours here. What is needed is some sense of the architectonic structure of deontology, consequentialism, and virtue theory. This can be achieved by noting how deontology and consequentialism can be understood as ethical strategies that emphasize different aspects of *phronesis*: deontological thought that emphasizes diagnosis, and consequentialist thought that emphasizes problem solving. Thus, the virtuous agent, in pursuit of acting well and living a good life, will treat individual ethical situations as individual problems whose treatment or solution must be tailor-made.

Deontological moral theories are a family of theories, which taken separately can appear to be quite disparate. There are theological deontic theories that say that what is right is what God says is right; and there are rules-based versions that say that there are moral rules, and what is right is what is according to the rules. Obligation-based moral theories say that what is right is what is obligatory. In rationality-based deontic theories what is right is what is rational, whereas other deontic theories are more psychological, wherein what is right is to act with a good will or with proper motives. But what seems to bind deontic theories together is their emphasis on why an act is performed: an act is morally correct if it is done for the correct reasons. The differentia of the species of deontic theories are found in what makes reasons "correct," but what is characteristic of their epistemology is what could be called their "etiological approach" to moral action. Deontologists consider an act to be good if it is the expression of the correct reasons for acting. In other words, one looks to the source of the act, or the reasons why it was performed, to determine its moral standing; what follows from the act or its consequences is of no concern.[11]

For some paradigm examples of acts that are right by the lights of deontology, consider learning that a friend is in need and, without a second thought, rushing to help; spontaneously smiling as a friend walks in the room; visiting a loved one in the hospital; or keeping a deathbed promise to someone who would never know if the promise were unfulfilled.[12] These are all acts that are to be performed without regard to the consequences (such regard is "one thought too many"); for example, if we were told that visiting a loved one in the hospital would be of no help whatsoever to the health of the patient, we still ought to go. There is no goal these actions seek to obtain; rather, they are spontaneous natural expressions of the person acting: they are good things to do, and they are such because they manifest the good will or the good reasoning or the goodness of the person who is acting. And when we observe someone behaving in these ways, we can recognize (sometimes) the good will of the person acting; we say that they did the right thing because they acted for the right reasons, not because of what the act would accomplish.

The epistemological aspects of deontology are related in a particularly close way to diagnosis, as an element of *phronesis*, insofar as when one is thinking like a deontologist all one must do is correctly assess the situation

11. This may appear to not sit too well with the versions of deontology that are propounded by Prichard (1912) or Ross (1930), for they hold that one does the right thing by doing one's duty, regardless of what one's reasons are for doing one's duty. This inversion of the good and the right complicates the story but does not change it. These issues do receive some (but not full) attention in the next chapter.

12. Some of these examples are from Michael Stocker's (1981) "Values and Purposes: The Limits of Teleology and Ends of Friendship," which I take to give the correct account of the kind of act that is good in itself, independent of its consequences.

and then act naturally. We assume that the good deontologist enters into ethical situations already having inculcated a particular form of deontology (has learned obedience to God, has learned the rules of obligation, has trained the will to be good, or has developed the proper motivational structures, etc.). After this, our good agent enters the situation, makes a proper diagnosis, and then reacts naturally. Here is an easy medical case and an easy moral case. The medical case: diagnosing hepatitis from jaundiced eyes. Doctors simply perceive that state, and what to do from there is clear. The moral case: one learns that a loved one is in the hospital, and one drops whatever is in hand and goes to the hospital. One simply perceives that circumstance and acts naturally. In more difficult medical cases, the symptoms may give contrary indications, and the relationships between the symptoms may need consideration in order to get to the root of the problem. In more difficult moral cases, obligations may be mutually exclusive, and the relationships between obligations may need consideration in order to determine which is the most primary (again, in an attempt to get to the "bottom" of the situation). As soon as our deontologist has correctly figured out what is going on, what needs to be done from there is "intuitively" evident. The epistemic work of the deontologist is done while taking in the facts of the situation, perceiving what the various reasons are for acting and evaluating them. Diagnose properly, figure out all these reasons, and the rules of deontology determine what one ought to do or what one's obligations are. Or perhaps, diagnosing properly and having a good will suffice for doing what ought to be done. In any case, the deontologist's epistemic work is in the reading of moral signs; what to do after that is to do what comes naturally. If people have inculcated deontology properly and properly assessed their current circumstances, this will be sufficient for them to perform the act they ought to perform. One reason it is virtually guaranteed that the right act will be performed is that the results of the act are of no consequence, and one need not even consider them or expend any epistemic energy on consequences in order to succeed in doing what one ought. Thus, the deontological strategy is to diagnose and engage the properly trained will.

It may be helpful to see this point from a different perspective. Deontological thought is concerned with coming to realize what may be called "the deep moral nature" of a situation, and this phrase is meant to cover the differences between species of deontology. For some, the deep moral nature may be about what a God wants or what rule this situation falls under. The deep moral nature could concern what obligations one has or maybe what the right reasons are for acting. We realize our obligations and, after that, act. Prichard (1912) would be the first to say that there is nothing to think about at all, after we intuit our obligations (thinking otherwise represents a failure of comprehension). Coming to realize that a rule applies is sufficient for knowing what to do. Rules may always be put in a conditional form, such as "anyone in situations Φ, ought to Ψ." Come to realize that you are in a situation that has a deep moral nature of the Φ kind, and no further thought is needed. By diagnosing that Φ is present, and thus which rule applies, Ψ-ing ensues. And, one might add, damn the consequences of Ψ-ing as being of no moral significance whatsoever. Deontological moral thought ignores these consequences.

This is in obvious contrast to consequentialist thinking. Consequentialism is the theory that holds that right acts are the ones that produce a specified outcome. Which outcome is specified is what distinguishes one version of consequentialism from the others. The specified end might be the greatest happiness for the greatest number, it might be the greatest happiness for me, it might be the most pleasure, and so on. What is distinctive about these theories is that it is irrelevant how this outcome is achieved. If an act is done unwittingly, and not as the result of a proper diagnosis or a properly trained will, or even if it is performed for exactly the wrong reasons or with bad will, the act may still be quite good, indeed. If deontology has etiological, backward-looking leanings, consequentialism is forward looking. The reasons one may have for acting are irrelevant.

The epistemic situation in general is more straightforward for consequentialists, for they are taken to perform quasi-mathematical calculations. The effects of performing a variety of possible acts are considered and compared for their ability to produce the desired outcome. Whether the right act is a calculation aimed at maximizing "hedons" or perhaps merely a rougher accounting of pros and cons, the correct act to perform is the result of calculating or accounting. This is the solution to the problem. And we can here begin to see how consequentialist thinking is closely related to the problem-solving aspect of *phronesis*. When we are thinking like consequentialists, we are thinking like impartial problem solvers. Why the problem exists and its underlying reasons or causes are epistemically relevant only insofar as they are needed to solve the problem. To put it crudely, if happiness is not being maximized, the only considerations that are important are those that help to correct this situation. Of course, consequentialists perform some sort of diagnosis in evaluating ethical situations, but the suggestion is that the epistemic processes that are distinctively characteristic of consequentialism are those processes by which the future course of action is determined. Whereas for deontologists the act that ought to be done presents itself naturally, so to speak, upon the completion of the diagnosis, for consequentialists, moral thought really begins only *after* the diagnosis is complete, when the results of different possible courses of action are being weighed against one another. Practical moral thought begins with the full knowledge of the present situation. From here the moral calculus is engaged, and the proper course of action is the result of the calculation.

To engage navigational language, deontology reckons up your past and this tells you your current location (or what your obligations or reasons are); consequentialism pilots one toward a goal so that, given reference to currently present landmarks or signs, you learn how you are faring on the way. There is no reason, however, why one must chose exclusively one moral methodology. Deontologists and consequentialists have both made the mistake of thinking that each had a complete account of practical rationality, or *phronesis*. On the contrary, all the information learned about reasons and how one is faring toward achieving a well-lived life may be more or less relevant or practical for one to figure out what needs to be done at any particular moment, depending on one's circumstances.

Sometimes what is called for is a spontaneous natural act of pure good will, and sometimes what is called for is a cold calculation and an act done without regard for motive, will, reasons, and so on. Consider situations in which we must choose the lesser of two evils. Of course, we perform some diagnosis; otherwise we would not know the unfortunate nature of the choice with which we are faced. We would not see, for example, that our obligations conflict. But when the straits are dire (someone is actually suffering in front of us, moment by moment), we should not be fixated on how we got there or why things are as they are. (If there is a lesson to be had, now is not the time to learn it.) When what is necessary is for us to get out of the mess we are in as best we can, when we are trying to minimize damage, when what we've got is a problem and we have to solve it—these are some of the times when consequentialist thinking correctly predominates.

There are also times when "how serious" the situation is is irrelevant; the numbers of people involved or who they are are trumped by the deontological "principle." Judges ought not to purposefully find the innocent guilty in order to prevent riots in the street, period. "Principle" may prevent one from acting in ways that will bring pleasure or gratification or some other desired end. Sometimes we must just do what we know to be right, consequences notwithstanding. It would be wrong to misconstrue this type of thinking by insisting that there is some subliminal or subconscious calculation taking place. Although there are times when it clearly would not be right to insist on principle alone, there are other times when our integrity demands that we stand by our principles (and no "alienation" from our ends need be involved). Thus, there are times when we do what we ought to do, even though we may "suffer the consequences" (martyrdom being the most extreme example).

Thus we can see the development of the different epistemic methodologies of these two ethical theories as capable of being roughly modeled on different aspects of *phronesis*. Different strategies have evolved for thinking about ethical situations. The character of the situation we find ourselves in is what will determine which strategy is most apt. This is not to say that consequentialists do not diagnose problems nor that deontologists do not solve problems. This is to say that the times when it is correct to think like a deontologist are those times when calculating is the wrong strategy to adopt; there are times when calculating consequences itself constitutes a moral failure (of having one thought too many). At other times, such calculation will be exactly what the situation demands. There are times to think like a deontologist, to diagnose and react, and other times to think like a consequentialist and calculate. Vernacular phrases such as "the lesser of two evils" and "let the consequences be damned" are evidence that commonsense morality has aspects of both consequentialism and deontology built in. In regard to the semantic issues that are the concern of the next chapter, we should not expect to discover that our moral terms exclusively or smoothly track the dictates of either consequentialism or deontology. Such a thought is merely a philosopher's fancy. Fancy aside, the virtuous person will be adept at both sorts of methodologies. Of course, there is no reason to assume that these are the only ways of thinking about moral situations that are open to the virtuous. Part of the skill of virtue will be knowing which strategy to adopt in any given case. Therein, perhaps, lies wisdom.

This model of articulated normative ethical theories will be developed further in the next chapter in a discussion of the semantics of "healthiness" and "goodness." Our present concern, however, is still epistemology and ethical forms of thought. And since many of the problems of defending moral realism have originated in the existence of extended moral disagreement between otherwise good people who epistemically "know all the facts," let us turn to this issue.

Stubborn Disagreement in Face of the Facts

The irresolvable nature of some moral disagreement has seemed to many to be an argument against moral realism. Stevenson (1937, 1949), Ayer (1952), and Mackie (1977), to name only a few, have all propounded such arguments. McDowell (1983) helpfully notes that sometimes this argument about disagreement is sometimes unhelpfully conflated with arguments about the diversity of moral views across cultures, and we should be clear that this is not what is intended. This sort of cross-cultural disagreement has already been discussed briefly in chapter 1, wherein relativity and conventionalism are shown to be consistent with moral realism. Moral realists are committed to saying that whenever cross-cultural disagreements exist that are not due to the kinds of relativity and conventionalism already discussed must be due to mistakes one of the parties is making about the moral facts. So, for example, when members of a culture defend their practice of involuntary gross excision of adolescent female genitalia as morally acceptable, we would conclude that either we or they (and undoubtedly they) are making some sort of mistake about what is good for human beings.

The idea we are concerned with, however, is not that people with different moral outlooks, points of view, or conceptual schemes may have seemingly irresolvable disagreements but that even within a single outlook such disagreements may arise. These moral disagreements must also be distinguished from possible semantic disagreement over the meaning of moral terms, which is taken up in the next chapter. The type of disagreement under consideration here goes something like this: it seems entirely possible that two people may be able to agree on all the empirical facts of a moral situation and yet still have a stubborn disagreement over the moral nature of the case and what to do about it. The conclusion often drawn from such situations is that at bottom, morality is not best interpreted realistically, that there is no "right answer," either because it is based on attitudes (hence Ayer, 1952, and Stevenson, 1937, 1949, and expressivism) or because moral discourse is, strictly speaking, all false (hence Mackie, 1977, and error theories).

It should be noted first that this presentation of the argument against moral realism from stubborn disagreement begs the question in its present form, for it takes as a premise the idea that all the "empirical facts" of the case have been settled and then goes on to "show" that all questions of morality are not thereby settled. A moral realist might respond by saying that it can be assumed that settling all the facts of a case fails to settle the moral issues only if it is also assumed from the start that morality is not at bottom factual; and this would not be an inappropriate response. It would, however, not respond adequately to the genuine worry that moral nonrealists have: it does seem as if there are cases in which "all the facts" are agreed on and yet the dispute rages on. To put this another way, one might say that it seems to be the case that rational debate about morality might be carried on indefinitely without resolution and without the disputants making anything that would amount to a cognitive error. And thus, it seems that we have a good reason to eschew realism about morality.

But do we really? Given the moral epistemology outlined above, there is a cogent way to respond to the argument. It proceeds first by noting that, in all discourses about skill, we can expect there to be intractable disagreement, even among experts, which persists in view of "all the facts," and that in such cases the dispute is chalked up to a difference in judgment and not to a lack of facts. For example, it is now fairly standard practice to get a "second opinion" on any serious and difficult medical diagnosis that has been made, and very often these opinions diverge. (For a doctor's personal anecdotes about second guessing and being second-guessed, see Groopman, 2000.) To take another example, if dead reckoning requires making regular adjustments for the effects of tides and leeward motion, then two experts might not be able to agree on their current position without this implying that they lack a definitive position. If morality is considered a skill, then we should expect these same sorts of disagreement in judgment to occur. Barring cognitive error, moral disagreements that persist are due to these differences in skillful judgment, not to a lack of moral reality.

We have already noted why we should expect disagreement between medical professionals. Not only are there differences in the ways in which medical problems are approached, but there are also going to be differences of opinion in the face of all the uncertainty that surrounds difficult cases. We expect medical experts to agree on the easy cases, but we also expect there to be moral agreement on the easy cases. One ought to eat well and to sleep regularly, and one ought not to cause needless suffering for fun. Those disagreeing morally about such cruelty have already, so to speak, fallen off the back of the moral train, and their opinion need not be taken seriously, much in the same way that those who maintain that cigarette smoking is not bad for one's health need not be taken seriously.

Easy cases aside, however, medical experts may disagree on their diagnoses and their prescriptions in at least three ways. The first way occurs in cases in which the differences make no practical difference in the outcome of the case; there may be more than one way to adequately "skin the cat", without this obviating the possibility for disagreements over technique. The second way occurs in cases in which one disputant has made some sort of undetected cognitive error in the appraisal of the case. Finally, and most important, disputes may arise in unusual and overly complicated cases, even when the parties to the disagreement have agreed on "all the facts" of the case. It is these last cases that are most similar to persistent ethical disagreement. Medical experts may agree on all the observable symptoms present yet disagree on what they amount to or what to do about them (presumably, this will happen more frequently the closer the case is to being "hopeless"). Medical experts may agree on all the symptoms that a patient is exhibiting, without agreeing on a diagnosis, and even if the diagnosis is agreed on, this does not guarantee that there will not be further dispute over what to do with the patient. It will often be hard to tell if these disagreements are due to cognitive errors or, for example, differences in "personal evidence thresholds."[13] The point is that, either way, we do not draw negative conclusions about the realistic interpretation of medical discourse as moral nonrealists would have us draw about moral discourse based on epistemically similar disagreement.

The purveyor of the argument by disagreement may not be satisfied, however, for it seems that moral disagreement may not concern particular cases but is, somehow, more global, even within the limits of a single moral outlook or perspective. So, one might point to Thrasymachus' debate with Socrates and suggest that there is no correlate to this in the sphere of medicine, for the very picture of health is not under debate between medical experts as it is in morality. And although this claim may be disputed by the moral realist, let us grant it. The suggestion seems to be that rational considerations alone may not bring all moral disputants into agreement, that it may not be possible to persuade everyone to morally agree sheerly by force of argument. Importantly, this seems to be so, and it may appear to point to a sui generis feature of morality. Even if it were assumed that there is a truth about justice, Thrasymachus may not be able to be rationally convinced that justice is not the interest of the

---

13. As Crispin Wright (1992) formulates the situation, it must be "*a priori* that differences of opinion formulated within the discourse, unless excusable as a result of vagueness in a disputed statement, or in the standards of acceptability, or variation in personal evidence thresholds, so to speak, will involve something which may properly be regarded as a cognitive shortcoming" (p. 144).

stronger, regardless of the arguments he is presented with. And this very fact may be a reason to think that such a truth about justice does not exist.

The first response here is to follow Phillipa Foot (1958–59), and to take Thrasymachus' position very seriously. If being just is not in one's best interest, then one has good reason to suspect that one ought not to be just. The moral realist may first respond by assuming the expertise of Socrates and denying Thrasymachus such a status, finding his expertise wanting just on this score. But abjuring from such a strategy (in the face of the inevitable charge of question begging), taking Thrasymachus seriously and engaging seriously in debate with him, does not mean that if we fail to persuade him that he is wrong then this indicates that there are no moral facts of the matter. We must remember, once again, the lesson taught us by Quine ([1951] 1953), mentioned in chapter 1: if one is willing to alter enough of one's belief structure, one may preserve the truth of any particular proposition in the face of any rational argument. Even if there is no real analytic-synthetic distinction to be drawn among propositions, one may continue to hold onto any given proposition if one is also willing to make enough changes elsewhere. If Thrasymachus held onto his theory of justice *come what may*, as if it were an analytic truth, there would be no way to persuade him that he was wrong. But we may not conclude from this anything special about moral realism. One could similarly insist that the world is flat or that the space trips to the moon were faked as a part of a propaganda conspiracy perpetrated by the United States to deflate Russian monetary reserves. One could insist on the Democratic or Republican Party national platform down the line. One could insist that God made the world in seven days or that there are no hidden variables capable of explaining quantum indeterminacy.

Importantly, intractable disputes arise in many areas of discourse, even within the "hard sciences." Debates rage over the proper interpretation of quantum physics, over the existence of quantum gravity, over the nature of biological function in general, and over the biological function of a neuron in particular. The disputants may agree on "all the facts" of the case, but the disagreement may still rage on. The case should close immediately after a moment's attention to theological debate. All the available facts are in on whether or not God exists. Either God does or God does not. (The reverse of the ontological argument is that if God does not exist, then God is not even possible.) We have our ontological debate par excellance; it has and always will continue to rage on. No one, however, thinks for a moment that its irresolvability inveighs one iota toward the conclusion that there is no truth to the matter, that theological discourse is not intended to be "fact stating," or that the debate is due solely to a clash of attitudes. Moral realism should not be held to a higher standard.

Perhaps that is quite enough for now, especially since we will return to disagreement again in chapter 3. Here is a quick closing argument for this section. The world is a complicated place, and morality is the most complicated of pursuits within it. We should expect some disagreements to go unresolved, for to expect otherwise would be to insist on a simplified view of morality and the human condition. Would the case be any easier for the moral realist if there were no unresolvable moral disputes? Well, there do not seem to be these sorts of disputes about table manners, but this is no argument for realism about etiquette or politeness. And, were we to imagine there were no ongoing moral debates, we could also imagine a diehard moral nonrealist in this case trying to make an invidious comparison of all these resolvable moral debates to all the unresolvable debates in theoretical physics, insisting that we think there are facts of the matter in physics even though the physicists themselves endlessly dispute which interpretation of (say) quantum physics to adopt, whereas the hypothetical lack of debate in our morality shows that we can just decide and agree on what is right and that alone is what makes right right. At this point, it seems as if our actual, unresolved moral debates could be an argument *in favor* of moral realism. In comparing morality with science and medicine, we should probably expect that getting moral matters right is going to be even more difficult than getting medical or scientific matters right, and these latter are difficult enough to inspire stubborn disagreement. We do not, as a result, thereby judge medicine or science unfit for a realist's interpretation, nor should we draw such conclusions about morality.

Aristotle's Rejection of Virtues as Skills

Aristotle discusses the similarities and the differences between skills and virtues throughout the *Nicomachean Ethics*.[14] As his account of the nature

14. In at least the following places: 1099b21–24, 1106b8–16, 1104a5–11, 1105a–26–b5, 1106b5–16, 1112a34–b31, 1120b13, 1122a34, 1129a11–16, 1133a14–16, 1140a1–b7, 1140b21–30, 1141b14–22, 1152b2, 1167b34, 1174a22–1174b2, 1179b33–1180b32.

of virtue often emerges out of a discussion of the nature of skill, in more places than not, Aristotle is discussing similarities between virtues and skill. An important example of such similarity, especially from an epistemic point of view, is that both skills and virtues are learned by experience and habituation. So, in the resulting Catch-22 puzzle "How can we become good without already being good?" Aristotle's (1985) solution models how a person becomes good on how a person becomes a grammarian or musician (1105a20). But, despite noting such a strong epistemological similarity between virtues and skills, it is quite clear that he does not think that the virtues are skills.

To jump to the quick: here is the passage that most clearly expresses Aristotle's (1985) opinion that skills are not virtues, where *techne* is being translated as "skill":

> Moreover, in any case what is true of skills is not true of virtues. For the products of a skill determine by their own character whether they have been produced well; and so it suffices that they are in the right state when they have been produced. But for actions expressing virtue to be done temperately or justly, it does not suffice that they are themselves in the right state. Rather the agent must also be in the right state when he does them. First, he must know [that he is performing virtuous actions]; second, he must decide on them, and decide on them for themselves; and, third, he must also do them from a firm and unchanging state.
>
> As conditions for having a skill these three do not count, except for the knowing itself. As a condition for having a virtue, however, the knowing counts for nothing, or for only a little, whereas the other two conditions are very important, indeed all-important. (1105a22–b6)

Putting aside for the moment the claim that the products of skills "determine their own character," we may break down the rest of the quote as follows: for a master to be practicing a skill, he must (1) know he is engaged in the skill, whereas (2) a virtuous person need not know she is engaged in virtuous activity. A master of skill (3a) need not "decide" on which actions to perform nor (3b) must perform them "for themselves," whereas (4a) a virtuous person must "decide" which actions to perform and (4b) decide on them "for themselves." Finally, a master of a skill (5) need not perform skillful acts from a "firm and unchanging state," whereas (6) virtuous acts must be done from such a state. Each of Aristotle's arguments has one of the following two problems: either the facts he musters to distinguish virtues and skills do not square with what we now think about virtues and skills, or where Aristotle succeeds in finding genuine differences between virtues and skills, these are consistent with the idea that virtues are a special subset of skills, so that the "differences" Aristotle points out are merely what makes virtues special skills.[15]

For the first type of problem, consider (1) in light of Archimedes' yelp of "Eureka!" after submerging himself in a tub. Surely, he did not know he was "engaged in his skill" as he realized that the ratio of volume to weight could be used to distinguish gold from fool's gold (or be used as a general measure of density). Those who are masters of a skill do not leave it behind in the workroom but, rather, live their skills. Solving a math problem while getting on a bus or waking up in the middle of the night with a solution in mind shows that skillful activity need not be knowingly engaged in. So, it is simply false to say, as (1) does, that practitioners of a skill must be aware of their engagement. And (2) is true for the same reasons that (1) is false: there is no reason that a temperate person need be aware of being virtuous or temperate while rejecting temptation. (This seems especially true when contrasting the temperate to the continent, where the appetites of the former need not be held in check like the appetites of the latter.) Similarly, one need not be aware that one is being just or virtuous when distributing resources justly. Also, if giving charity or being benevolent are considered virtues, being conscious of being virtuous while being charitable or kind is, as the Williams' saying goes, "one thought too many." It would be wrong to make virtuous action necessarily self-conscious in these ways. Thus, an inspection of (1) and (2), far from serving to distinguish virtues from skills, shows the two to be of a piece.

Jumping ahead to (5) and (6), we realize that (5) says that an expert in a skill may make a correct move by accident (i.e., it was not done from the "firm and unchanging state" of expertise), and yet this move, from the point of the view of the skill, would be perfectly satisfactory because the outcome would be correct. For example, consider taking a car to a mechanic because it is not running well, and the mechanic fixes the automobile by accident. From the point of view of the consumer, who just wants a running car, what we have is a job well done. This is what Aristotle (1985) is referring to in the first half of the remark, that "the products of a skill determine by their own character whether they have been produced well; and so it suffices that they are in the right state when

---

15. The second type of weakness mentioned here is roughly similar to a type of defense of the "craft analogy" found in sections 47–48 of Terence Irwin's (1995) *Plato's Ethics*. Irwin and I differ, however, over the *praxis-poiesis* distinction's success in differentiating skills from virtues.

they have been produced. But for actions expressing virtue to be done temperately or justly, it does not suffice that they are themselves in the right state." One can produce something skillful by accident (5), but one cannot perform a virtuous action by accident (6). Thus, virtues are not skills. Agreed all around is the truth of (6): virtuous acts cannot occur by accident. But do we really have good reason to think that skillful actions may occur by accident? I submit that whereas a consumer (with only a single car problem) might not care if the mechanic fixes the car by accident or from a firm and unchanging state, to an expert mechanic's evaluation of the work, a car fixed by accident is not a job well done. To think otherwise is to conflate luck with skill. Aristotle thinks that skills are valuable only for their products (whereas this is not so for virtues). But this is only true if we ignore the value of the skill to the expert and only consider skills purely from the point of view of consumers. There is no reason to do this, however. Just as we must consider the value of virtuous acts to the agent who is performing them, we must also consider the value of a skill to the expert who is engaging in it. If we do so, we see that (5) is false: a correct move made from something other than a firm and unchanging expertise is not a skillful move. The value of a skill is *not* only in its products. From the point of view of the master artisan or expert, the value of a skill is as much in *the doing* as in *the making*. In fact, perhaps, *the doing* is even of more value, for we often find experts fairly apathetic toward their past and completed projects and singularly engrossed in the current one.

And so, we now find ourselves face to face with Aristotle's notorious distinction between doing and making. In passages other than the one just quoted, Aristotle (1985) argues that perhaps the most basic way in which skills and virtues differ is that the former are concerned with production, *poiesis* (1140a1), whereas the latter are concerned with action, *praxis*, performed "for itself" (1105a32). We have seen reason, contra Aristotle, why we cannot look merely to the quality of the product in judging skills, for they alone do not determine a job well done from the point of view of the expert. But if Aristotle can make the claim that if an expert is engaging in a skill this is purely making, but when a virtuous agent is engaging in a virtue it is purely doing, and there is an important difference between them, then he has shown us good reason to think that virtues are not skills. The argument might be summarized as follows: as noted above, we learn skills and virtues by the same means, namely, by performing actions or engaging in the activity that is the object of the skill or virtue. We learn to be a builder by building, and we learn to be temperate by performing temperate actions (1103a32–b2). Still, "production has its end beyond it; but action does not, since its end is doing well itself" (1140b6–7). Therefore, since skills are concerned purely with production and virtues with action, the virtues are not skills.

We begin with Aristotle (1985) on production: "Now building, for example, is a skill, and is essentially a certain state involving reason concerned with production; there is no skill that is not a state involving reason concerned with production, and no such state that is not a skill. Hence, a skill is the same as a state involving true reason concerned with production" (1140a6–11). Although Aristotle's opinion has obvious authority, we should not just accept it blindly, and in this case even a commonsense view of expertise shows Aristotle to be wrong: engaging in a skill does not entail involving reason for the sake of the particular product of the skill. Counterexamples involve both practicing a skill for the sake of becoming better at the skill and practicing the skill for the sake of experiment or enjoyment or even for its own sake. When an expert practices, this may be in the spirit of a rehearsal for a performance, and in this sense of practice, one may say that the practice is done for the sake of a product (where the product is the performance). But one need not practice in the sense of rehearsal; one can practice a skill purely for the sake of wanting to become more proficient, without any sense at all that one is rehearsing for the sake of a future product. Or one may simply want to exercise one's skill for its own sake, because it is relaxing or pleasurable, or because learning new skills may improve one's mind or life. Experts may also experiment while engaging in their skill: trying new materials, new instruments, and new techniques is surely all part of the nature of skill, but one need not be doing so for the sake of future products. It is true that the raison d'être of a skill is the production of something and that practicing and experimenting may in some oblique way be concerned with production. But such an oblique intention cannot be seen as necessarily being a reason concerned with production or motivation of each skillful act. Consequently, we must conclude that skilled action need not be concerned with production. Indeed, we find that experts, while most deeply engaged in their skills, are not thinking at all about a future product but are fully engaged in the present moment. Thinking of the future while in the middle of a task can be seen as the nonmoral correlate to Williams' "one thought too many"; thinking in this way may interfere with performance. This is the state that modern psychologists refer to as "flow" (Csikszentmihalyi, 1990), a concept that we certainly cannot hold Aristotle accountable for being ignorant of. But, in any case, engaging in a skill is not necessarily a state that involves reason concerned with production.

Moreover, similar remarks may be made about virtue. Just as we can imagine practicing a skill for its own sake or for the sake of "honing" one's skills, we can certainly imagine temperate or self-controlled people (*sophrosune*) who are testing themselves to make sure they are not getting lax or tending toward *akrasia*. (Can the smoker who has quit go into the smoky bar and not yearn to light up?) Similarly, we may imagine those dissatisfied with their cowardice to deliberately place themselves in situations where they must practice "facing their fears" for the sake of becoming more courageous. The virtuous may practice being virtuous for the sake of becoming more virtuous, just as an expert in a skill may practice (engage in one's skill) for the sake of furthering one's expertise. And here we must note the relationships between virtuous action and the good life (*eudaimonia*). Though it seems to contradict his thought that virtuous acts are "doings" and not "makings," Aristotle (1985) does recognize that our virtuous actions are done for the sake of producing *eudaimonia* (1097b2–6), even if virtuous action should not be done with one's *eudaimonia* in mind, for this would be thinking "one thought too many." Formally considered, virtuous actions are productive of *eudaimonia*, even though *eudaimonia* (in many cases) cannot be the direct intention of a virtuous act.[16]

Aristotle (1985) says, "[Wisdom, virtue] is not knowledge of skill, because action and production belong to different kinds. The remaining possibility, then, is that wisdom is a state grasping the truth, involving reason, concerned with action about what is good or bad for a human being" (1140b3–6). It is to the point to note that just as health is the *telos*

---

16. For a detailed discussion of this formal relationship, see Annas (1993). For a discussion of how an end like eudaimonia can produce motivations that are independent of the production of that end, see Schmidtz (1995). Irwin acknowledges this sense in which virtue is concerned with the production of *eudaimonia* (see Aristotle, 1985, p. 385). Here is the quote mentioned above at 1097b2–6: "Honor, pleasure, understanding and every virtue we certainly choose because of themselves, since we would choose each of them even if it had no further result, but we also choose them for the sake of a well-lived life [*eudaimonia*], supposing that through them we shall flourish [*eudaimonia*]. Eudaimonia, by contrast, no one ever chooses for their sake or for the sake of anything else at all." I resist translating *eudaimonia* as "happiness" because of how misleading this can be.

of medicine, *eudaimonia* is the *telos* of virtue. Moreover, we would be right to insist that if wisdom or virtue is a state concerned with action "about what is good or bad for a human being," it would be invidious to say that skill is concerned with production but virtue is not; that, for example, medicine is concerned with what is healthy or unhealthy for a human being and is thus concerned with production, but that virtue, while it is concerned with what is good or bad for a human being, is not concerned with production.

So, I take it that the *praxis-poiesis* distinction does not do the work Aristotle thought it did, for it is not clear that the distinction can be made cogent; and even assuming it can be, we still find that a proper understanding of skills must account for *the doing* of the expert, and a proper understanding of virtues must account both for practice and rehearsal, which is *the making* or honing of virtue, as well as for the sense in which virtues are productive of *eudaimonia*. Thus far, we have yet to find a reason to doubt that virtues are skills. There is, however, another type of consideration Aristotle discusses that is supposed to differentiate skills from virtues.

We gain access to these by returning to (3) and (4) of the analysis of the first quotation. To repeat, masters of a skill (3a) need not "decide" on which actions to perform, nor must they perform them "for themselves" (3b), whereas (4a) a virtuous person must "decide" which actions to perform and decide on them "for themselves" (4b). The truth of (3a), that the masters of skills, such as doctors, need not decide on which actions to perform, will depend on what is meant by "decide." Presumably, what Aristotle is trying to get at is the idea that a doctor may react (even from a firm and unchanging state) with some sort of automaticity, or without reflection, and still succeed quite well in curing the patient, whereas virtuous people must "make decisions," presumably in a reflective or at least conscious manner (4a). If the sense of "decide" has been understood correctly here, then (3a) does seem to be true, for, as noted above, experts in skills often cannot retrospectively report accurately on why they did what they did, even if what they did was founded on their correct understanding of the *logos* of their skill. Let us assume that (4a) is thus true, and those who are virtuous [although not always conscious of what they are doing (2)] can always retrospectively report, via introspection, accurately on their reasons for action. Now, since the virtuous seem to have the ability to retrospectively give accurate accounts, via introspection, of why they did what they did, and experts in skills do not

always have this ability, we may have found an important difference between virtues and skills.

Let us proceed by first taking a step back and remembering that the
topic here is moral epistemology. The thesis being explored is that virtues
are skills, in the hope that if this is true, we will have a moral epistemology
that can show how moral knowledge is epistemically on a par with medical
knowledge. Aristotle, at this point, argues that virtues are not skills, for
whereas our inability to introspect the reasons behind skillful behavior
does not show it to be any less skillful, an inability to introspect the
reasons behind prima facie virtuous behavior would show it to be non-
virtuous. But why should this difference in ability to be introspective be
relevant? Why need an expert be necessarily articulate in this fashion? If
we found a doctor who was always able to report reliably on her reasons
for action, this would not be grounds for saying that she knew medicine
better than any other doctor unless she also had a higher success rate in
curing patients. *Ex hypothesi*, skills come with sufficient intellectual structure (logoi) to ground claims to knowledge of a skill. No one is questioning the existence of medical knowledge (qua example of a skill). An
ability of a doctor to be introspective in the relevant way gives us further
proof of the doctor's knowledge, but third parties can judge when a putative doctor has medical knowledge by combining what this person says
about medicine (even if she cannot always say why she does what she
does) and by the reliable results of this person's actions. (Reliability is
necessary to rule out doctors or mechanics who cure or fix through luck.)
The question seems to be whether the same standard applies to virtue, or
if virtue demands a higher standard, namely, an ability to reliably discover
by introspection reasons for action. But, for the following reason, this is
the wrong question to be asking.

The most important point is that however this question is answered,
we have plenty of room for the possibility of moral knowledge. Importantly, for Aristotle to reject the thesis that virtues are skills, it is necessary
for him to find differences between the two that are not consistent with
the possibility that the virtues are a subset of skills. Virtues may be special
skills, requiring "talents" (if you will) not required by other skills, but this
obviously does not show that the virtues are not skills. If the virtues are
a subset of skills—so that for the skills that are virtues a different, higher
standard applies—Aristotle has not found a distinction that shows that
the virtues are not skills (see also, Annas 1993, p. 68). What will make
moral knowledge a subset of knowledge gained by skill will be for it to

be based on a logos, to be acquired by experience and in accordance with practical rationality. If a high degree of reliable introspection is an extra demand that we place on moral knowledge (as we are assuming, if only for the sake of argument), we cannot conclude from this that the virtues are not skills.[17] This would be logically equivalent to concluding that *Homo sapiens* are not primates because we can speak. So, in response to Aristotle, we might say that even assuming that he has lit onto a difference in introspective abilities of humans engaged in virtues and skills, this fails to be a reason for thinking that the virtues are not skills.[18]

17. I do not, as an ethical theorist, agree that this black-and-white sort of introspectibility criterion is apt in the case of justifying moral knowledge or knowledge of skills in general. I think that virtuous people reconstruct their reasons for action after the fact as much as doctors do but that they do so with a higher reliability, which is required because of the added difficulty of being virtuous. The more difficult the skill, the higher a person's introspective reliability must be. Courageous people might act on reflexes and do so for the right reasons. We cannot assume from this, however, that the courageous, in answering our post facto queries, are not reconstructing what their reasons *had to be* any less than did the doctor. For an opinion on the general need for introspectibility in accounts of epistemic justification, that is, the internalist-externalist debate in epistemology, see Bloomfield (2000).

18. Another of Aristotle's arguments is consistent with virtues as a subset of skills and not a different beast entirely. At 1140b22–24, he argues that an expert in a skill who makes mistakes deliberately is "choiceworthy" or "preferable" to one who makes mistakes by accident, whereas the opposite is true for the virtues. Presumably, Aristotle is here saying that it is better for people to accidentally do moral wrong than for them to do so deliberately, and so we are less likely to hold their accidental wrongs against them than their deliberate ones. On the other hand, if experts are going to do something wrong, we will count it against their expertise more if it is accidental than if it is deliberate. If a doctor kills a patient by accident, we think less of the doctor's skill than if the doctor killed the patient on purpose. This is a very interesting and insightful thought, but once again we must wonder at its relevance. Our concern is whether virtues and skills have the same intellectual structure, and there is no reason to assume that our evaluative practices of praising and blaming (or "choosing" or "preferring") have any bearing on this concern. If bad luck or an accident keeps both a virtuous person and an expert in a skill from being successful in their endeavors, we may hold it against them differentially, but this has more to do with what we find valuable than it does with the intellectual nature of virtues and skills. In the same vein, if an inept doctors kills someone as a result of his ineptitude, we *may* find this more blameworthy than if a fool kills someone as a result of foolishness. But this does not show us that medical knowl-

The same type of move is appropriate as a reply to Aristotle's (1985) final argument against the idea of virtues as skills. This is also perhaps what is really driving his argument about how *praxis* and *poiesis* differ. The excellence of a building lies in the building itself, not in the way it was produced, whereas the excellence of a virtuous action must take into account the nature of its motives. So, the thought continues, acting virtuously requires not just the knowledge of what to do but also the proper motivation to do it. Whereas skills are just concerned with knowledge and are mere capacities (1129a11) and do not, so to speak, come with motives built in, the virtues do come with motivation built in. If a doctor sees someone who is sick, the doctor can choose to help or not; but if a temperate person is tempted toward gluttony, the temperate person's motivational structure keeps him or her from so indulging, on pain of intemperance. If one is virtuous, one has no choice but to act virtuously. In terms of our ability to continue to pursue the development of moral epistemology, three points should suffice to justify putting aside this final concern of Aristotle's. First, at 1095b32, Aristotle says that a virtuous person could "remain asleep or inactive throughout his life," and this does not square well with the thought that a virtue is something more than a mere capacity.

Second, whatever motivational structures allow *Homo sapiens* to do what they do is a contingent matter, independent of questions of justification and the nature of the intellectual structures of virtues and skills. If there are some skills that are so difficult for humans that they cannot be mastered unless *every* opportunity to exercise them is taken advantage of, then were one to endeavor to be an expert in such a skill, one would have to develop a motivational structure identical to the ones we find involved with the virtues. Consider the dedication that goes into being a consummate chess player or athlete. Presumably, the more difficult such an endeavor is, the more one must dedicate oneself to being a master of it. Presumably, as well, there is nothing more difficult than becoming morally good or wise. So, we should not be surprised to find exactly what we do in virtuous people: they recognize what morality demands and they are automatically motivated to act. They have become, have been taught, or

---

edge is justified in a different way than wisdom is. Consider, contra Aristotle, this: a doctor who deliberately makes mistakes is not preferable to one who makes them by accident, and a judge who makes mistakes in justice by accident is not more preferable than one who makes them deliberately. Mistake for mistake, they are all of a piece.

have trained themselves to be psychologically determined to be moral. (This will be discussed in much greater detail in chapter 4, where the topic is moral motivation.) If such motivational dedication is what is required by the virtues and no other skills demand this, then so be it. The virtues are then special skills, which should not be especially surprising, if they are skills at all.

Finally, in response to Aristotle is an argument from authority: presumably, the ancient Greeks were far more familiar than we are today with the hypothesis that the virtues are skills, as well as being more familiar with Aristotle's arguments. If these arguments convinced no one back then, besides himself and his followers, and it has been shown that there is some reason why these arguments are even less persuasive to us today (if only because we know more empirical psychology than he), then this should weigh into our deep questioning of Aristotle's rejection of the thesis that the virtues are skills. The strengths and benefits that accrue as a result of accepting the thesis far outweigh any doubts Aristotle's arguments might encourage.

THREE

Moral Language

The "Good" Rules

Following the Linguistic Turn

So far, we have seen how understanding goodness as modeled on health-iness produces a moral ontology that helps us make sense of the kind of property to which moral properties belong. And we have also seen how an ontology of this kind can be mated to an epistemology that places moral inquiry among other epistemically unproblematic endeavors like medicine, navigation, engineering, and chess. And from the point of view of pre-twentieth-century philosophy, with its debate over the primacy of either metaphysics or epistemology, satisfying both of these philosophical needs alone might be an adequate defense of moral realism. But the for-malism that was introduced to philosophical methodology in the late nineteenth century forced the clear recognition of the importance of lan-guage per se as an area of empirical data to which philosophical theories must answer. Of course, from Socrates, we learned of the need for a good definition, and from Aristotle we got an understanding of truth that the most modern minimalists appeal to as authoritative. One might see Locke's distinction between real and nominal essence as presciently antic-ipating Kripke's (1972) and Putnam's (1975) work on causal theories of reference and the necessary a posteriori. But there are few clearer harbingers of the full-on linguistic turn in analytic philosophy than Moore's ([1902] 1988) investigations into the meaning of the word "good" and the importance of understanding this, at least as a separate and perhaps prior issue to a query into the nature (or nonnature, as the case may be) of goodness itself.

Such an approach seems to make philosophy of language first philosophy: whereas Descartes, overturning Aristotle's science of *being qua being* as first philosophy, saw the metaphysical project as necessarily bound by the epistemological limitations of inquiry, the linguistic turn takes the view that since the medium of both epistemological and metaphysical inquiry is language, then our philosophical pursuits must begin with an investigation into it. So, we find the pithiest corner of the linguistic turn coming in Quine's (1969) formula that "to be is to be the value of a bound variable." If we can become clear about the logical structure of a discourse, capturing it in a formalized notation (where variables standing for entities are "bound" by quantifiers), then we can determine the metaphysical commitments of the discourse by determining which entities cannot be "paraphrased away" within that notation. A similar but less formal project is now referred to as the "ordinary language school of philosophy," which was found mostly in the Great Britain of the 1950s. Ordinary language philosophers thought that we could solve certain philosophical problems by looking closely at the way in which we talk about them in the vernacular. And despite the help this type of linguistic philosophy has been, say, in understanding sense data, it is today generally thought within analytic philosophy (I hope) that the emphasis on language has perhaps been a bit too great. Language is indubitably important to philosophy. But however important it may be, there is more to the world than how we represent it and interact with each other within it, even though we most frequently do this through the medium of words and language. One will not have a complete understanding of moral practice without an understanding of the language of the practice, but the language does not exhaust the practice. Still, if we wish to have a complete picture of morality, we must have a grasp of how moral discourse works.

We have learned that our words have functions that are quite different from describing or representing things in the world. Perhaps this is not so profound, but we may perform actions by saying things with words; for example, we may make promises or commitments, as when one says "I do" at a marriage (Austin, 1962). We may "give voice to," or express, emotions or attitudes (Stevenson, 1937). We may command others to obey our will or attempt to persuade or proselytize. And when coming up with a satisfactory moral epistemology stumped the moral realists of the earlier part of the century, forcing a reconsideration of moral realism per se, metaethicists began to explore the possibility that they had been pursuing the wrong project: the crucial question did not concern the nature of goodness but rather the use of the word "goodness." It was thought perhaps that calling x "good" was not an attempt to describe some attribute of x but (roughly) to express a positive attitude about x or to commend x to others. Indeed, the likelihood of such a hypothesis is buttressed by observing that we are generally attracted to the things we call "good," just as one would expect if calling x "good" was commending it (Darwall, Gibbard, Railton, 1992). Similarly, calling something "bad" would be condemning it. And if, aside from certain complicated items of moral discourse, commending and condemning were all there were to the language of morality, then a further exploration into the nature of goodness would be spurious: goodness, understood as a property of a person or perhaps an act, is otiose. Everything there is to be understood about our moral practices was thought to be exhausted by an analysis of the uses of moral language, like praising and blaming. Thus, moral nonrealism was the dominant metaethic of the twentieth century.

There have, of course, always been problems. Some of the complicated bits of moral language, such as "I think x is good, but I may be wrong," seem to resist being straightforwardly understood without recourse to the property of goodness. And it seems unlikely that when we hear of "the perfect murder," our speaker is commending the murder (indeed, it being "perfect" makes it more condemnable). But despite these sorts of problems, it does seem likely that at least one of the functions of moral speech is the expression of attitudes such as commendation and condemnation. The question remains, however, if moral language has other uses. And if, in the analysis of moral language, we find that there are rules to the use of the word "good" that are analogous to the rules found in nonmoral discourses, which themselves are committed to the description of objects (above and beyond any attitudes one may take toward those objects), then there is reason to think that these linguistic forms of moral nonrealism are not able to capture all the facts there are to be captured.

It just so happens that there are both semantic and syntactic rules for "good" that have analogs to our everyday uses of "healthy." Though we may be expressing pro-attitudes or negative attitudes toward people or food or a pulse rate when we call these things either "healthy" or "unhealthy," we are certainly doing more than expressing these attitudes: we are describing or ascribing the properties of healthiness or unhealthiness to these things. It is these properties toward which we have the attitudes that we do. (For the moral analog, see A. N. Prior, 1949 [p. 82 ff.], where he gives quotations from Reid's *Essay on Active Powers*, V.vii., and Sidgwick's *Method of Ethics*, I.iii.1–2.) We typically commend that which is healthy and condemn that which is unhealthy, but we cannot infer from this that there is nothing more to our discourse about health than the expression of these attitudes. The same holds true for moral discourse.

One caveat is in order. What is to come may seem like a descent into ordinary language philosophy, for we are drawing conclusions about goodness from how we speak about it. And taken in a certain way, this is not misleading. What we are engaged in is an inspection of how we speak about goodness that is supposed to reveal data that support a hypothesis that goodness can be helpfully understood by attending to health. True enough. In what follows, however, these data are used differently than is typical of ordinary language philosophy, for two reasons. First, no attempts will be made to give a reductive definition of "goodness". Second, the arguments to follow can be taken as only confirmatory evidence for the present version of moral realism; this is not an attempt to "read reality off language" or to pull a metaphysical rabbit out of a linguistic hat (to borrow a phrase of Salmon). Here, the strategy adopted is one typically employed by those arguing *against* moral realism: the thesis that goodness can be modeled on healthiness establishes certain predictions of how we should talk about goodness, especially in contexts where there is disagreement about whether *x* is "good" or not. This is the methodology of Horgan and Timmons (1991, 1992a, 1992b, 1996a, 1996b) in their series of articles that demonstrate a basic sort of problem, one that plagues a variety of versions of moral realism. The problem they establish for these particular realists is to my mind decisive, but the model of goodness that is drawn on healthiness does not engender the problem. Far from being an attempted resurrection of ordinary language philosophy, there is still the need to preserve the grain of truth in the lesson to be learned from that methodology: error theories aside, the metaphysics of a discourse ought to be able to make some sense of the rules of the language of that discourse.

This chapter is split into two halves, one on semantics and one on syntax. "Semantics" here refers to a model that establishes guidelines for different uses of the word "good." These are rules for determining which kinds of situations are fit for being described in terms of "goodness" (or "badness"). An example of a semantic model is the way in which a "possible world semantics" helps us make sense of the kinds of situations in which modal speech is used: a proposition is necessarily true if it is true at all possible worlds, and a proposition is possibly true if it is true at a possible world that is "relevantly similar" to, or "accessible" from, our own. Such modal propositions are set off from other uses of language by their syntactic features, though we may use semantic models to help us organize and understand those features. Determining which propositions are modal and are thus fit to be considered in terms of possible worlds is a matter of syntax. Very roughly, we note that the modal operators "necessarily" and "possibly" function in the grammar of the propositions that contain them in ways that are importantly dissimilar from propositions in which only what actually obtains is described (which is why some modal propositions are called "contrary-to-fact" or "counterfactual" conditionals). We cannot point to anything in the actual world that can serve completely as a "truth-maker" for propositions with these modal operators, so we have developed semantic models that, in one way or another, posit these possible worlds that are capable of helping us to organize our intuitions about which modal propositions are true and which are not. So, semantic models can help us make sense of propositions with differing syntactic structures produced by using "theoretical" terms (where moral and modal speech are considered to be theoretical). Which propositions are of the modal type is a question of syntax; how to make sense of this type of proposition is a question of semantics.

We begin with the semantic model of "health" that was most fully developed by Aquinas (though Aristotle had something in it himself). This shows "health" to have a primary meaning and two secondary, "analogical" meanings. After laying out this semantic structure for discourse using "health" and revealing the same structure in discourse using "good," we will then see how the problems of semantic disagreement raised in the cited articles of Horgan and Timmons can be avoided. If Horgan and Timmons have raised the largest problem for the semantics of moral realism, there is an equally large problem that has historically caused problems for the syntax of moral realism. This concerns the prescriptive elements of moral discourse, the grammar of prescriptions, and whether they are capable of being true. There is some reason to think that sentences that contain a prescriptive "ought" are best thought of as a type of command and thus are no more capable of being true than a command such as "Shut the door." Many of these problems stem from a syntactic distinction drawn by Hume between propositions that contain "is" and those that contain "ought." In response to these criticisms, an analysis of prescriptions will be presented, showing them to be syntactically different from "is" statements in the same way that modal propositions are different from descriptions of the actual world. Thus, if modal assertions are capable of being true or false, then the same ought to be said of prescriptions. Finally, this analysis will be shown to provide an explanation for the normativity of prescriptive language.

Semantics

Of "Health"

We have discussed in chapter 1 the fact that healthiness, as a property, is invisible and empirically nondetectable, but a moment spent on the semantic consequences of this is in order before we begin. Healthiness is transcendental in ways that are analogous to moral goodness, as discussed in the transcendental argument of the introduction. But as an intermediary between the property of health and the predicate "health," consider the concept *health*. If health (the property) is nonobservable, then a conceptual analysis of *health* will not be able to be completed in terms of other concepts that are themselves completely observable. (This in itself is an argument against the reducibility of health.) Semantically, this means that "health" is not capable of empirical definition, if by "empirical definition" one means a specification of empirically observable conditions that, when present, warrant a predication of the term defined. It could be argued that it was considerations just such as these that led Moore ([1902] 1988) to conclude that "goodness" (because of its indefinability) must be simple and nonnatural. (Jackson, 1998, has a similar reading of Moore.) Such reasoning leads quickly to the absurd in the case of "health," however, for the idea that health is either a simple or nonnatural property simply will not do. Accepting the conclusions of philosophers of biology, we find that "health" can be understood in terms of "proper function." As noted in chapter 1, the philosophers of science have not been able to reduce "proper biological functioning" to observable consequences because they do not seem to be able to completely eliminate the notion of "purpose" from their accounts, and purposes are not something empirically observable. There will be no identification of the "true nature" of "health" forthcoming, where by "true nature" we mean the sense in which being H_2O is the true nature of the stuff we call "water." Put in another way, there will be no necessary a posteriori knowledge gained of an identity that holds between health and some other specifiable set of empirical conditions, in the same way that we have discovered a posteriori that being Hesperus is being Phospherous or that being water is being H_2O. There was never a particular phenomenon that served as the "object of baptism" of "health," to which all our present predications of "health" are now causally linked. "Health" is neither a proper name nor a descriptive name of something that may be ostended, nor for any (perhaps infinitely long) specifiable collection of properties (where either of these kinds of names is understood as Kripkean rigid designators, entailing a modality of necessity indexed to the actual world).[1] Because healthiness has transcendental elements, "healthiness" is (in some sense not completely clear to me) a theoretical term—more theoretical, in some sense, than "subatomic particle" (for reasons Harman, 1988, points out), less theoretical, in some sense, than "number," for numbers are abstract and health is not. One upshot here is that there are limits to what we can expect in explicating the semantics of "health." We will not get to the bottom of the meaning of "health" by a definition, but we can gain some insight into the semantics of "health" by investigating the kinds of situation we describe as "healthy" and the differences among them.

Whereas it seems as if Aristotle was onto the different ways that different kinds of thing could all be healthy, it was Aquinas who clearly formulated semantic rules for speaking differentially about health, and he understood these rules as a part of a larger theory of language.[2] His difficulty revolved around how we could meaningfully speak of the Christian conception of a "personal" God: how could God be rightly called a "person," given how different God is from people? Or, given how different humans are from God, how could both a human and God "love" each other or "believe" some proposition to be true? Aquinas answered these questions by saying that with language we may "analogically predicate" certain terms from common applications (predications) into applications

---

1. It may seem odd to think of a predicate like "health" as some sort of name. I take it that the sense in which "health" is not a name is what makes it different from terms, like "red" or "sweet," that can be taken as names of either sensations or causes of sensations. In this way, "red" and "sweet" can serve as rigid designators of actual colors or tastes, insofar as (for example) if atmospheric changes were to cause all apples to appear to normal viewers to be purple, one may remain warranted in saying that "apples are red." The logic of the modal operator in use when predicating rigid designators is technically discussed in Davies and Humberstone (1980); see especially the section entitled "The Necessary 'A Posteriori' and Other Applications."

2. Here I draw mainly from Alston (1993).

of which we are less familiar while still succeeding in speaking meaningfully, still succeeding in making sense. It turns out that there are many different types of analogical predications, and not all of them are primarily religious. Aquinas uses the example of "healthy" in demonstrating a certain kind of analogical predication whereby a term may be meaningfully used or applied in contexts that are only related to the primary use of the term. His thought runs like this: the basic or primary predication of "health" is to organisms, organs, or tissues, but there are two other kinds of analogical predications as well. We also call "healthy" both the causes and the signs of an organism's "health" (in the primary sense). To keep all these straight, let's name these three predications "b-health" for the basic predication, "c-health" for causes of health, and "s-health" for signs of health (excuse the use-mention slippage). We may then say that food is c-healthy if it promotes or causes one to be b-healthy, and elastic skin tone or blood pressure within a certain range is s-healthy if these turn out to be signs, symptoms, or indications of the b-health of the skin or cardiopulmonary system, respectively.

The property of health in the most primary sense of "health" was the object of our attention in chapter 1, and so the discussion there was carefully limited to the predicate "b-health." As a property, b-health, is instantiated by living or biological tissues, organs, or organisms when they are functioning properly. In the broadest and most metaphysical terms, b-health is a way of being and is found at the junction of being and becoming.[3] That is, b-health is the efficient living actualization of inherent potential energy within matter: a living item is "b-healthy" if it is "functioning properly," where the "properly" is really of the first significance. A function may be either performing poorly or well, or it may be malfunctioning or functioning properly. Although it was mentioned above, it is important to emphasize here that this does not make the property of b-health a functional property; it is best understood as a property of a function. Perhaps the simplest argument for this is as follows: malfunctioning and proper functioning will have the same status, in respect to being a way of functioning, and if the malfunctioning of a function is not itself a functional property, then neither is proper functioning. The prop-

---

3. Consider that nothing lives in a single moment, but life must be understood as a diachronic process. Entropy, as well, is a property that can only be defined as a change in the state of an system across time; infinitesmals aside, at a single instant nothing has entropy. The deepest mysteries of life—process, potential, being, and becoming—will not be addressed here due to author's ignorance.

erty of b-health is instantiated by living systems and is a way of being alive. When a function is a living function, as the function of a heart is a living function, and it is performing properly, b-health is instantiated. There is a sense in which this is to give a definition of "b-health" in terms of "proper living function"; but note that this sense of the definition makes "b-health" neither a proper name of the property of a living thing when it is properly functioning nor a descriptive name of such a property. Neither "proper function" nor "b-health" is the sort of term that can be defined but are both, instead, terms for which one must have a (philosophical) theory. (See also notes 2 and 5, chapter 1.)

For now, we may say that the semantics of "b-health" can be understood in terms of being guided by the presence of the property b-health as instantiated by tissues, organs, or organisms. It is found in propositions such as "It [She, He] is healthy," where "it" may range over anything alive, and "she" or "he" may range over individuals (typically animal and not vegetable) of the female or male sex. Also b-health may be predicated over groups of individuals, where it may refer to a statistical norm of health of the group as a whole: "It's a [b-]healthy herd of cattle." Since definition is impossible, let it suffice to say that, although bordering on metaphor (or worse, perhaps catachresis), tissues, organs, and organisms are "b-healthy" when they are "robust," "strong," "flourishing," or "doing well" from an evolutionary or biological point of view. A "b-healthy" organ is one that is "doing what it ought to do," in the sense of having a "job" or "function" to perform and "doing so proficiently," "efficiently," or "properly." Beyond this, perhaps the most important fact about predications of "b-health" is that they are highly relativized or indexed. This is most clearly revealed in the syntax or grammar of statements in which b-health is ascribed to an object through a predication of "b-health." The underlying syntax of such statements is identical to that which analytic philosophers of biology have found to underlie function statements. Considerable attention to an analysis of this syntax will be paid in the second half of this chapter; for now, let us simply say that when an object is "b-healthy," it is "functioning properly."

The semantics of "c-health" are perhaps the easiest to grasp because of the existence of antonyms that give fairly clear insight into its meaning. If "c-health" is predicated on causes of b-health, then its antonym would be either "toxicity" or "poisonousness." These are found in propositions such as "Chicken soup is [c-]healthy food" or "Mercury is poisonous." Now, here we have a property on which a realist can readily find purchase; no one with the strength of one's convictions can survive while denying the reality of the existence of toxic or poisonous substances. Thus, there are substances that are properly, truly, called "[c-]healthy." It is not surprising that a list of these substances is impossible to adduce, if only because of the relativity of "c-healthy" and "toxic." At the very least, these are relativized to species, so that for cows, eating grass is c-healthy but is not for humans, and to certain individuals, so that iron-rich diets are c-healthy for those with anemia but not in general. Interestingly, what counts as "c-healthy" or "toxic" can even depend on amounts and context, so that large amounts of arsenic are toxic for humans, but in certain instances of sickness (b-unhealthiness) small amounts of it may be used as c-healthy medicine. Whereas an antonym for substances that are "c-healthy" is "toxic," there are behaviors that can be called "c-healthy," such as exercise, but there do not seem to be behaviors that can be called "toxic." Being slothful is not toxic for a person, but it is not c-healthy either. Sloth can lead to the buildup of toxic substances that would otherwise be purged through exercise, but not exercising is still not properly called "toxic." (Smoking cigarettes might be considered a "toxic" behavior, but this is in virtue of the toxic substances contained in tobacco.) The same may be said of other deficiencies in what is c-healthy: a prolonged lack of vitamin C causes scurvy, but not eating vitamin C is not properly called "toxic," even though consciously not doing so will kill a person. In the same way, not eating mercury is not properly called "c-healthy." It may be the case that some of these semantic intuitions about what to call absences of "c-health" or "toxicity" are not generally shared by all English speakers, but this is not quite to the point. What is most important is to note that we have at least some clear notions about when to predicate "c-health" and when to predicate "toxic"; whatever further debates exist, they rest on a shared understanding of some easy cases, and disagreements about other cases are thus substantial (empirical, a posteriori) and not merely semantic (conceptually analyzable, a priori).[4]

---

4. An important insight into how normative ethics should handle pleasure and pain can be seen by noting that c-healthiness and toxicity are orthogonal to pleasure and pain. There are bitter pills that are c-healthy and toxic substances, such as heroin, that when ingested induce the heights of pleasure. What this implies is that the effects of certain substances on one's b-healthiness cannot be judged by attending to how they feel. Sometimes one must do what is painful for the sake of one's b-healthiness. Again, one's b-healthiness transcends what can be subjected to introspection. Applying this lesson to goodness inveighs deeply against hedonic conceptions of the good life.

In our third use of "health," we find it being predicated of signs or symptoms of b-health and in propositions such as "You have a healthy complexion." We get some insight into the kind of situation in which this term is used by attending to what Grice (1957) says about how "natural" and "nonnatural meaning" differ. The former is at play when we say that "those spots mean measles" or that "the tree having x (number of) rings means that it is x years old." Neither of these propositions can be restated by following the verb "mean" with a phrase in single quotation marks (e.g., "Those spots mean 'measles' " makes no sense). Nonnatural meaning is at play when we say that "those three rings on the bell (of the bus) means 'the bus is full' " or that "he is telling you he loves you when he says, 'Be careful.' " So, to begin with, we may say that when x is a sign of y's b-health, we may say that x naturally means that y is b-healthy. If x naturally means y is b-healthy, then x is s-healthy. If x is the elasticity of y's b-healthy skin, a doctor might say to a medical student, "Elasticity such as this is [s-]healthy." As discussed in chapter 2, the relationship between y's b-health and a sign thereof is most often a causal relationship, as in the case of spots and measles, but it may also be a merely logical relationship, as when we say that "the leg's being bent like that means that it is broken" (there is only a logical distinction to be had between the bend and the break). As far as nonnatural meaning goes, there is no commitment to a Gricean theory of semantics or nonnatural meaning. As a predicate, "s-health" (like "b-" and "c-health") has an indefinitely large extension; again, this is the case, given the number of possible species of living organisms and the fact that every individual's b-health will itself be individualized, and thus the signs of every individual's b-health will also be individualized. Two individual conspecifics might have the same blood pressure; for one this would (naturally) mean that the cardiovascular system is b-healthy, whereas for the other this might mean there is a great risk of an imminent heart attack.

So, there are three different types of predications of "health." And we find the answer to our third riddle in the introduction, the semantic riddle, by noting that "good" has three structurally parallel predications. Remember that this riddle asked what sort of rules could govern the application of the predicate "good," given that things as diverse as people and acts are all called "good." In view of the linguistic turn of our century, a moral realist is obliged to say something about the meaning of the word "good" (or the meaning of propositions that contain the word), above and beyond noting that "good" is commendatory (pace Stevenson, 1937, and other expressivists). A moral realism that models its ontology of goodness on healthiness has a semantic structure for the meaning of "good" served up on an Aquinian platter. And the recognition that "good" can be used in three different ways, all analogous to different senses of "health," is even more intellectually satisfying when one notes that these three senses of "good" are all archetypal semantic expressions of the three normative ethical theories discussed and articulated in chapter 2. We have found that each normative ethical theory has a distinctive way of thinking about different aspects of morality: virtue theory is concerned with the goodness of lives of agents, whereas deontology and consequentialism are concerned with different behaviors (acts) and how these can be used to diagnose or solve problems. It makes sense for us to expect to find that these theories use the word "good" differently. Here is how our expectations are satisfied.

Of "Good"

To jump precipitously to the conclusion, all the pieces fit together like an interlocking puzzle: the semantics confirms the metaphysics, which confirms the epistemology, which confirms the semantics, and so on. One cannot complain that the reasoning is circular, for eventually all reasoning is, and the point is that the circle is large, is informative, and involves a variety of discourses. (It has a "wide cosmological role"; see Crispin Wright, 1992.) And if this is so, then the prescient might see where we are headed. If goodness is like healthiness, then we should expect to find the same sorts of semantic rules applying to each. For example, they should both handle negation in the same way. We have at least some reason to look askance at a metaethic that modeled the semantics of "good" on "water," if only because "not good" comes in degrees (like "mediocre") but "not water" does not. "Goodness" does seem to have the same semantic shape as "healthiness," at least in negation. The similarities do not end at such broad generalities, and all vague predicates handle negation in the same way,[5] but we find the same deeper, tripartite structure in the semantics of "goodness" as we find with "healthiness."

---

5. Consider what might be regarded as a moral Sorites paradox, beginning with the Aristotelianism "One swallow does not make a summer" and its application, that one virtuous or vicious act cannot make a person good or bad (virtuous or vicious, *eudaimon* or non-*eudaimon*). Well, a fool might think that there isn't anything wrong with doing any single vicious act, nor can there be reason for doing any single virtuous act; and the paradox is off and running. Similar

Now, if goodness is like healthiness ontologically, and we can thereby expect their similarities to be captured in ordinary language, then we will see that the primary predication of "goodness" will be to agents and not to acts, just as we found with "healthiness."[6] Just as the primary predication of "health" (b-health) is to tissues, organs, or organisms, so too the primary predication of "goodness" is to people (or perhaps lives). The secondary, analogical predications of "health" are to causes or signs of b-health. And we find two forms of secondary and analogical predications of "goodness" as well, for both consequentialists and deontologists use the word differentially: the former to capture acts that cause goodness (in the primary sense), and the latter to capture acts that are signs or expressions of the agent's good will or goodness (also in the primary sense).

To follow the lead of "healthiness," let's distinguish between b-goodness, c-goodness, and s-goodness (again, forgive the use-mention slippage). The first is found in propositions such as "Socrates was a [b-]good person" and "The only thing good in itself is having a [b-]good will"; the second is found in propositions such as "Doing charity is [c-]good for a person"; and the third is found in such propositions as "It was so [s-]good of you to help." Taking these in turn, we begin with predications of "b-goodness." Saying that the primary predication of "good" ("b-good") is the name of a property instantiated by agents does not by itself commit one to much ontologically, for at the very least, the thought poses further problems about what kinds of thing agents are. There is a variety of possible answers, each corresponding to a particular theory of personal identity. (A similar point came up before, at the end of the discussion of supervenience.) In looking for an understanding of moral agency, we cannot avoid other ongoing metaphysical debates that are conducted independently from moral theory. So, one might identify objects by saying that they are identical to particular four-dimensional

---

thoughts are found in Confucius' commentary on the *I Ching* (1950) hexagram Shih Ho ("Biting Through"): "If a good does not accumulate, it is not enough to make a name for a man. If evil does not accumulate, it is not enough to destroy a man. Therefore, the inferior man thinks to himself 'Goodness in small things has no value' and so neglects it. He thinks, 'Small sins do no harm' and so does not give them up. Thus, his sins accumulate until they can no longer be covered up, and his guilt becomes so great that it can no longer be wiped out."

6. This semantic priority begs no questions at the level of evaluating normative ethical theories, for there we judge by how good our theories are at making us be moral, not by how well they comport with our speech.

space-time "sausages" (Heller, 1990), that some of these "sausages" are people, and that it is they who may have instantiated moral properties like b-goodness and warrant predications of "b-goodness." The Cartesians and dualists (if not lately shamed into silence) will say that "b-goodness is predicated of immaterial minds"; spiritualists (rarely feeling shameful) will predicate it of souls; and error theorists, about the self (Hume, at one point), will say that since there are no selves in this sense, the property of b-goodness is never instantiated at all. A nonrealist about the self would end up with an error theory of our predications of "b-goodness" insofar as they are all, strictly speaking, false. Psychologists, about the mind, will strike personal identity up to psychology, though exactly how the identity of a person is related to the actual brain matter in the head remains contentious. Given other theories of personal identity, b-goodness and b-healthiness are instantiated by the same kind of objects, so that "b-goodness" is properly predicated over the same sort of entity as "b-healthiness": biological organisms (Olsen, 1997).

What is crucial here is not the fact that such debates are unresolved but that they proceed as if everyone (at least roughly) understands their subject matter. A debate over the proper object of predications of "[b-]goodness," be it an animal organism, a psychology, a will, or a soul, are substantial debates that cannot be settled by a third party who is suggesting that the disagreements are merely semantic and that "[b-]goodness" is equivocal in these cases. The disputants are not merely talking past each other but are questioning the workings of b-goodness and the proper uses of "[b-]goodness." We may say that although there are some disagreements about the use of the term, there is overriding semantic consent that any differences in use are a result of (something like) differing theories about a single thing: b-goodness.

Note how different the situation would be if one person said, "Arnold is a healthy human"; another said "Tofu is healthy food"; and a third accused the first two of having a substantial argument over the kind of object of which "health" may be properly predicated. Here we would say that there is, in fact, no substantial argument between the first two people and that the dispute is merely semantic: they are not exactly equivocating between these two uses of "healthy," for their meanings are related (analogically), but there is no ontological dispute to be found between saying that both Arnold and tofu are healthy. The same situation applies in cases of talk about b-goodness and c-goodness. If doing something causes there to be more b-goodness, then to that extent it is called "c-good," just as medicine or tofu are called "c-healthy." Thus, one might say that "doing charity is [c-]good for people, insofar as it may make one more sensitive to the difficulties that many live with, and this is something to which [b-]good people are sensitive." One particular person might be c-good for another (say, if they love each other well), but exercise can also be c-good for one's character (perhaps instilling a sense of temperate life-style); so we may predicate "c-good" of both objects (for people in this sense are objects) and acts or events. Moreover, whether or not something is c-good for a person will be dependent on facts about that person. Whether or not one takes the night off from working either might be c-good for someone who doesn't get out enough or might not be for someone under an important deadline. This is consistent with the possibility that there may be some things that are always c-good for human beings, such as loving one's children, as well as consistent with there being some things that are always c-bad for human beings, such as causing needless suffering. It is importantly not consistent with absolutism about all of ethics; it may always be c-bad for human beings to cause needless suffering, but whether or not lying is c-bad or whether or not one ought to lie in a particular situation is (contra Kant) a matter in need of sensitivity to cases, which is at odds with a full-going absolutism. Thus, "c-goodness" is a relativized, nonabsolute predicate.

There is another semantic fact about "c-goodness": it is normal for it to take a particular preposition, namely "for." And it is here that it becomes useful to begin seeing how "c-goodness" is a predication that is distinctive of consequentialist discourse. In the previous chapter, consequentialism was described as a type of normative ethical theory, which says that we ought to do the act that brings about a certain specified consequence, and exactly which consequence we ought to do our best to bring about will depend on which version of consequentialism we are considering. But typically, when we describe an act as being "good for" some particular end, we are talking about c-goodness. This is not just revealed in propositions such as "Charity is [c-]good for a person" but is also related to the notion of instrumental value, which is typical of consequentialism. "For" in this sense is used to indicate the presence of "purpose or destination," and the *Oxford English Dictionary* takes many columns to spell this out in full. We have seen how thinking like a consequentialist embodies a problem solving thought process, and the outcome of such a process will be a decision to act, where the consequentialist will say that the "c-best" act is the one most likely to cause the most amount of b-goodness or the least amount of b-badness (as the case may be). Insofar as an ethical theory is teleological in structure, acts will be c-good insofar as they are "[c-]good for" bringing about some specified end.

To see a further link between c-healthiness and c-goodness, imagine trying to teach a reluctant child the value of family in a situation in which a visit to elderly relatives is expected but the child would rather stay home to watch television. A parent might say in such cases, "You're going to go, because it is [c-]good for you whether you know it or not, and you'll go whether you want to or not." The hope here is that by making the child visit, the child will eventually learn why such visitations are important. At the beginning, we should note that such treatment for the child is the analog of a "bitter pill," as indeed are all situations in which we decide on a course of "tough love." What is c-good for people might very well be completely disengaged from any of their actual desires or motives, in the same way that what is c-healthy for someone is disengaged from what is pleasant or painful (cf. note 4). There is, therefore, reason to think that in considering what is c-good for humans, attending to what is seen to be desirable or pleasurable at best provides a very fallible access to what is actually c-good for them.

It is in distinguishing acts that appear virtuous from those that actually are that leads us into the deontologist's dialectic, for at least some deontologists wish to draw a distinction between acts that are right because they are in accordance with duty and those acts that are good because they are done from a sense of duty (Ross, 1930). The sense of "good" in the previous sentence is "s-good," where an act is s-good if it manifests or is a sign of a person's b-goodness. An s-good act naturally means (a là Grice, 1957) that one is a b-good person (even though one swallow does not make a summer); an s-good act is a single piece of evidence that indicates that a person is b-good.

This feature is manifested in the semantics of deontologists in a manner reminiscent of the consequentialist's talk of acts that are "[c-]good for" some end; the deontologist's predication of "[s-]good" typically comes attached to either the preposition "of" or "from," indicating that the act's causal genesis, or its etiology, begins in a person's b-goodness. Thus, we speak of "acts *of* [b-]good will" and "an act that was done *from* the [b-]goodness *of* one's heart." It is the deontological aspect of Rawls's (1957, p. 659) theory of justice that is under consideration when he speaks (at the earliest) of "a sense of fair play." We also speak of kind or s-good acts "done from the heart." The "of" or "from" indicates what we think provides the causal springs of the act, and hence is indicative of the act's etiology. Alternatively, the deontologist's discourse may be cast in terms of motivation; thus, an act is right (in Ross's, 1930, sense) if it is in accordance with duty but s-good if it is done because of the b-good motivational structure of a person. When a person's motives are b-good, then his or her acts are s-good; if an old friend hears of our troubles and offers assistance, we give our thanks by saying, "It was so [s-]good of you to think of us." We take such acts to be expressions or manifestations of a person's moral character or will, just as a doctor will take someone's pulse or blood pressure to be an expression of that person's state of health.

A single act can be both s-good and c-good, as well as both s-bad and c-bad. So doing charity work may be c-good for one's character insofar as it helps to make one a more sensitive, better (in the sense of b-good) person, but charity work may also be s-good insofar as it may be done from a sense of b-good will or as a manifestation of the b-goodness that has already become part of one's character (much like our well-reared, once-reluctant child). And that very same charity work may be c-good for the people on the receiving end of the charity. Alternatively, in *Gorgias*, Plato (1994a) has Socrates argue that causing others to suffer is worse than suffering, and if this is right then its converse will also most likely be true: it will be better to bestow benefits (gifts) than to receive them. As for causing someone to suffer, a single act of this can be s-bad insofar as it manifests something b-bad in one's character, like maliciousness; it can be c-bad (for the person who is causing the suffering) insofar as it can do further damage to one's character. If Plato is right, then this will always outweigh the damage that the same act causes to someone else's life. We begin to see how ethicists may speak past one another unwittingly by noting that some acts may be mixed: a single act may be s-good, insofar as it is an expression of a b-good will, but c-bad if it goes badly awry, and so on.

And so there are three different ways that "good" is ordinarily used: it can be predicated of agents and of acts that are either causes of or signs of an agent's moral standing. It turns out that the semantic structures that regulate our varied uses of "good" are quite complicated, and it is because this very complexity can be so accurately modeled on the semantics of "health" that we find strong evidence of being on the right track. Moreover, further confirmation is found in the current literature on the semantics of moral realism. Terry Horgan and Mark Timmons have written a series of articles that demonstrate a fairly widespread and very serious problem that is infecting the semantic aspects of the versions of moral realism currently most popular in metaethics. If we find that the present theory is immune to these semantic problems endemic to other versions of moral realism, we will have found one more reason to think that we are making progress in the successful defense of moral realism.

Horgan and Timmons and Moral Twin Earth

Here is a story about the word "good" that has been promulgated by empirically minded metaethicists who live, more or less, near Ithaca, New York. (See, e.g., Railton, 1986; Boyd, 1988; Sturgeon, [1985] 1988.) These "Cornell realists," for want of a better name, typically use a causal theory of reference to explain how the word "good" gained its reference, or got its meaning, employing the persuasive moves that Kripke (1972) and Putnam (1975) used to explain how "water" got its meaning. A two-sentence summary of the familiar story is that there was an intention of a linguistic community to refer to water, the physical material that turned out to be H_2O, with the word "water." Thus, it was H_2O that causally mediated the use of the word "water" even before we discovered that water is identical to H_2O.[7] When we discover water's identity to be H_2O, we will be said to have knowledge that is necessary a posteriori. If the Cornell realists are right, then there is a property or group of properties that causally mediate the use of "good" (or "right"), even if we, as empirical investigators, have not yet discovered which properties these are. When we do eventually make this discovery, presumably ending the debate that constitutes normative ethical theorizing, we will find that goodness is necessarily identical to those properties, just as water is necessarily identical to H_2O. And as our knowledge that water is H_2O is necessary a posteriori, our knowledge of what good is will have the same status.

If this is the case, then our discourse should have certain semantic commitments about what we are willing to say about things like water and goodness. Unfortunately for the Cornell realists, it seems as if our intui-

---

7. This is to tell the Putnam-Kripke story in a way that keeps "water" being univocal. An alternate reading, found in Chalmers (1996) and Jackson (1998; also discussed briefly in notes 9 and 10 of chapter 1), employs two senses or intensions of "water": "A" or "primary" intensions and "C" or "secondary" intensions. I will be assuming that "serious metaphysics" is concerned with centered possibility only, insofar as we want to know about our world and what is possible *given* it. Thus, insofar as A intensions are not coextensive with C intensions, I take them to be irrelevant to metaphysics. This is, I believe, the traditional reading of Putnam-Kripke.

tions about the semantics of "water" match up with what we would expect if water were (necessarily) identical to H_2O, but the same cannot be said about the semantics of what is morally "good." The semantics that follow from the moral ontology of the Cornell realists is not the semantics that we ordinarily employ in our moral discourse. If this problem is generalizable to every version of moral realism, then realism is in grave trouble. If, however, there is a version that avoids this semantic difficulty, then this speaks strongly in its favor.

The problems with using the causal theory of reference in this way have been made very precise in an ongoing series of articles by Terry Horgan and Mark Timmons.[8] If we encounter a Twin Earth with stuff that very much looks like water but is actually XYZ and not H_2O, most people (so it seems) would think that the word "water" has two different meanings on Earth and Twin Earth because the word tracks two different kinds of stuff. "Water" on Earth and "water" on Twin Earth are merely homonyms. But consider the analogous case with "good": suppose that here on Earth we make the discovery that the properties actually mediating our use of the word "good" are those that traditional consequentialists have maintained. "Good" then would be necessarily identical to (roughly) "maximizing happiness." We proceed to Twin Earth and, lo!, find that Twin Earthlings have discovered that the word "good" is mediated by the properties that deontologists have maintained, and "good" is (here?) necessarily identical to (roughly) "acting from the motive of duty." It seems unjustified to say that the Twin Earthlings got the meaning of "good" wrong, whereas we here on Earth got it right; we have no more right than they to accuse the other of being *necessarily* wrong. (Remember, everyone's discoveries are necessary a posteriori.) Thus, the empirically based moral ontology of the Cornell realists, along with their account of how "good" gets its meaning, fails: ordinary moral discourse would say that we have (at the very least) a semantic disagreement with the Twin Earthlings about the meaning of "good," and we would not say the same about "water" about which there is no disagreement at all. It cannot be the case that goodness is nec-

---

8. Terry Horgan and Mark Timmons, "New Wave Moral Realism Meets Moral Twin Earth," *Journal for Philosophical Research*, 16, 1991, pp. 447–465 (this seems to be most general treatment of the problem); "Troubles on Moral Twin Earth: Moral Queerness Revived", *Synthese*, 92, 1992a, pp. 221–260; Troubles for New Wave Moral Realism" *Philosophical Papers*, 21, 1992b, 153–175; "From Moral Realism to Moral Relativism in One Easy Step", *Critica*, vol. 28, no. 83, 1996, pp. 3–39.

essarily identical to both maximizing happiness and acting from the motive of duty, nor would we be satisfied with thinking that "good" here and "good" there are merely homonyms. If "good" were like "water," then we should not find these differences between them. The semantics of "good," putatively modeled on those of "water" (as hypothesized by the Cornell realists), fails to comport with ordinary moral discourse.

The problem can be made quite precise, but it is a remarkably flexible problem, which can be modified in different ways for different versions of moral realism. The problem was formulated with the Cornell realists in mind, for they originally tried to secure meanings for moral terms based on the relationship of "water" to H_2O. It turns out that other versions of moral realism have analogous problems. Michael Smith's "metaethical rationalism" has similar troubles (Horgan and Timmons, 1996b). There is some reason to think that Frank Jackson's (1998) recent work on moral realism faces the same difficulties;[9] and there might very well be a version of the problem for those holding that values and colors have the same ontological status, namely, as secondary qualities equally fit for a dispositionalist's treatment (see McDowell, 1988; Wiggins, 1991). Briefly, the problem arises for the secondary-quality theorists as follows: a dispositional analysis of "red" must fix or rigidify the meaning of "red" to the actual practices or judgments of normal (or ideal) observers in normal (or ideal) conditions (for rigidification, see Davies and Humberstone 1980). If "actual" practices differ on Earth and Twin Earth concerning the meaning of "red," rigidification will not cause any problems: there will be no disagreement between us and the Twin Earthlings about the meaning of "red" because it will unproblematically have different referents for each place. (There is no problem in saying that "red" for us and "red" for them are merely homonyms.) Rigidification might very well be a problem, however, when we are considering the meaning of "good": if the practices of judging "goodness" on Earth and Twin Earth differ, and both they and we rigidify over our own practices, we are faced the same basic problem that faced the Cornell realists. Moral realism is in need of an ontology that does not engender these semantic worries.

Moral Twin Earth Gets Real

So, we go to Twin Earth, and we find that they say, for example, that different things are c-healthy for them than we think are c-healthy for us.

---

9. Based on discussions with Terry Horgan and Mark Timmons.

How is the dispute to be resolved? Ideally, it is solved empirically. We must find out if the evolutionary processes on Earth and Twin Earth have really left their inhabitants in the same state. If the physiology of the two sets of peoples are really identical (or at least functionally equivalent), then if, for example, they use "[c-]health" differently than we do, there are four possibilities. First, we are mistaken about what is c-healthy; second, they are; third, the differences in predication do not map onto any significant differences in benefits or detriments in the b-healthiness of the populations (the cat is skinned equally well in both worlds, so to speak), and so these differences can be seen as merely conventional; fourth, we are *all* wrong. On the other hand, it may be possible to find out that there are slight differences in the physiologies of the populations. (As mentioned in chapter 1, this is what Blackburn, 1993, calls a "releasing condition.") If this were the case, and we assume a good medical understanding of the differences, then we should see these differences mapping onto differences in the way "[c-]health" is used. So, for example, if H_2O makes Twin Earthlings sick, then it is not c-healthy for them, even though it is for us. In cases such as this, it may even turn out that we all say that two particular substances are both equally [c-]healthy, when in fact we ought not to because of the differences in our physiologies; that is, we may both think that there are no functional differences in c-healthiness between Earthlings and Twin Earthlings in drinking either H_2O or XYZ, but we may be wrong. There may, perhaps, be a subtle difference we are not detecting. Similarly, there may be a single substance that is equally c-healthy or toxic to both them and us and all our beliefs about this substance may be false. What is crucial for our purposes is noting that c-health is relative to b-health, which is itself relative to the particularized and contingent facts about physiology that happen to obtain.

Concerning the relevance of moral disputes to metaethical theorizing, we may note that making these determinations about physiology, b-health, and c-health would be empirically very difficult and would involve complex and detailed epidemiological studies of the two populations, and such studies themselves are open to theoretical disputes about the validity of various possible methodologies. For example, here on the actual Earth, it has been very difficult for us to establish the status, amounts, and kinds of cholesterol that are desirable for good b-health (for actual humans). (Even when only one planet is involved we have trouble resolving such medical questions.) But despite the epistemic difficulties of doing such complicated empirical work, we expect that there are answers to these questions; the epistemology is difficult, but the metaphysics are not suspect. Ongoing and difficult disputes about what counts as "healthy" do not engender doubt about the reality of health.

What is crucial is that we never assume that (even) if we can find properties that the word "health" actually succeeds in tracking, then we have "discovered" the meaning of "health." We always leave open the possibility that our medical practices are mistaken or could be improved. The obvious move to make is toward convergence on the truth. We will (some may think) converge on learning the truth about medicine, and when we do, then we can define "health" in terms of the properties it tracks, given the medical theory on which we have converged. Convergence is an unfortunately large topic.[10] It should suffice for now to note that as an actual case that involves medical theory, we might either converge on a theory that recognizes the existence of *chi* (as Eastern doctors currently think) or we may not. We are not, however, necessarily guaranteed to get it right. We might not ever be able to figure out a test to determine whether or not *chi* exists and then, like good scientific verificationists, therefore conclude that it does not exist. We might, however, be wrong (thus the difficulty of proving a negative existential). At least when it comes to health and medical knowledge, there is no necessary connection between what our practices contingently converge on and the reality those practices are trying to describe or understand (more on convergence and morality in a moment).

Unsurprisingly, at this point, the same strategies for the various predications of "healthiness" in the Twin Earth case apply equally well in answering the semantic problems attending "goodness" that are generated by Horgan and Timmons's Moral Twin Earth case. Unfortunately, the epistemic problems are even larger in the moral case than in the medical ones, for if there can be disputes about what counts as "healthy," we can surely count on there being disputes about what is "good." (Even today, when our knowledge of morals and medicine are limited, it is more difficult and rare to find a truly wise person than a truly good doctor.) Despite the rise in epistemic uncertainty when entering into the moral domain, there is no reason to think, at this point, that we will find that

10. Moral realists of various stripes have employed a notion of convergence to ground their theories; these include both moral functionalists like Frank Jackson (1998) and secondary quality theorists like David Wiggins (1991). It is, I think, also covertly working for the Cornell realists, insofar as they assume that knowing which properties our moral language tracks (has converged upon) yields knowledge of the meanings of moral terms.

it ought to engender doubt about the metaphysics of the case. If the inhabitants of both planets are really *Homo sapiens* (or functional equivalents), then the same options we had for "healthiness" apply to disputes about predications of "goodness"; either we are wrong or they are or the differences do not map onto real moral differences. Finally, we may all be wrong. The differences may be purely conventional, if there is a functional equivalence in regard to the differences; that is, if there are differences in what counts as "[c-]good" between us and them and these do not amount to differences in the b-goodness of both populations, then we may view them as morally irrelevant. They would have the same status as differences in what side of the road to drive on or on which side of the plate a fork belongs.

The real escape from the problem set up by Horgan and Timmons comes when noting that moral realism should be committed to the idea of global moral error. Everyone could be wrong about some particular moral facts, even though there may be universal convergence on what is in fact an error. We have in the past converged on false moral beliefs, such as that women are inferior to men or that people of other races are inferior to our own. (The former example was believed by women, as well as by men, and the latter did not depend on who "we" were; everyone thought themselves similarly superior.) We may well converge in the future on other false moral beliefs. Assume that some sort of liberal democracy really is the fairest and best sort of human government; still, in 1000 years, we may all be living under, say, Chinese totalitarian rule (with no nicely universalized "rule of law") or we may even have adopted the culture of today's Afghani Talibhan, preventing women from working or going to school. The idea that we, humans in the actual world, will necessarily converge on the moral truth is ludicrous: our moral practices are only contingently correct.[11] So, in a Talibhan world, where they have converged on the idea that "good" sometimes refers to "properly domesticated" women, we would (upon encountering them) say that they are wrong, despite the fact that their word "good" actually may track "properly domesticated" women. This does not, however, mean that we have rigidified the meaning of our word "good," saying it necessarily refers to

11. All humanity could have exploded in a nuclear armageddon in the early 1980's, when Ronald Reagen was squaring off against Yuri Andropov. We all might still explode at some point in the future. What do we say about necessary convergence upon moral truth in cases (in possible worlds) such as these? See also introduction, note 5.

what our practices say it refers to, for the same possibility of mistake that holds in the Talibhan world holds in our actual world as well. What is good for humans is good for humans, and this is quite independent of what humans think is good for humans. Our epistemological access to the contents of the actual world is in this way contingent.

To think that our practices necessarily get things right (even at the limit of inquiry) is to move away from realism. Our practices may aim at getting things right, and we may call or predicate all sorts of things "good" or "bad" by the lights of our own practice. A real realist, however, is always going to put the world in the causal driver's seat, so to speak. The world sets the standard for the theory to meet, not vice versa. To summarize this point in the terms of Plato's *Euthyphro*, even if we idealize our practice, our moral predications, which say that "*x* is good," will not be true because we have judged *x* to be good (by the lights of an idealized theory). Rather, even if we have an idealized theory, to say that "*x* is good" will be true because *x* is good, independent of our judgments; the theory is (merely) ideally suited to what it purports to be a theory of. The contents of an ideal moral theory do not determine the contents of moral reality; rather the contents of moral reality determine the contents of the ideal theory. To accept that we have found the definitive meaning of "good," when finding that we use the word to track properties of a certain sort, is to accept the idea that our practices are definitive of the contents of moral reality. This is not realism but rather a subtle form of projectivism, wherein we "stain" the world with our (ideal) practices. Whether or not our practices get it right is not determined by what we think of those practices, nor by the substantial conclusions we converge on, nor by anything else except the actual contents of the world.

This is crucial, so to put this in other words, the claim that is being denied is the one many moral realists have made (and Horgan and Timmons take advantage of): if it turns out that the word "good" actually tracks, say, deontological properties, we cannot from there infer the fact that the meaning of "good" is so fixed and that deontology is therefore the "true" moral theory. This puts the practice before the world, the semantic cart before the metaphysical horse. Moral realists should not look to the world to confirm a moral theory that is supposed to be known (necessary) a posteriori, nor should they think that the ability to use the word consistently guarantees that what is being called "good" truly is good. That the world fulfills our expectations does not, by itself, confirm our theories of the world. (This is especially true if data are always so underdetermined that we can use any set of datum points to confirm any theory we like.) As realists, we should be doing our best to make our theories fit the way the world (actually) works, not searching for the best ways in which to "discover" the world confirming our theories.

Thus, we can imagine Twin Earthlings all being in error or learning from them that we are in error or discovering from our disagreement that everyone is wrong or that there really is no difference worth disagreeing about. Or we might realize that Twin Earthlings are, contrary to appearances, not (functional equivalents of) *Homo sapiens* and that what in fact is good for them is not what in fact is good for us. This sort of relativization allows both of us to be correct, though the same behavior might be good for us and bad for them. Moral Twin Earth is not a problem for moral realism's account of "good": our semantic intuitions about "good" are not the same as they are about "water" (nor should we have expected "good" to act like a substance term), but our intuitions of how "good" works can be made sense of by looking at how "health" works, and no ("new wave") semantic problems arise.

A final word is wanted on the case of Moore's ([1902] 1988) famous "open question argument." Moore says that any proposed definition (analysis) of a moral term like "good" is going to leave an "open question" about whether the analysis works for any particular (and seemingly apt) predication of "good." If I say "good" means "pleasurable," then whenever I predicate "good" of something, x, it is still open for me to ask, "Yes, x is pleasurable, but is it really good?" Thus, the open question. With the tools we now have in place, we can, very briefly, explain why the question rightly remains open, for Moore is certainly onto something here (and it has nothing to do with his misbegotten "naturalistic fallacy"). Importantly, his claim is both descriptive of the philosophical evaluation of moral judgments and is a normative claim about moral judgments in general. For any definition we could conceivably come up with, we (qua realists) are, *and we ought to be*, open to the (epistemic) possibility that any particular circumstance in which the word "good" seems apt may, in fact, be one of two errors. Either it could be a case in which x is an exception (in the sense spelled out in chapter 2) to a rule, such that it is not what it seems. In cases like these, x is not, in fact, good. Or it could be a case in which x is a counterexample to our definition, disproving (or bringing evidence against) the particular normative ethical theory that we had "discovered" to be true and had yielded our definition. Here we decide that x is good and our definition was not; what is good turns out to be something other than what we had been calling it. The open question is insurance that the world (with moral reality as a part) is in the metaphysical driver's seat, not the semantics or the analysis or the theorizing. This is being a realist. We, qua *Homo sapiens* (a fortiori qua philosophers), should never be so cocksure of ourselves that we stop questioning our particular moral judgments.

Two parting shots: (1) there is also an open question, albeit a much less open one, that our definition of "water" as "H_2O" is false in any and every instance. It is possible (as an epistemic modality) for us to be mistaken about chemistry as a whole and the real essence of water in particular, and we should not become blind to this. (Locke was quite right here.) The correlate to Moore's (1902) open question in normative scientific discourse is "always question your assumptions." Thus, Einstein asked the scientifically open question "Is what we call 'mass' really invariant to how fast it is moving?" Nevertheless, the question about the definition of "water" will always seem to be less "open" than that about "good," if only because chemistry seems to be easier, at least more concrete, than ethics and morality. (2) Another reading of the open question argument puts it in the same general territory as Kripke's interpretation of Wittgenstein's rule following considerations: consider the use of the words "good" and "plus." How can we be sure that a present usage of a word is in accord with our past usage? If "quus" is the mathematical function that yields the answer "5" as the correct output of "68 quus 57," we may quote Kripke (1982) on Wittgenstein:

> The sceptic doubts whether any instructions I gave myself in the past compel (or justify) the answer "125" rather than "5" [to the problem of 68 plus 57]. He puts the challenge in terms of a sceptical hypothesis about a change in my usage. Perhaps when I used the term "plus" in the *past*, I always meant "quus": by hypothesis I never gave myself any explicit directions that were incompatible with such a supposition. (p. 13)

Thus the open question argument can be framed for "plus" as easily as it can be for "good." What is important for us is that any of these interpretations of the open question argument shows that it poses no special problem for definitions of "good" per se but indicate problems far more widespread.

Syntax

Grammar, Modality, and the "Is"-"Ought" Distinction

In the history of moral philosophy, the syntax of moral language has posed larger problems for moral realism than has moral semantics. If

Moore (([1902] 1988) inaugurated the modern semantic problems for moral theory, it was Hume who brought us the syntactic problems. It was he who noticed an important grammatical difference between central elements of moral language and normal descriptive speech: in particular, he noticed that when one describes something in the world one tries to tell it like it *is*, but when we engage in morality we often talk about how something *ought* to be. The latter is really quite another matter from talking about the former, and this gap has proved most interesting. But why try, almost certainly to fail, to outrun the eloquence of *A Treatise of Human Nature*? As the man, himself, famously says,

> In every system of morality, which I have hitherto met with, I have always remark'd, that the author proceeds for some time in the ordinary way of reasoning, and establishes the being of a God, or makes observations concerning human affairs; when of a sudden I am surpriz'd to find, that instead of the usual copulations of propositions, *is* and *is not*, I meet with no proposition that is not connected with an *ought* or an *ought not*. This change is imperceptible; but is, however, of the last consequence. For as this ought, or ought not, expresses some new relation or affirmation, 'tis necessary that it shou'd be observe'd and explain'd; and at the same time that a reason should be given for what seems altogether inconceivable, how this new relation can be a deduction from others, which are entirely different from it. But as authors do not commonly use this precaution, I shall presume to recommend it to the readers; and am persuaded, that this small attention wou'd subvert all the vulgar systems of morality, and let us see that the distinction of vice and virtue is not founded merely on the relations of objects, nor is preceiv'd by reason. (([1739] 1978, pp. 469–70)

One can only applaud the acute attention required to discern such an imperceptible change. [Yet one may also wonder if Hume himself gives an argument here that starts with a premise about the way in which we actually do speak, an "is" premise, and finishes with a conclusion (a "recommendation") about how we ought to speak.] The distinction between the *ought* and the *is* is certainly one that must be accounted for by any system that aspires to transcend the vulgar. Although countenancing the validity of the distinction Hume so rightly sees and acknowledging the burden of accounting for it, one might nevertheless be dissatisfied with Hume's diagnosis of the situation.

Hume saw the difference between the *is* and the *ought* to be a reflection of the fact that we cease to use reason alone when thinking about an *ought*, when reason is sufficient for thinking about an *is*. The above quotation is set in a context in which Hume is trying to show that morality is something other than science (which is in the business of describing only what is). "Moral distinctions [are] deriv'd from a moral sense," where this moral sense is one in which the work is done by our sentiments or reactions to the world, reactions derived from passions. Thus, according to Hume, an *ought* is distinct from an *is* because, roughly, any *ought* is to be some sort of output of our passionate nature, and this is something distinct from the project of describing nature or how something *is* said to be. Given this line of thought, no amount of deducing from what *is* the case can yield a conclusion about what *ought* to be the case, for the *ought* requires the input of the passions, which have no place in the determination or description of what *is*. What *is* is determined by the facts of the matter; what *ought to be* is determined by how we feel or think about those facts (in some special not-fully-cognitive sense of "think").

The issue is syntactic, as Hume notes in calling the "is" and the "ought" "copulations." The syntactic distinction he draws is meant to be a linguistic sign that we are thinking differently when engaging the *is* and the *ought*. One might wonder, however, if this difference in thought is really captured best by how Hume explains it. One may (with Hume) think that the very role of language changes in going from *is* to *ought*: we go from a fact-stating discourse to a discourse in which commands or demands are made or attitudes are expressed. Indeed, since Hume, this is the most popular interpretation of the distinction. (The most developed form of the command theory of "ought" is Hare's, 1991; for expressivism one must attend to Blackburn, 1993, and Gibbard, 1990.) But Hume's reaction to the distinction he has noticed is quite radical. It is a bit surprising, in fact, to find that this "imperceptible" syntactic difference marks such a dramatic change in the very use or semantics of the language of the speaker, a change from assertion to command, say. The distinction's subtlety is a testament to Hume's acumen, no doubt, but if it really marked such a dramatic change in how we think and talk, would it really have gone unnoticed for so long by so many? We may assert that "the door is still open" and we may make a command of the very same words, and we do typically know the difference, as do our listeners, if they are not dim. We typically do not confuse our assertion that "our team is the best" and enthusiastically cheering them on with words. Perhaps Hume's diagnosis of the situation is right, but it is not the only possible one. If there were a more conservative diagnosis of the distinction, we should be happy to learn of it. And if this conservative diagnosis of the *is-ought* distinction is drawn from another part of Hume's thought, then so much the better. In fact, such an alternative exists.

Hume is also the philosopher who has made us think twice (and three and four times) about causation and our inability to see a "necessary connexion" between cause and effect.[12] Indeed, his criticisms of such a connection are very similar to his criticisms of thinking that morality is a fully factual matter. Although the dictum "You cannot derive an 'ought' from an 'is' " has gained some currency because it is easily coined, Hume's empiricism regarding causality (including his critique of induction) could as easily be recognized by intoning, "You cannot derive a (causal) necessity from an actuality." In making judgments about what is causally necessary, we find, as Hume says, that the "mind has a great propensity to spread itself on external objects" ([1739] 1978, p. 167); and that we erringly go "beyond our immediate impressions" (p. 155) in considering necessary connection. In making moral judgments we are "staining the world with our sentiments," and we should note that we may "take any action allow'd to be vicious: Wilful murder, for instance. Examine it in all lights, and see if you can find that matter of fact, or real existence, which you call *vice*" (p. 468). He could have said the exact same thing about necessary connection.

Now, it is not the place here to enter into a full discussion of Hume's critique of causation, but what must be noted is the fact that there is a syntactic distinction to be found between saying what *is* the case and saying what *is (causally) necessarily* the case. To use the jargon, we move from normal quantified logic, where the quantifiers range over either some of what is or all of what is, to modal logic, where we also have operators that range over what is (causally) possible or (causally) necessary. Hume is right to say that we cannot deduce what must be the case from what is the case. Putting this thought in linguistic terms, we have a syntactic distinction, captured formally by the modal operator, which is indicative of there being a different kind of proposition than we have when we are merely saying how things are. This syntactic difference has semantic consequences, and these can be organized by using "possible world semantics" to capture these syntactic differences: we may say that the actual world is only one possible world, and to follow Hume, we may say from there that we cannot reason from how things are at the actual world to how

---

12. The reading of Hume that I am about to give seemed so natural to me when it occurred to me that I assumed I could not have been the first to think of it, and, indeed, I am not. See Lewis White Beck, 1974, who notes (in his first footnote) that this reading lends credence to Kemp Smith's conjecture that Book III was written before Book I. I thank David Owen for the reference to Beck.

things must be or to what is necessary or true in all possible worlds. What statements of causal necessity give us are statements of how things are in other possible worlds, and Hume is right to point out that this move from what *is* to what *must be* is problematic. Nevertheless, we make the move.

Most people are not Humeans about causation. It seems that the idea that there is nothing more real to causation than constant conjunction is far too strong a conclusion to come merely from the recognition of our inability to observe necessary connections between causes and effects. Causal theorizing aside, however, what we learn from Hume's challenge to causation is that there is a better, less drastic analysis of the *is-ought* distinction than the one he, himself, gives us. The *is-ought* distinction is not one that marks off a wholesale change from one use of language to another: the better interpretation of the distinction is that it is syntactically a modal one. Both *is* statements and *ought* statements are assertions; the difference is that *is* statements are assertions about how things actually *are*, and *ought* statements are assertions about how things *ought to be*. What is marked off is a modal distinction. Statements about what ought to be are statements that pick out how things are in some other, possible world. Which possible world? Well, the tautologous (and smart-aleck) answer is to say, the world where what ought to be actually is. We can do better than this, however. And we will do so later in the chapter.

The present point might be made in this way: even if one were not impressed with the slogan that " 'ought' implies 'can'," one might still find it quite natural to say that the way things ought to be is merely one of the ways things can or could be, one of the ways it is possible for them to be. It is also possible for things to be as they ought not to be. "Ought" does not signal a different way of talking than "is," that is, a different use of language; rather, "ought" merely signals the fact that we are talking about a way things might not actually be but a way things could be, a way things would be, if we all were only to be good (and do as we ought). "Ought" statements are modal statements, not commands or expressions of attitude. For the sake of Humean apologetics, it might also be worth noting that the strides taken in the last hundred years or so in formal and modal logic make it much easier for us to see this fact than it would have been for Hume, who had no formal notion of a "quantifier," modal or otherwise.

Before we move on to the syntax of prescriptions, however, it may be worthwhile to see a different way of approaching the same problem. Nonrealists, like Hare, Blackburn, and Gibbard, argue that moral language is not fact stating, or it does not consist of assertions about how things are. It is fairly easy for them to give an account of the "ought" side of the *is-ought* distinction. These are the easy cases for them because when we prescribe a course of action, when we say what ought to be, such as "You ought to be kind," we are doing something quite different from saying how things are, as Hume rightly pointed out. "You ought to be kind" seems close enough to a command or an exhortation of kindness for these nonrealists to think it is not an assertion. These nonrealists find their problem in trying to account for the "is" side of the distinction: the more difficult pieces of moral language for them to explain are propositions such as "X is good" specifically because these look a lot like assertions such as "X is square" and not much at all like commands or exhortations. Indeed, much ink has been spilled concerning how it might be that something that looks so obviously like an assertion (i.e., "X is good") is actually not. Given a theory of moral realism, on the other hand, statements like "X is good" are easy to account for syntactically; such statements come out clearly as assertions that are stating the facts of the matter. The tough cases of moral language for the realist are prescriptions, for these are not clearly "mere" assertions, stating the facts of the matter. If a realist can make out the sense in which prescriptions are fact-stating assertions, then the realist can be taken to have given an account of the most difficult aspects of the syntax of moral language. The key is to see prescriptions as a subset of assertions, namely, a particular, modal subset.

Here is a final note about the "different use of language," which many nonrealists are quick to point out accompanies much moral speech. No one at this point would deny the nonrealist's contention that moral speech is sometimes used for purposes other than assertion or description (Falk, 1953; Schmidtz, 1995). Of course, this happens all the time as we moralize. The realist may easily acknowledge that when one utters a prescription, it might be attended as well by an attitude or by a desire to persuade or even to coerce listeners to do as they ought; but this is not necessarily the case. For example, Fred might tell Joe what he thinks Joe ought to do and not care in the least whether or not Joe in fact does it. In fact, if Fred is bitter or petty or vindictive and also dislikes Joe for some reason, he might even hope that Joe does not do as he ought and will thereby suffer for it. As a matter of what the bare language conveys, an ought statement, "You ought to be kind," is merely a description of one possible way you could be. It does not, ipso facto, encourage you to be kind.

The Structure of Prescriptions

The full scope of this topic is far broader than one would think because the best model for the logical or syntactical structure of a prescription comes from literature in the philosophy of biology. In particular, we will be concerned with the "normal form" of a function statement as presented by William Wimsatt (1972) in the context of a more general theory of the language of functions. If one wants to become completely clear on the questions of this language, however, one must engage the rather extensive literature on the nature of functions themselves; this leads quickly to deeper topics in the philosophy of biology because biological functions seem to imply natural purposes, and explaining what seem to be natural purposes is no mean philosophical feat. Perhaps needless to say, the full story about biological function quickly gets more complicated at an exponential rate. Here, we'll abjure from these depths and stay as close as possible to questions of syntax and grammar and the barest of theoretical frameworks needed to understand them. More details are available in Bloomfield (1998) and, of course, a much fuller treatment of the work is in Wimsatt's original (which is, by the way, a model of philosophical analysis).

A caveat to start: the argument is not to suggest that prescriptions, moral and otherwise, are actually function statements, only that these forms of speech have the same implicit grammar as one another and thus can be understood as the same parts of speech. Importantly, if function statements are fit to be either true or false, as we normally think, and prescriptions deserve the same syntactic treatment, then prescriptions are truth-apt pieces of language. This is the minimal claim, which is quite ambitious enough. To demonstrate that prescriptions *are* function statements would demand comparative semantic analyses of both, which seems difficult at best. Regardless of the final outcome of such an analysis, there are some semantic similarities between prescriptions and function statements that may be useful for pumping intuitions about the syntax.

Consider the following when I evaluate the workings of the brakes in my car, I may make many assertions—"They're old and no good; they're malfunctioning (not functioning properly); they're not doing what they ought to do; the calipers are leaking brake fluid and so aren't doing their job; I really ought to set aside an afternoon to fix them soon." These assertions are not part of moral discourse, yet the *grammar* is identical to that which we find in morality. Prescriptions, or prescriptive "ought" statements, can, with little infelicity, sometimes be replaced by function statements (and vice versa). The links between these two types of sentences can most easily be seen by noting the employment of the idea of a "job" or a "role" in each. A function statement is an ascription of a job to an individual item, based on a theory (in a way to be described below). If a heart's function is to pump blood and it is malfunctioning, we may say, "It isn't doing its job; it is failing to do what it ought to do" in place of "It is malfunctioning." To see a prescription boil down to a function statement, compare "A borrower ought to return what is borrowed" with "It is the job or the role of the borrower to return what is borrowed." The latter statement, about jobs, is a general assertion about the nature of borrowing: returning what is borrowed is what distinguishes "borrowing" from something more akin to "theft." What it is to have a job is to have something to do. The normativity comes through clearly by noting that it is implicit though tautologous, that qua one's job, "One ought to do one's job."[13] It is merely a quick step from jobs to functions, as the job of the heart and its function seem (at least) very similar. So, though perhaps a bit odd to the ear, one may say, "It is the function of a borrower to return what is borrowed" in place of "A borrower ought to return what is borrowed," *salva veritate*.

If any of this is not too ear jarring, the chord may only be struck better after more discussion of the implicit syntactical structure shared by prescriptions and function statements. So jumping right in, with the normal form of function statements as laid out by Wimsatt (1972), we have:

(1) $F\ [B(i),\ S,\ E,\ P,\ T] = C$

This is to be read as the following (somewhat clumsy) sentence: "A theorem of background theory T is that a function of behavior B of item i in system S, in environment E relative to purpose P is to do C" (p. 32). For example, roughly, "According to biological theory, a function of the beating of the heart in a human in normal conditions and environments, relative to the purpose of exchanging O_2 for CO_2, is to circulate the blood." Instead of explaining the variables by referring only to function statements (following Wimsatt), we may do so in tandem with the normal form of a moral prescription, thereby encompassing the two normal forms with one explication:

---

13. Thus, A. N. Prior takes up Hume's challenge to derive an "ought" from an "is" as follows: "From the premise that 'He is a sea captain' we can validly conclude that 'He ought to do whatever a sea captain ought to do'." This is attributed to Prior by MacIntyre (1984, p. 57) but no reference is given.

(2) $O [B(i), S, E, P, T] = C$

This is meant to be read (so to speak) as follows. "A theorem of background theory T is that when i has role B in situation S in culture E relative to purpose or goal P, i ought to C." For example, roughly, "According to moral theory T, when an agent makes a promise, in a systematized understanding of promise making, set within the context of Western culture, relative to the purpose of [maximizing happiness, or being a member of the kingdom of ends, or achieving eudaimonia (as indexed to T)], the agent ought to keep the promise." Now, obviously, when function statements or prescriptions are used in the vernacular, much of the content above is left implicit or tacit, most likely in the spirit of a conversational implicature (though speakers may be ignorant of some of the relevant factors). In any case, to make either function statements or prescriptions absolutely unambiguous, all the information referenced in (1) and (2) is necessary.

In both (1) and (2), i is the variable that represents the item, the heart, or the moral agent involved, and B represents the behavior of that item to which the statement refers. In (1), we want to know the function of the beating of the heart; in (2), we want to know what someone who makes a promise ought to do. It is important to note that although we often talk about the function of an item, which particular item or agent involved is only secondary to the behavior in which that item or agent is engaged. It is the beating that has the function, not the thing doing the beating. This distinction between i and B is needed, to start, because the heart may engage in behaviors other than beating that may have different functions. Furthermore, if there was an evolved backup organ or pump for a failed heart and that item could take over for a failed heart in emergencies, then the behavior of that item, the pumping, would have the same function as a heart. Functionally equivalent behaviors have identical functions, regardless of the item involved. The corollary to this in (2) is of great moral import, for here we find an insight into the universalizability of prescriptions. To quote Hare (1991) one more time, prescriptions are universalizable, based on this fact:

> one cannot with logical consistency, where a and b are two individuals, say that a ought, in a certain situation specified in universal terms without reference to individuals, to act in a certain way, also specified in universal terms, but that b ought not to act in a similarly specified way in a similarly specified situation. This is because in any "ought"-statement there is im-

plicitly a principle which says that the statement applies to all precisely similar situations. (p. 456)

Thus, we find within the analysis of function statements in the relationship between i and B a model of universalizability, which is often taken to be the central defining feature of prescriptions. It is not the particular agent involved that is important, but the relevant facts of the case that determine the characteristic nature of acts of B-type. Hare has notoriously had problems in explaining which facts count as relevant or which situations count as "precisely similar"; universalizability has been threatened with the triviality of being able to say only that "cases are alike [and ought to be treated as such], morally or in any other respect, unless they are different."[14] Ideally, we would like to have some way of knowing to whom the prescription applies and to whom it does not, and we will return to this problem of fixing the scope of a prescription below. For the moment, having noted the relationship between i and B, as well as the fact that it can explain the origins of universalizability, we proceed with the explication of (1) and (2).

Biological functions take place within certain biological systems, so that the very same behavior can have two different functions. The behavior of swallowing serves in both the gastronomic system and the system that regulates pressure in our aural canals, as we may swallow during an airplane's takeoff (note that one could also be eating at the same time). So, in devising a "normal form" of function statements that hopes to disambiguate the function of a particular behavior from another other possible function, we must include a variable in the formula: hence, the S. We must also do this for prescriptions. Agents each play a role in the moral situations in which they are involved, and so what they ought to do is affected by the particular role they play in that particular situation. (It is here that we begin to see some of the detail of the metaphysical relativity that was introduced in chapter 1.) If I make a promise to someone else, then in determining what I ought to do, we must take into account that I am adopting a particular role in a promise-making situation. And whereas normally adopting this role would mean that I ought to keep my promise, not all promise-making situations are created equal;

---

14. This is perhaps the grossest understanding of the triviality criticism. But this and many other, more fine-grained trivialities are discussed by D. Locke (1968). Thanks here to Ron Milo. Mackie (1977, p. 83) notes a similar triviality.

in a few of them I ought not to keep the promise, say, in some cases of conflicting obligation. In determining what one ought to do in a particular moral situation, it also might make a difference if the promise was made to either a parent or a stranger. Given the plausible thought that a moral situation can be understood as a system of interacting items, or agents, constructing the normal form for prescriptions, we have to include a variable, S, that describes the particular situation or context in which the agent's behavior is to take place.

We may not rest here, however, with our contextualization. The very same behavior, performed in two systems or situations describable in the same way, might still merit different prescriptions, given the broader environment or culture in which the system is existing. As noted in chapter 1, if I unwittingly insult someone, there are cultures in which I ought to apologize and others in which any further mention of my insult will only make matters worse. These are the sorts of differences, also noted in chapter 1, that concern cultural differences in ways of being courageous. We thus need a variable to denote these environmental differences—hence, the E. In the case of function statements, the E is required because there are cases in which the operation of a certain item serves different functions in different environments. Wimsatt's (1972) example is a lungfish, which has an air-filled bladder that serves as a rate of climb indicator when the fish is in the water but serves as a lung in times of drought. In the environment of water, the bladder does not play a role in the fish's aerobic system, and obviously it indicates no ascent when the fish is stuck in the mud.

Moving through the elements in the normal form, we see that it is the role of a purpose that has the most philosophical significance. Purposes, as noted, bring in difficult issues regarding the philosophy of biology. The question is open whether biologists can tell the whole story about functions in a way that reduces the notion of a purpose (or what the behavior is for) to a set of properties that are directly observable. The argument of the appendix is designed to mitigate the force of such worries by pointing out that the same problems affect the paragon of "hard science," namely, physics, as these scientists try to reduce the unidirectional and aysmmetric second law of thermodynamics to the symmetrical laws of statistical mechanics. The conclusion of the argument is that morality, biology, and physics all share the same sort of problem with reduction; noting this does not solve the problem, of course, but it puts moral realism in the same company as scientific realism (which is all the moral realist could hope for). In any case, there is reason enough at this point to keep a place in our analysis of function statements for purposes. This seems especially true given that the explanandum of biological function is answering the "What is it for?" question (L. Wright, 1973), which is most readily done by appeal to a purpose. (See also note 3, chapter 1.)

As for why purposes need to be included in the analysis of prescriptions, this is no more or less straightforward. Many normative ethical theories are quite comfortable with the idea that there is a purpose behind every prescription. Of course, what that purpose may be will depend on which theory we are considering. Virtue theorists, or those moved by the ancient Greek eudaimonistic systems, obviously avail themselves of purposes, for these assume the final end, which is the "that for the sake of which" all our actions are performed but which itself is not for the sake of anything else (see, e.g., Aristotle, 1985, 1097b2–6). This end, goal, or purpose, is presumably *eudaimonia*, a well-lived, or excellent, life. The *suum bonum* of the consequentialists, perhaps the greatest good for the greatest number, by their lights gives purpose to all moral action. Some action theorists might argue that the very notion of a "purposeless act" is nonsense (or oxymoronic, at best). Others, however, see a split between deontological and teleological moral theories as falling precisely along the lines of which theory requires purposes; in particular, those with a deontological bent say that certain kinds of moral value can only be understood by an evaluation of acts that transcends purposes or teleology.[15] There is some reason to think, however, that those acts that transcend purpose are precisely those that cannot be prescribed, for which the prescription is either otiose or "one thought too many."

So, the role of purposes in morality arises in the deontology-teleology distinction, but they are probably more commonly thought of as the crux between categorical and hypothetical imperatives. Typically, categorical

---

15. As noted in chapter 2, Stocker (1981) holds that some acts that cannot be evaluated in teleological terms are those acts that do not seem to have a purpose, such as smiling spontaneously when one sees a long-lost friend. True, the existence of a purpose behind the smile sullies its value; but note also that if such an action is the result of a prescription, it is likewise sullied. Therefore, not all acts of moral worth can be prescribed, and presumably what is most crucial about these particular acts is the motives behind them. Motives may not be prescribed, but neither are motives purposes (for it makes no sense to prescribe a motive). The problem here is that one cannot prescribe acting from love or respect, for such motives are not under the needed kind of short-term voluntary control. As interesting as these issues are, they do not present a problem with the analysis of prescriptions given above.

imperatives are understood as imperatives that apply to all individuals, independent of any end they might (hypothetically) have. The issue is not resolved, however, by merely noting that categorical imperatives lack hypothetical purposes. Assuming that there are categorical imperatives, this leaves open the possibility that they presuppose categorical purposes. And, indeed, it seems they must. As deeply as one may want to go into Kantian deontology, it should rankle to think that there is no purpose in acting according to maxims that could be willed to be laws or that we should behave according to rules that are purposeless. The purpose might be derived from our rational nature, it might be becoming a member of the kingdom of ends, it might be an expression of respect for the law or God, but there must, for a deontologist, be a perspective (transcendental or otherwise) from which the act is reasonable and makes sense. The purposes that make our acts reasonable may be categorical, but they are purposes nonetheless.[16] So, we may conclude that by the lights of any of the major normative ethical theories out there, purposes are required in the analysis of a prescription. (Note, that these may be left implicit, and making them explicit could be "one thought too many"; but that which is left implicit is still present, if unaccounted for.)

So, there is reason to include a variable for the purpose of the act, P, in the normal form of a prescription, for at the very least it provides purpose, or a final, categorical, or hypothetical reason for the act. And our explication of (1) and (2) is beginning to round itself out. What we are left with is the role of theory, which is needed to understand the truth conditions of both function statements and prescriptions.[17] It is at this point that malfunction enters the picture and, through it, some insights into the modal nature of prescriptive language and the beginnings of an understanding of normativity.

16. Kant ([1785] 1959) says, "To that [universal] realm [of ends] we can belong as members only when we scrupulously conduct ourselves by maxims of freedom as if they were laws of nature" (p. 463); at a more technical juncture, "The logical interest of reason in advancing its insights is never direct but rather presupposes purposes for which they are to be used" (footnote at p. 460).

17. Although it may be clear from the text, I am assuming a theory of truth that is significantly more inflated than both deflationist and minimalist theories. I am taking seriously, though I cannot explain it fully, the idea that certain (though perhaps not all) discourses are representational, that their raison d'être is to describe reality accurately, as it is, much in the same way that a good map represents the world as it is. This may, and probably does, entail some notion of correspondence.

That theory plays a role in making prescriptions should not come as a surprise at this point. Moral and medical theories issue prescriptions, and biological theory ascribes functions or makes function statements. The theory-dependence of function statements becomes apparent when we note that the purposes for which a heart beats if given a biological theory might be different than the purposes for which it beats if given an evolutionary theory: in the former, the purpose may be to exchange O_2 for CO_2; in the latter, the function may be to aid in survival and procreation. (Ends may be packed into systems like Russian dolls.) Introducing theory into the picture begins to give us some insight into when a function statement is true because one requirement for its truth will be that the theory that issues the function statement is itself true. Now, it may not be completely standard to talk about "true theories"; we do not generally speak of theories as having truth values. Normally, we think a theory is constituted by certain propositions (or some other sort of linguistic item), and it is these that are supposed to be one of the *relata* for the truth relation (the other *relata* being the world). But if we may speak loosely about how some theories "get it right," where this is perhaps understood in terms of accuracy of description, so that some theories get it right but others do not, then we might say that the true theories are the ones that get it right: they describe that portion of the world they intend to describe, and they get it right by describing it accurately or well. For example, it is not too odd (I think) to say, "The Copernican theory of cosmology is true but the Ptolemic theory is false."

We may, for the sake of our argument, assume that modern biological theory, for the most part, gets it right, or is true, and this is required for the truth of any particular function statement that issues from it.[18] A

18. There is a problem with Wimsatt's discussion here that was pointed out to me by José Benardete. Note that (i) The function of the heart is to pump blood and (ii) According to theory T, the function of the heart is to pump blood are different. Assuming that theory T does say that the function of the heart is to pump blood, (ii) is trivially true. Of course, (ii) might be false as a report of the contents of theory T, and so it is not completely trivial, as a tautology is. Still, it is facts about hearts that make (i) true, and it is facts about theory T that make (ii) true. Wimsatt is correct in holding that function statements are somehow relative to a theory, or are indexed to a theory, yet saying that function statements implicitly refer to a theory changes their truth conditions.

The problem arises because Wimsatt builds theories into his analysis just as he builds in behaviors, systems, and other factors: it seems as if any given function statement is referring to a theory in such a way that the whole content of the

second requirement is that the function statement really does issue from that theory; the empirical application of theory to world must not contain some sort of error. In applying these thoughts to moral theory, we begin by noting (again) that biological and evolutionary theories may each yield their own function statements. We may then consider moral theories and note that, in large part, the prescriptions they yield are quite similar (though the theories often go their own ways in extreme examples). Deontologists, consequentialists, and virtue theorists may all agree that "one ought not to cause needless suffering," though each sort of theory will explain why the prescription is true in its own terms, or based on the content of that particular theory.[19] Note that these theories may be functionally equivalent, insofar as each (even by its own differing lights) prescribes behavior that is, or makes people, morally good. We may say the same, for example, about Eastern and Western medical practices today, which in many cases are equally successful at making people healthy. Whatever the full truth happens to be about human medicine or morality and whichever normative theory completely captures them, different theories that are not fully correct in detail may, nevertheless, be equally capable of "getting the easy cases right."

If one is still a bit puzzled at the thought of a true prescription, one should consider an example such as "Parents ought to care for their children." *If our going moral theory is even roughly correct, then there are

---

theory is built into each function statement. The result is that we end up saying something like (iii) A theory T which contains theorem t, contains theorem t. We can keep function statements from being trivially true while acknowledging that they are theory-relative by not building the content of the theory into every function statement, while still indexing the function statement to the theory. This indexing cannot be made a part of the *internal* logical structure of a function statement; nevertheless, it is a part of the context in which any function statement is uttered. Function statements issue from theories: they are theorems of theories. Therefore, the only way to mention the relation of function statement to theory is in a metalanguage in which we are talking about the theory, not using it. So, we must remove the reference to theory T from within the logical structure of function statements, as Wimsatt has it, while acknowledging that any understanding of such statements cannot be complete without noting the relationship between the function statement and the theory from which it emerges.

19. This seems roughly equivalent to the situation in quantum physics in which the same physical data are interpreted in a variety of ways, which are the different "interpretations" of quantum physics (e.g., the Copenhagen interpretation, many worlds theories, and hidden variable theories).

objective standards of evaluation by which parent-child relationships can be judged, and a particular relationship will "make the grade" or not. It will be good, bad, or mediocre; parents will be good, bad, or mediocre parents. It is true that parents ought to care for their children because this is the only way for the relationship between them to be good. The standards of evaluation used in making judgments of individual parents are part of the moral theory itself; the standards are part of the empirical content of the theory. If this seems unlikely or mysterious, simply compare the moral prescription with a function statement like "The function of the heart is to pump blood." *If our going biological theory is even roughly correct, then there are objective standards by which we evaluate the workings of hearts, and a particular heart will make the grade or not. There are good hearts, bad hearts, and mediocre hearts. Our biological theory sets the standards for how these evaluations are to be made. The moral language at the first "*" above is grammatically isomorphic to the biological language at the second "*."

As an introduction to the notion of malfunction, recall again that there is a sense in which the term "proper function" is redundant; if an item is functioning, even at a mediocre or average level, it is still functioning as it ought, or properly. There is, however superior functioning, as well as malfunctioning. A heart that is malfunctioning is one that is not successfully pumping blood, and it is thereby a bad heart, a bum ticker not doing its job. Parents who are not successfully caring for their children are thereby bad parents, or just plain bums who are not doing their job.

Normativity and Modality

Let's assume both that Thrasymachus lived by his convictions and that the moral theory he believed in was false; it does not "get it right." Let's also assume that we know the moral theory that actually does get it right. (These assumptions are quite weak: the argument to follow works equally well even if it is actually true that Thrasymachus' theory gets it right and morality is the interest of the stronger.) From these assumptions, it follows from the prescriptions that are issued by the true theory that Thrasymachus often did what he ought not to have done. Or at least, he often did not do what he ought to have done. If we know that Thrasymachus is in a particular moral situation, we could then predict what he will do, based on the (mistaken) theory that we know he employs, or we could prescribe what he ought to do, though we may know that he will not actually do it. How, one might ask, are we to understand the truth conditions for a prescription understood as a description of behavior that never actually occurs? How are we to explain the truth conditions for the proposition that "Thrasymachus ought to act less selfishly" though we know he will not?

The answer is found by looking at how we understand the truth conditions for descriptions of an item's malfunctioning and the truth conditions for function statements about that item. When we see something malfunctioning, we say, "It is not doing what it ought to be doing." We may also say what the item's function is, note that it is not doing that, and conclude that it is malfunctioning: a heart's function is to pump blood, and that heart that is not is therefore malfunctioning. The key to understanding these statements is by noting an implicit modal component within them. When we say that this particular malfunctioning heart ought to be pumping blood, that its function is to pump blood, even though it is not working, what we are saying is that there is a possible world in which the heart is actually pumping blood, though this possible world is not ours. Which world is it? Well, of course, it is the world where the heart is properly functioning, or pumping blood as it ought. Function statements, as well as statements of malfunction, are implicitly modal. When something actually is functioning as it ought, then the possible world where it is properly functioning is the actual world.

One cannot automatically deduce the function of an item from what it is doing, for if it is the kind of thing that has a function, then it is also the kind of thing that can malfunction. A description of an item's actual behavior does not yield a description of its function. To determine an item's function, one must discern the type of thing of which it is a token and then appeal to a theory of that type of thing to determine the function of that type's tokens. Typically, the theory ascribes purposes to the item (or behavior, within a system, etc.), and the function of the item is to contribute properly to particular systems, within environments and so on, to the achievement of those purposes that are characteristic of the items described by that theory.

To sharpen up the modal relations here and some of their logical structure, note that by saying what an item's function is we are saying what it is going to do if it is working in the way the theory says it ought. It may not be working in this way, however; it may actually be malfunctioning, and in this case the function of the item can be understood in terms of what it is doing in another possible world in which it is actually functioning properly. Call the other possible world, in which the item is functioning properly, *F*. Call the actual world *A*, remembering that actuality is an indexical, such that the world you and I happen to be in is the actual world. [*A* is one of an infinite number of possible worlds because what is actual is also possible. *A* contingently happens to be the actual world; if another possible world had been the actual world, then the world you and I refer to as "*A*" (i.e., our world) is merely possible.] *A* is the same as *F* in those cases in which an item is functioning properly; *A* is not *F* in those cases in which the item is malfunctioning. And it is contingent whether or not *A* is *F*. In other words, one cannot deduce a true function statement for an item based solely on a description of how it is actually behaving. If it were necessarily the case that things functioned properly, then we could deduce an item's function based solely on a description of what it is doing. But such a deduction is impossible. This problem for function statements is identical in structure to Hume's problem for deducing an "ought" from an "is." Function statements pick out a possible world at which the item is behaving in the way the theory of those items describes, in which case it is it functioning properly. Sometimes the possible world that the function statement picks out is the actual world; sometimes it is not.

Ought statements also pick out a possible world at which the agent is behaving in the way moral theory describes; this is the world at which the agent is doing what he or she ought. Sometimes the possible world that the *ought* statement picks out is the actual world; sometimes it is not. Nevertheless, we cannot deduce a true *ought* statement for an agent based solely on a description of how he or she is actually behaving. If it were necessarily the case that agents did what they ought to do, then deductions of "ought" from "is" would be unproblematic. Since it is always contingent that agents do as they ought, we can never deduce an "ought" from an "is."

Thus, again, we can account for Hume's famous distinction without making the radical move of saying that moral speech is something other than assertoric. "Ought" statements implicitly make reference to other possible worlds, and this accounts for why descriptions of the actual world cannot fully account for "ought" statements. Modal speech is, in general, very difficult to understand fully; the literature that investigates its mysteries is huge. What we find here, importantly, is that normative speech, speech that prescribes or says what ought to be so, is syntactically of the same sort as standard modal speech. Indeed, it is a subset of modal speech, insofar as it is the part that implicitly refers to that particular possible world at which one does what one ought. Normative discourse, far from presenting some sui generis problem in the philosophy of language, merely presents the same problems that plague any other discourse with modal import. (Keep in mind that every dispositional property requires counterfactuals, or modal speech, to be understood. The philosophical challenges here are not specific to morality or biology but to physics in general.) This is the most parsimonious explanation of Hume's *is-ought* distinction to date.

We can now return to the problem that Hare (1991) faces: if prescriptions are universalizable, this means they must apply to all situations that belong to a particular type. What we wish to know is how we are to cut these types, or how to fix the scope of prescriptions. Cut them too wide (absolutism being the widest possible), so that, for example, one ought always to return what is borrowed, and we find them falsified by obvious exceptions (such as when our distraught friend wants his sword back). Cut them too narrow, and they will have to be specified so much that they will only apply to the unique situation in which the prescription is uttered. Hare says that prescriptions apply to all situations that are "precisely similar," but his theory has no resources to help us figure out which situations those are. The present analysis makes some progress, for it tells us that prescriptions apply to all situations that are similar in terms (along the axes) of situation, culture, purpose, and so on, where we refer to the elements found in the normal form for prescriptions given above in (2). These variables fix the parameters against which situations must be deemed "similar." This point can be made precise in a more technical jargon: in terms of possible worlds, these parameters are those that map out the logical space of possible worlds. "Relevant similarity" (Lewis' phrase [1986]), which is required by the accessibility relation between possible worlds, is determined along the parameters given in (2). Thus, a prescription will pick out a set of possible worlds, relevantly similar across the variables found in the normal form of prescriptions, at which, in each world, the agent does what the agent ought to do. And it is contingent whether or not the actual world is a member of this set. We can even say a little something more about how similar situations must be across these parameters in order to be within the scope of a prescription.

The relation of similarity, a two-place relation in which x may be similar to y, is the subject of an ongoing research project in metaphysics.[20] If any have criticized Hare (1991) for not being able to make sense of similarity, this would be unfair. Hare has as much right as any to bank on

---

20. See, for example, Quine (1969, pp. 114–38), Armstrong (1978), and Lewis, (1986).

the promissory note of the metaphysicians who work specifically on this topic. Still, although the general problem of similarity remains, it would be preferable to be able to say something more about the role of similarity in universalizabililty than that situations have to be "precisely similar" in order for a prescription to apply to all of them. One thing we do know about similarity is that it comes in degrees, from the wholly dissimilar to the identical. The present analysis makes headway where Hare cannot, for it helpfully tells us that the degree of similitude a prescription implies can be understood in terms of "functional equivalence": a prescription will apply in all functionally equivalent circumstances, from the moral point of view. In informal terms, if it makes no sense to say that one "ought to do it this way rather than that," because both ways solve the problem equally well, then from the moral point of view these ways are "functionally equivalent" or "relevantly similar" to one another. To connect this (again) to the result of the preceding paragraph, a prescription will apply to all situations in which the *S, E, P,* and so on of the prescription are describable in functionally equivalent terms. True, this puts the burden of the analysis on understanding how similar things have to be in order to be functionally equivalent; at this point the burden has not been shouldered, for no one has a full analysis of "functional equivalence" in place. But perhaps the materials for a complete and substantive answer to the problem of universalizability are in place, insofar as one can now understand "relevant similarity" in the moral sense as "functional equivalence" is understood in the biological sense. The scope of moral prescriptions is no broader or narrower than the scope of functional equivalence.

And finally, to round out the chapter, we can begin to say something about the origins of normativity, though not all questions can be resolved. The word "normative" itself is unfortunate jargon. Neither "normative" nor "normativity" is to be found in common parlance. Therefore, saying what these words mean will always be a bit tendentious and theory laden. If there is any colloquial sense to "normativity" at all, it has to do with norms of behavior or mathematically statistical norms. Etymologically, we are in the territory of the "normal." At least insofar as they can fail to be met, norms are typically standards of achievement of some sort within a particular field of endeavor. So, when metaethicists are debating the nature of the standards we use in making moral evaluations, we are debating the nature of norms. But not only moral discourse is normative. Logic is normative insofar as validity is a standard by which arguments may be evaluated. [The quick and dirty deduction of the reality of normativity is that there are facts about truths, facts about truth-preservingness (validity), and therefore facts about which are good arguments and which are bad arguments or which arguments we ought to employ and not employ.] Epistemology is also famously normative, insofar as its central concept, *justification*, is a standard that gives license or warrant to certain beliefs and not to others; there are some belief-forming mechanisms we ought to use (veridic perception) and others not (wishful thinking).

Of the sciences proper, it seems that all the applied aspects of mathematics, physics, chemistry, engineering, and so on have normative import; there are ways in which one ought to proceed and not proceed as well. The same may hold true for the theoretical branches of these sciences, but it is not clear. Whether the subject matter of theoretical math or physics has normativity built into it (beyond the logic involved) is hard to say. But certainly normativity arises in "metadiscourse" even about the most theoretical and least applied sciences: whenever there is talk of theory selection based on parsimony, simplicity, elegance, explanatory power, and so on, these scientists are choosing their theories according to normatively laden criteria, presumably a type of normativity closely related to epistemic normativity. In this fairly commonsense way of looking at things, investigating numbers, subatomic particles, electromagnetic radiation, oxygen and the other elements, and all of the interactions of all of these sorts of items will not yield any evidence to even be able to speak meaningfully about the X-ray not doing what it ought to do or the chemical reaction failing to proceed as it ought.[21] One cannot make any sort of prescription for items of this kind, and insofar as this is true, then it seems as if mathematics, classical and quantum physics, and chemistry have nothing to do with normativity.

If we stick to biology, which is normatively laden insofar as it is committed to a function-malfunction (or fitness-unfitness, survival-extinction) distinction, there may nevertheless be a sense in which one may say that in biology everything always does what it ought to do, and this is the sense in which one believes that there are no such things as miracles. Insofar as the causal laws of nature are "obeyed" automatically, "everything does what it ought." A heart, the arteries of which are virtually all blocked, in that condition will or will not have a heart attack, and it

---

21. One can make predictions, and if things don't turn out as predicted, it may be said that "that ought not to have happened"; predictions are interestingly different from prescriptions, in particular in the employment of purposes. For more of a beginning on these topics, see Bloomfield (1998).

makes little sense to say after the attack that "it ought not to have happened." Indeed, perhaps there was no (nonmiraculous) way it could have been avoided. But insofar as the notion of a function is at play, we have the notion of malfunction, and thus we can give some sense to talk about what hearts ought to do. Biology is thereby shot through with normativity. This might be most obviously the case with evolutionary biology, where the norm or standard involved is survival and procreation. But one need not appeal to phylogeny; one may look to ontogeny. Here, one may ask of an individual organism if it is developing as it ought. Organs and tissues have purposes and either are able to help promote those purposes or not. If they do, they are doing as they ought. If not, not. Proper function is a biological norm (related to survival of the fittest).

Importantly, despite the fact that normativity arises in so many different discourses, this does not by itself give us a reason to think that there is more than one kind of normativity, especially if it seems to arise in the same ways across the lines of discourse (in ways outlined above and below). Nevertheless, it does not seem to be the case that all normativity is of the same sort: the normativity that attaches to etiquette seems to be different than that found in biology. The metaphysics of a discourse will determine the nature of its normativity (if it is normative at all). Thus, given our thesis about goodness and healthiness, the normativity that runs through morality is the same as the normativity that runs through the biological sciences. To put this in explicitly linguistic terms, the normativity in the "ought-ought not" distinction is identical to the normativity in the "function-malfunction" distinction.

This has, so far, proceeded at a fairly intuitive level, but some of the machinery put in place above will help give our understanding of the origins of normativity more precision. Theories are descriptions of some domain, and some theories employ the notion of a purpose whereas others do not. Of those that do, we may say that these theories ascribe purposes to the type of item it is describing. Hearts, as a type of item, have certain purposes. If a particular token of that type is incapable of behavior performed for the sake of the purpose ascribed to it by the relevant theory, then that token is not doing as it ought. (There are caveats needed here to rule out accidental furtherance of purposes, but such complications are left aside.) Normativity, therefore, arises when it is possible for a token item or agent, call it x, to act in ways that are contrary to the purposes had by items or agents of the type to which x belongs. Call this type X. When theories quantify over tokens of a type X and describe them as having purposes or ends, and it is possible for a token x to fail in achieving those ends or act for other ends entirely, then that theory has normative import.

One might want to say that having purposes or ends alone might suffice to establish a norm. This would be to say that it is possible for there to be a discourse or subject that describes a type of thing, the tokens of which always, perhaps necessarily, do what they ought. So, it might be argued that one need not appeal to the possibility of malfunction (things not going as they ought) in order to understand function. If, for instance, there were some final end toward which all objects were inexorably headed, then perhaps even if nothing could avoid that end there would still be normativity. If this is the case, then thermodynamics is normative, insofar as the heat-death of the universe (or maximum entropy) is inevitable. If, however, one thinks that "ought" necessarily entails the possibility of "ought not" or one thinks that there is no proper function without the possibility of malfunction, then one will be led to think that normativity is limited to parts of reality in which things can go wrong and not be as they ought to be.

We may wrap up by returning one final time to Hume's claim that one cannot deduce an "ought" from an "is." No one has ever had a problem thinking that "if it is my goal to get out of the woods in which I am lost, there are things I ought to do and others I ought not to do. I ought to try to follow water; I ought not to walk in large circles." These seem to be true statements. Common sense tells us that it is true to say that if you want to get out of the woods, you ought not to walk in large circles. What could be more true? I perform the following practical inference: "I am lost in the woods. If I walk in large circles I will not get out. I want to get out. Therefore, I ought not to walk in large circles." Have not we deduced an "ought" from a bunch of "is's"?

Not so fast, our defender of Hume would rightly say. The third premise of the argument mentions a desire or a want of mine, and this implies some sort of affectivity, some "facts" not grounded in reason. Where there is affectivity, there are no facts of the matter, and this (according to the Humean theory) is the source of normativity. Normativity in this view comes from what we desire, our purposes, and there are no facts about what we ought to desire and no facts either about what our purposes ought to be. Therefore, although the "ought" does not appear until the conclusion of the argument, it is packed into the premise about what is wanted.

One might respond by saying that, in any logical deduction, the conclusion cannot "go beyond" the premises, and deduction can only unpack information that is already implicitly there. Let's, however, try a different, less dialectical route. The problem with the defense of Humeanism here is in thinking that there are no facts about what our purposes ought to be. Consider this thought in light of evolutionary thinking in which humans are naturally invested with certain talents, drives, and instincts. Isn't there some sense to the claim that we ought not to make incest our purpose? More generally, there is nothing more natural than a biological system that is struggling to survive where failure is the difference between life and death. If there are facts about what makes a human flourish and live a good life (above and beyond mere survival), because of the kind of creatures *Homo sapiens* are, then so be it. If parents who abuse their children are also hurting themselves morally, preventing their lives from being as good as they could be (as they are in another possible world in which they do as they ought and love their children), then this is just something that we have to learn about ourselves as empirical objects of study. The Humean will no doubt counter that if I choose to scratch my little finger rather than save the world, then there is no factual mistake I am making. But, of course, at this point we can see that there must be: perhaps I am mistaken in thinking that a human being can be happy or live well, or live a life of *eudaimonia*, knowing that I have scratched my little finger at the cost of the lives of others; perhaps I am mistaken about what will cause the greatest amount of happiness; perhaps I am mistaken about what a person with good will would do. I can adopt purposes other than those I ought to adopt. Just because this is possible, it does not mean that I cannot make a mistake in doing so. There are facts about what we ought to want, normative facts; the true (normative) theory of morality will describe the purposes that humans ought to attain, just as the true biological theory will describe the purposes that hearts ought to attain.

One cannot deduce an "ought" from an "is" if all one has to go by are how people actually behave. If, however, one looks at human nature, one sees that there are some goals truly worth working for, purposes or plans toward which one ought to aim, and others one ought to avoid. These are facts about us, special normative facts but facts nonetheless. If we were different creatures than we are, we would have different aims or purposes, but we are not and therefore do not. "Ought's" are a subset of "is's." One can never deduce that a member of a particular subset obtains from the fact that a member of the general set obtains. Some of the things that are are necessarily so; but one may not deduce what necessarily is from what is. Similarly, one cannot deduce an "ought" from an "is." There is, however, no more linguistic, logical, or metaethical hay to be made from the "is-ought" distinction than there is from the "primate–human being" distinction.

• • •

FOUR

Moral Practicality

Externalism sans Magnetism

The Absurdity of Magnetic Tofu

The last chapter ended with a discussion of the source of normativity, or at least of the sort of discourse that admits of normative distinctions. A normative discourse is one in which an item that falls within the discourse's range may fail to behave in a way consistent with the ends or purposes that that discourse ascribes to that item, in virtue of its being a token of a certain type. In those instances, one may say that it is not (actually) behaving as it ought to behave. The theories that have normative content are those that ascribe purposes to agents (items) such that if those agents fail to act in a way consistent with those purposes, then they are failing to live up to standards that all such agents ought to live up to. The standards are based on the nature of that type of agent (item). Moral theory is, of course, paradigmatically normative. And as far as morality is concerned, saying exactly which purposes we, human beings, have and ought to be pursuing is the subject matter of normative moral theory (for

My thanks to the participants of the Bled 2000 Philosophy Conference, in particular Paul Weirich and Kirk Ludwig, for warnings about the proviso to claims (3) and (4).

Kantians who typically eschew purposes, see pp. 139–40). For this reason alone, we may say that moral theory is practical: a moral theory that fails to give any guidance or help to a person who wishes to live well (or better) is a failed moral theory. To put this point in the language of the last chapter, the practical aspects of moral thinking are (at least one of) the purposes of such thought.

The fact that all parties to the debate agree that morality is practical is, however, quite different from all parties agreeing on what this means or on how morality achieves its practicality. How morality can be practical is the last of the riddles presented in the introduction. Puzzling through this is an old pursuit, and a discussion of Plato's answer will be discussed below. To get to the bottom of things (to diagnose the problem), we've got to explore the connections between knowing what is good (and right) and being motivated to pursue it. To make this into a problem specific to us humans, we need to learn about the links between our knowledge of what is good and our being motivated to act in accord with it, or to do as we ought. It has seemed to many philosophers that, in some way to be explained, knowing what is good automatically (necessarily) brings about, or causes or entails, being motivated to act in accord with that knowledge. The riddle to be pursued runs as follows: is an agent's recognition of what is good sufficient for that agent to be at least somewhat motivated to pursue that good, or might an agent see what is good and not be motivated at all by that knowledge? Or, does knowing what you ought to do entail that you are (at least somewhat) motivated to do it?

Given the present position on moral realism, the natural answer to the question is to adopt the position lately called "externalism" and say no. Many, perhaps most, philosophers have adopted the "internalist" position, answering yes. Much of the chapter will be devoted to why so many have (mistakenly) thought internalism to be true. The reason that moral realists should answer the question with no is given by John Mackie (1977), though he thought himself refuting realism. Mackie's unhappily named argument against moral realism is the "argument from queerness": if goodness (or moral properties in general) is to exist in the way a realist thinks, then in order for the recognition of goodness to be sufficient for being motivated to pursue it, this property of goodness must have some sort of "to-be-pursuedness" built into it, some sort of magnetism or mysteriously attractive power or (to put it in moral terms) an effective authority over us and our motivational structures. Mackie said that these moral properties would have to be very unusual properties indeed, and we should not believe in such things.

For one who thinks that goodness can be understood via healthiness, Mackie's (1977) argument is perfectly sound, up to this point. The difference is that his *modus tollens* is the realist's *modus ponens*. Both agree that moral properties, if they really exist as external features of the world, cannot also have to-be-pursuedness somehow built into them; moral magnetism must be mysterious and denied philosophical respectability. Goodness, if it exists, cannot have a snake-charming power over us. Mackie, however, holds onto a positive, yes answer to the riddle, accepting the "internalist's" position that recognized moral considerations necessarily motivate. He argues from there to a conclusion that moral properties cannot be "out-there" externally in the world. Contra Mackie, this book argues that moral properties are out there in the world. If there are real moral properties, and Mackie is right in thinking that there is no magnetism, then we are led to a negative, no answer to the riddle: we may recognize a moral consideration and fail to be motivated by it; it is out there but lacks built-in motivational power. We are only contingently motivated by the moral considerations we recognize. (To put this point in terms of "reasons for action," moral properties give us reasons for action independently of what may contingently motivate people.)

Admittedly, this has been put in abstract terms, but matters get more concrete quickly because, as should not be surprising, the relations between what is good and being motivated to pursue it can be modeled on the relations between what is healthy and being motivated to pursue it. You recognize that *x* is good. To understand whether or not or how automatically you are motivated to pursue *x*, consider the following: you recognize that *x* is healthy. Are you thereby or automatically motivated to pursue *x*? The answer is surely no. No arguments should be needed (though there are many to come) to see that there is nothing so perfectly natural, nothing so all together too common for a person to hear in our day and age, than for someone to say, in all due sincerity, "I know that everyone ought to exercise and eat right, but I'm just not motivated to do these things at all." If so, then it is false to say strictly that knowing what one ought to do (in every case) entails being (at least somewhat) motivated to do it. Whether or not a person is motivated by the considerations of health is a contingent matter based on the psychological makeup of that person. One might wish to protest that morality is somehow special, that moral knowledge is somehow different than other sorts of knowledge. One might think that the "moral ought" has sui generis motivational features. Of course, the burden of proof would then be on those claiming such a special status for morality. The following arguments show that the burden has not heretofore been shouldered successfully. And by now, we have enough reason to think that a reasonable fall-back position is that the property of moral goodness is only capable of motivating us in the ways in which the property of physical healthiness is. The contingencies involved regarding the motivation to be healthy are the same as those regarding the motivation to be good. One must agree with Mackie (1977): it would be rather absurd, would it not, to believe that tofu was magnetic?

Intuitions behind Internalism

The moral realist can at this point only applaud. Thank goodness that no one (we may hope) has much invested in defending the idea that properties affecting our health necessarily motivate us. The empirical evidence alone seems to indicate that people can recognize how their behavior may positively (or negatively) affect their health and not be motivated by this or care in the least. Some of us are brought up by our parents and culture not to care about keeping fit; others just find themselves that way as adults, without thinking about it much at all. In any case, empirically it seems that we can be motivationally left cold by the rational recognition of the healthiness of eating tofu. If "internalism" were the name of a (type of) theory that posits tight connections between rational considerations of health and our actual motivational systems, internalism would be in pretty sad shape.

Far more plausibility has been found, however, in the case of a type of internalism concerning moral motivation. Here people have taken very seriously the idea that recognizing a moral consideration entails having a motive to act in accord with it. Typically, a caveat is appended that says, "insofar as one is rational," "other things being equal," or some such notion. The idea is that if agents sincerely recognize that, for example, it would be good to help old ladies across the street, recognizing that we ought to do so, such a recognition entails being at least a little motivated to help. The motive need not be overriding, but it must be present. Failing to be motivated, being "left cold," would by itself constitute a reason to think that one really did not know that it would be good to help the old lady. (Contrast this with being absolutely left cold by tofu.) Roughly put, many have thought the degree to which we are rational is the degree to which we are motivated to do what we ought. The idea is that somehow reasons for acting have motives built into them, so that recognizing the reasons ipso facto causes one to be motivated.

The intuitions for such a position go back at least as far as Plato. And unsurprisingly, Plato's metaphysics of universal forms is at the center of his picture about how we become motivated to be good. For the sake of argument, it should be safe to assume that these forms or properties are in some sense abstract, as opposed to concrete or particular, entities. Plato, however, thought that some abstract objects could, so to speak, command the attention and draw the mind to them. Thus, goodness was an abstract object that had the further, some would say "queer," quality of being something that is motivationally magnetic. Once goodness got hold of the mind (outside the cave in the light of the sun), most likely (and perhaps exclusively) via philosophy, people are drawn ineluctably to emulate goodness, thereby becoming good themselves. This thought explains why there was such a high premium back then on coming up with philosophical arguments that could get people to see what is truly good for their lives. The attention was to be moved by the argument to a point where the mind was directly being illuminated by the light of the form of the good— at which point one would automatically strive to become goodness itself, as one "participates" in the very form of goodness.

This is a strikingly beautiful picture, no doubt. Unfortunately, as mentioned above about Mackie (1977), there are problems with it. We cannot imagine a way for abstract universals, similar to numbers and sets, to have some magnetic influence on the motivational structures of the brain. If the form of the good is going to be different from the referent of "5," then some story must be given about why some universals are different in this way from others. And no such story is forthcoming. There is simply no way to get motivational (magnetic) forces out of abstract objects so that they may affect our brains, making us motivated in certain ways. Without appeal to scientifically unrespectable, nonnatural or supernatural forces, one cannot explain how abstract objects could produce such effects.

Even if Plato's account of how we can become motivated to be good has some problems, still there is the part of the story that I think accounts for much of its beauty and attraction: this is the underlying thought that if people could only be made to see what is good for them, they couldn't help but to be motivated by it. So, moving toward a specification of the content of the internalist's claim, we can begin by contrasting three different claims. We can call the following "the normative claim":

(1) The recognition of a moral consideration ought to motivate one to act in accord with it.

It seems safe to assume that all parties to our metaethical debate think that the normative claim is true (at least insofar as one thinks it is possible for ought statements to be true). The second claim could be called "the moral claim":

(2) Morally good people are motivated (perhaps overridingly) to act in accord with the moral considerations they recognize.

Again, it seems safe to assume the truth of the moral claim; indeed (2) might be pretty close to analytic, insofar as the meaning of "being morally good" is virtually synonymous with that of "acting in accord with moral considerations." Claim (3), the internalist's claim, is more clearly synthetic:

(3) People are motivated to act in accord with the moral considerations they recognize.

Claim (3) is meant to describe relations that exist between our rational and our motivational capacities: the moral reasons we see and the motives that move us to act. Claim (3) is taken by internalists to be necessarily true (not merely *de dicto* but *de re*). Thus the claim more explicitly reads,

(4) The recognition of a moral consideration entails (necessarily) the presence of a motive to act in accord with it.

Now we must be very careful at this point. As noted, it is common to add to (3) or (4) a *ceteris paribus* clause or a proviso that reads "insofar as people are rational." The reason we must be careful is that it is all too easy to add clauses that end up being equivalent to (1) or that beg the relevant questions. If one accepts as a tautology that "being rational entails being motivated as one ought to be," then insofar as one is rational, one will be motivated by moral considerations. Given this tautology, adding "insofar as one is rational" to (4) yields (1), which is not in dispute. This is merely to point out the fact that most often "rationality" is itself normative, so that building it into the internalist's claim changes the claim from being one that describes how we actually are to one that describes how we ought to be. (Note the subtle slippage from "is" to "ought"; more on this later in this chapter.) The same may be said of a *ceteris paribus* clause: such a clause is unproblematic, unless the only way to spell out the conditions under which "all other things are equal" is by specifying exactly those conditions in which we end up being motivated as we ought to be. In general, adding such clauses to (3) and (4) is fine, as long as the resultant claim is one that applies to moral agents in general and not just to those moral agents who are motivated as they ought to be. In order to not beg questions, it will be taken as an open question whether or not rationality entails that one will be motivated as one ought to be; we leave open the possibility that someone may be rational and yet unmotivated by morality or, to go even further, rational and yet evil. The internalist's claim is that these possibilities are really impossible.

For the moment we can, in rough-and-ready terms, understand internalism as a theory about the ways in which moral reasons are capable of motivating us to act in accord with them. Perhaps what counts as rational for a person is determined by facts about what that person desires or prefers, or perhaps it is determined by facts about rationality per se. In either case, internalism says that reasons and motives are necessarily conjoined: what we have reason to do will motivate us, all we must do is see it. Again, the claim is not (merely) that we ought to be motivated by the moral considerations we recognize (on pain of being irrational) but that we actually are motivated by the moral considerations we recognize (on pain of being irrational). The claim is that we necessarily, and hence actually, are motivated to do as we ought insofar as we are capable of recognizing what we ought to do. Reasons necessarily (though perhaps not overridingly) motivate those who recognize them.

Now, internalism is obviously a very complicated topic. Indeed, there is no single canonical formulation of internalism, and laying out in detail the conceptual geography of variations would take up too much space. (In a recent article Robert Audi, 1997, makes an argument by cases against internalism, finding problems within each of almost 20 different versions and families of versions of it.) Among the internalists themselves, however, there are only two main competing, traditional themes about how best to understand their own internalist intuitions. Seeing the failure of internalism begins with investigating these two traditions, the Humean and the Kantian, and showing how both founder.

Hume and Williams Meet Thrasymachus

We begin with the Humean tradition, the modern exemplar of the view being Bernard Williams (1981, chap. 8); I'll call this the HW view. Hume took it to be the case that rationality, as a faculty, is incapable of motivating us by itself and that all motivational force ultimately derives from our passions. Reason is, famously, the slave of the passions. Now, prima facie, this may seem contrary to the tenor of internalism as discussed above, but in fact it is not because, in the HW view, what counts as reasons for a person is determined by that person's passions. To use Williams's terminology, we each have a "subjective motivational set," call it S, made up of "such things as dispositions of evaluation, patterns of emotional reaction, personal loyalties, and various projects, as they may be abstractly called, embodying the commitments of the agent" (p. 105). In this view, then, one will have a reason to ϕ, if and only if ϕ-ing is related to some element of S as causal means to an end. Thus, recognizing that one has a reason to do something automatically engages a person's S, entailing that one will be motivated to act in accord with the reason, and we have internalism.

What this implies, however, is that if ϕ-ing will not further the pursuit of an element in S for an agent, then there cannot be any reason for that agent to ϕ. (There are no reasons for the agent external to this set, no so-called "external reasons.") This is problematic, and we can see why by reconsidering once again (our old friend) Thrasymachus. We assume that Thrasymachus is under what might be called "ordinary optimal conditions": these are conditions in which he is not drugged, asleep, or hypnotized, conditions in which he can think calmly and rationally and is not overlooking readily available information (Rosati, 1996). Pretheoretically, we think these are the conditions in which Thrasymachus is going to be most capable of thinking accurately and correctly about the contents of his subjective motivational set. We can also assume that, in these conditions, he will not make invalid inferences or think along forms of thought that are "irrational." In these conditions, Thrasymachus has the best sort of access to the contents of his S as any human could hope for. We know he believes in a (false) theory (or a theory we disagree with) that says that morality is the interest of the stronger and that morality is therefore only for the dupes who are not smart enough to benefit by immorality and go uncaught. We then put Thrasymachus in a situation in which he is able to do an injustice for which he will not be caught (for whatever reason; perhaps he has found Gyges's ring), and this injustice will further his pursuit of some element in his S. The problem is that in the HW view, there is a reason only for Thrasymachus to do the injustice and no reason for him not to. And as if this were not troubling enough, if it is the case that prescriptions require reasons to back them up, there is no true prescription saying, "Thrasymachus ought not to do the injustice."

One may try to insist that Thrasymachus has, perhaps latently or in an undeveloped fashion, elements in his *S* that give him reasons to be moral even if he cannot recognize them as such. Thus, one might think all Thrasymachus needs is some education about what he *really* thinks is valuable, and the problem seems to go away. Perhaps the HW view can account for the following example; perhaps it cannot. Consider the case in which an agent begins a practice of φ-ing because it furthers the cause of a preexisting element in the agent's *S*; call it *e*. After a time, however, our agent begins to see φ-ing as valuable in itself, independent of its contribution toward attaining *e*. The agent then begins to φ for its own sake. Now, one might think that this, all by itself, disproves the HW view: what this shows is that the agent had a reason to φ all along, independent of its contribution to *e*, even if it would have been psychologically impossible for the agent to comprehend this any earlier.

The problem here is not that an agent may fail to recognize a consideration as a reason when it is presented; the problem is that, in this view, that consideration is not a reason if it fails to bear the proper relationship to some extant element in the agent's *S*. Perhaps, however, a more charitable interpretation of the HW view might be able to accommodate this sort of case. No advocate of the view is going to think that the contents of an agent's subjective motivational set are static. We are developing, dynamic creatures and what concerns us, what we value and what we care about, changes as we experience more in life. Let's assume the HW view has a way to account for the sort of change outlined in the preceding paragraph. Does this help with the case of Thrasymachus? The answer is no.

We must remember that Thrasymachus, despite his many moral failings, is no fool. In ordinary optimal conditions, he makes no rational mistakes in thinking about himself and the contents of his *S*. He has his theory of how things work, and he, we may imagine, accepts this theory with a "come what may attitude." As in the introduction, this phrase "come what may" invokes Quine's ([1951] 1953) "Two Dogmas" and his demonstration of the futility of trying to draw a sharp boundary between analytic and synthetic propositions. Thrasymachus may rationally take it as analytic or true by definition that "morality is the interest of the stronger," so "morality" means (for him) "the interest of the stronger." At this late date, it should not surprise us to find that any given belief—

even a pretty crazy one, such as that the Earth is flat—but perhaps most likely a moral belief, can be taken to be a central and indisputable element (taken as "analytic") within a web of beliefs, a belief such that, automatically, any argument showing it to be false is taken to be a reductio ad absurdum of that argument. If Thrasymachus or anyone for that matter, wishes to hold onto a belief that morality or justice is the interest of the stronger, "come what may," there may very well be no way to rationally demonstrate to him the errors of his ways. As argued throughout this book, it might well be the case that there is simply nothing anyone could possibly say or do to get Thrasymachus to change his view. He could be intractably bad, even in "ordinary optimal conditions." If this is the case, then in the HW view, Thrasymachus has no reason to change. In considering how practical morality is to be, it would normally be intolerable to think that the more wayward and mistaken people are about morality, the less reason they have to change, yet this seems to be the conclusion.

The HW view could be spared this problem if it were the case that at some very deep, perhaps at the deepest, level we cannot be wrong about what is good for us. If we were incapable of this sort of error, then whenever we encountered a Thrasymachus-like person, we could say (were we to tend toward such presumption), "Oh, you have reasons to be moral all right, reasons that resonate with your deepest values, and this is the case even if you can't ever see them." But the problem with this solution is that we, *Homo sapiens*, are actually capable of being wrong, at the very deepest level, about what is good for us: we are capable of just this sort of error. We can be irrevocably wrong about what is good for us, and if we are, we will then be incapable of being motivated by what is in fact good for us. The HW view may be right in thinking that motivation comes from what we care about and value, and so on. But it certainly gets wrong the connection between motives and reasons: we can fail to be motivated by what we have reason to do. In the HW view, if it is impossible for us to be motivated by something, then there cannot actually be a reason to do it. This simply cannot be right.

We must be very careful here to contrast this result with the perfectly commonsensical thought that we ought to be motivated by what we actually have reason to do, regardless of our subjective motivational set. [This is a normative claim, in the spirit of (1) above.] For this to be the case, for such a perfectly acceptable thought to even be coherent, we must recognize that it makes perfect sense to think that we can have reasons (for action) that are incapable of motivating us; it makes perfect sense to think that what counts as a reason for an agent does not necessarily depend on what can possibly motivate that agent, namely, the elements of *S*.

To continue in a normative tone for a moment, we might tell Thrasymachus what he ought to do. If it is impossible for us to convince him that he is wrong about morality, then, again, in the HW view, he will have no reason to do as he ought to do. Note, however, that he will have a reason to do what it is *he thinks* he ought to do, given what he rightly sees are the actual constituents of his *S*. So, in the HW view, he actually does have a reason to do what, in fact, he ought not to do. He will not, on the other hand, have a reason to do as he ought. And at this point, the HW view has becomes quite absurd.[1]

It is possible to have reasons that one is incapable of being motivated by. If one is, like Thrasymachus, incapable of being motivated by certain reasons, then one becomes incapable of actually doing what one ought. Therefore, one cannot always do what one ought. And this deserves the briefest of digressions, for if it was Hume who taught us that "is" does not imply "ought," it is remarkable here that it was Kant who has foisted

---

1. The point here is obviously that common sense disagrees with the Humean, insisting that morality must give us reasons for action or tell us what we ought to do, independent of what our desires happen to be. There is another divergence of the two, though the argument is so crude it barely merits a note. I hope the reader will forgive the possible impropriety of the example, but its strength is required to make the point clear. The Humean thinks something roughly as follows: for the doing of any *x*, such that a person *y* desires to *x*, this desire is sufficient for *y* to have a reason to *x*. Common sense says this is too much. Consider the example of a person who desires to eat feces. The Humean seemingly is forced to say that people have a reason to eat feces if they so desire. Now, in the vernacular, there is a sense of "reason" that admits of there being good and bad reasons, and insofar as this is so, then it might be said that one has reason to eat feces if one so desires, but this will surely be a bad reason; I take it without argument that common sense is committed to saying that there are no good reasons to eat feces, anyone's desires notwithstanding (ignoring the special pleading for cases in which, e.g., a madman says, "Eat shit or die"). The Humean thought is not, however, that desires give rise to either good or bad reasons but that they give rise to good reasons alone, reasons that are capable of providing some measure of justification for actions based on them. Common sense does not allow that all desires give rise to good reasons; therefore, the Humean view does not comport with common sense. The confusion has been due, I think, to a conflation of reasons that explain action but do not justify it (bad reasons) and those that explain and also justify (good reasons).

on us the dictum that "ought" implies "can." But just because we all morally ought to have motivational structures that preclude acting from sexist or racist motives, this does not imply that everyone can have the motivational structures they ought to have. Some people may be irredeemably sexist or racist, actively and persistently being motivated to resist any attempts to change the situation. For such people, given how they actually are (and not how they could have been if things had been different), it may be impossible for them to do what they ought. If Thrasymachus (or the murderers of James Byrd, Jr.) believes his false moral theory in a Quinian "come what may" manner, he would then be incapable of being or doing as he ought. And this situation seems all too easy to imagine.

The probable falsity of Kant's dictum is interesting but is, in the end, beside the present point. It does serve nicely, however, as segue into the discussion of the second traditional version of internalism, for it, too, comes to us from Kant.

Kant, Nagel, and Korsgaard Meet Anscombe

It was in regard to the First Critique that Kant recognized Hume as the one who shook him from his "dogmatic slumbers," but we must see Kant as responding to Hume in the present context as well: it is almost impossible to imagine Kant not losing sleep upon reading Hume's eloquent arguments for the idea that reason is merely the "slave of the passions." Indeed, it is at the very center of Kant's moral philosophy that reason alone is both necessary and sufficient for one to be moral and actually do what is right. For Kant, rationality, all by itself, is practical; it can get us to do things, to perform acts. Desires, for Kant, have nothing to do with the motivation to be moral; passions, one expects, even less. Reason alone can tell us what we ought to do, and insofar as we are rational we will necessarily (and overridingly) be motivated to act appropriately. Truly, we have here a grand and awe-inspiring conception of rationality and morality.

Luckily, there is no need for a full survey of Kant's moral philosophy. What needs to be focused on is the necessary relationship that Kant thinks he sees between the recognition of a reason and the motive he thinks it (actually always) succeeds in inspiring [keeping in mind that this is different from unproblematically thinking that there is a necessary relationship between the recognition of a reason and the motive it *ought* to inspire, our normative claim (1)]. In particular, we must look at the modality of the relationship between reason and motive, the nature of the necessity of it. No one would want to claim that we are never motivated by the reasons we recognize; the contentious bit comes when Kant goes modal on us. To take the plainest route toward understanding how this is supposed to work, we need to introduce some more modern thinking on the subject, that of Thomas Nagel (1970) and Christine Korsgaard (1985). I'll call this position the KNK view.

We begin with the notion of a theoretical, or purely logical, inference; examples would be any classic syllogism, such as

(5) All humans are mortal.
(6) Socrates is a human.
(7) Therefore, Socrates is mortal.

Such an inference or syllogism is said to be valid because the structure of any argument that has the same logical form necessarily preserves truth from premises to conclusion. And we often say that insofar as a person is rational, that person will necessarily draw the conclusion given by the premises. If one is rational, then the recognition of the premises entails making the inference to the conclusion. Indeed, we are even drawn to think that this is a constitutive claim about what it is to be rational. We may say that rationality commands us to draw the inference once we have recognized the premises; insofar as one is rational, one cannot help it.

But there is another kind of inference, which was introduced in chapter 2. This is the practical inference, and we learned about its formality first from Aristotle. Here, typically, the logic goes from premises that describe the case at hand to a conclusion traditionally taken to be an action (not merely a proposition that describes what action ought to occur; rather, the action itself is the conclusion). Although not exactly in Aristotle's form, a clear and easy example with the requisite marks would be an inference from the following premises:

(8) If one is thirsty, drinking water will slack it.
(9) I am thirsty and this is water.

We arrive at a conclusion in which I actually take a drink of the water. Now, we cannot be precise here and say that the inference is "valid," for there is no truth in the conclusion, given that actions are not capable of being true or false. Nevertheless, we may confer on the inference the approbation of being rational. The situation is more complicated than this, however. We do sometimes have competing interests, and we want to leave open the possibility that it is not a failure of my rationality if I do not drink water, though I recognize (8) and (9) to be the case; I may be busy or have more pressing demands on my time that do not allow a pause to slack my thirst. Aristotle took care of this problem by placing all such inferences within the context of a person's life taken as whole, an agent's *eudaimonia*. Complications of *akrasia* aside, he may well have thought that given the context of an agent's whole life, the inference operative within the agent's current circumstances would overridingly produce the action that ought to occur (at least insofar as the agent is rational). This is not, however, quite the way in which the KNK view handles it.

In the KNK view, instead of having a conclusion that is an action, a practical inference has a motive as the conclusion. If I recognize that (8) and (9) are the case, then insofar as I am rational, I will be motivated to drink the water. I may not actually drink it, but this may be no failure of rationality. I will not necessarily be overriddingly motivated by the recognition of (8) and (9), but I will necessarily be motivated (to some positive degree). The argument seems to be something like this: just as rationality necessitates the drawing of the conclusion in theoretical inference, it also necessitates the forming of a motive as the conclusion of a practical inference. Thus, insofar as one is rational, one will be motivated by rationality. Rationality commands the formation of motives in the practical sphere, as it commands the drawing of valid conclusions in the theoretical sphere; and the necessity that attaches to the latter attaches to the former as well. Reason is thus practical insofar as it is capable of motivating rational people. (See Nagel, 1970, pp. 20–22.)

So, whereas the Hume-Williams view holds the thought that what reasons we have are dependent on the kinds of thing that are capable of motivating us (namely, the elements of our various *S*'s), the Kant-Nagel-Korsgaard view holds that rationality alone can determine what reasons we have and that these are capable of motivating us all by themselves. Both agree that the recognition of a reason necessarily entails having a motive, and we have already seen how this thought collapses for the HW view. Seeing how it collapses for the KNK view requires the inspection of an argument developed by G. E. M. Anscombe.

Anscombe's ([1974] 1995) argument, which I call the "time-gap argument," is found in "Practical Inference," which came up earlier, in chapter 2's discussion of the logic of practical inference. It is a marvelous and marvelously difficult essay. The time-gap argument itself, just a part of the larger article, was not explicitly written with the internalism-externalism debate in mind but as part of a response to an article by von Wright in which he stumbles over himself a bit in trying to explain how the making of inferences can lead to action.

Anscombe ([1974] 1995) takes up the suggestion that the necessity that connects inference and motive is of the same strength as that which obtains between the premises of a theoretical inference and the conclusion of such an inference; and so we find ourselves addressing something very much akin to the KNK view. Anscombe reasons as follows: the distinction it is crucial to notice is the one between the inference, as it stands "timelessly" composed of propositional entities and their logical relations, and the actual employment of the inference, which takes place in a person's brain or mind within time.[2] All humans are mortal; Socrates is human and therefore mortal. The validity of the inference is what we can call "timeless": it has always been valid and it will always be valid. This validity is not dependent on anyone ever actually thinking it through; rather, when we do think the inference through, we may confer approbation on the thinking by calling it "valid," but this will always be in virtue of the fact that the timeless inference is valid in a manner quite independent of both our thinking it through in the head or our calling this thinking "valid." So, there is the inference that is valid in a timeless manner and the employment of the inference, which takes place in time, that is as an event in someone's brain. Presumably, whenever people run through the inference in their heads, this is an event that can be timed (it has duration); and the moment at which the inference is drawn, the moment in which the mind moves from a consideration of the premises to a drawing of the conclusion, is a moment we could (in theory) pinpoint (were we to have the technology to "read" brain activity). The inference, as it stands timelessly, cannot be divided in the same fashion. Timeless validity entails a necessary truth-preserving structure of propositional contents, but this same timeless validity cannot have any sort of effects at the pragmatic level of what is going on in someone's brain or mind.

2. The time-gap argument is not committed to any particular theory of the mind and works whether or not materialism is true. All it needs to get going is the plausible assumption that thought occurs in time (sequentially). This could get tricky, given Kant's First Critique commitment to the empirical nature of time and the transcendental nature of the mind. One may doubt the consistency of these two commitments for reasons that have nothing to do with pracitcal morality. My thanks here to Lawrence Pasternack (Mid-South Philosophy Conference, Memphis TN, February 25, 2000).

Anscombe ([1974] 1995) now suggests that the only necessity involved in the situation is that which comes in because of the validity that exists within this timeless structure. Although the employment of the inference in the head may deserve the approbation of being called "valid," this is a sort of validity that does not create a necessary bridge to span the gap between the consideration of the premises and the drawing of the conclusion. The inference in the head can be considered as *necessarily* truth preserving only in virtue of the timeless logical structure it manages to recapitulate or instantiate. The diachronic structure of the instantiation, or the inference as it is in the head, is contingently constructed in time. The inference in the head may preserve truth, but it only does so contingently. No *strong necessity* can be found in the employment of the inference in the head because something could always interfere in the moment between the consideration of the premises and the drawing of the conclusion. Such interference could be either external—were one, say, to be distracted at the crucial moment—or it could come from some internal, psychological source. (One might insist on a *ceteris paribus* clause, which would rule out such interferences, but the difficulties of doing so without begging the question have already been addressed.)

The words "strong necessity" were used two sentences back, and the modalities here are admittedly slippery. But we must leave open the possibility of what could be called "psychological determinism" and so admit that the brain's movement from mental state to mental state may be in this sense moved with some sort of necessity or determination. This is a very weak form of necessity, and in fact it is the same level of modality discussed above in relation to Thrasymachus' intractability. Taking this time an example of being good, consider a particular person, like Socrates. Socrates might have been the kind of person who has developed (perhaps consciously, perhaps not) psychologically necessary connections between his reasoning and his motivational structures. Indeed, Socrates might find himself compelled or necessitated to perform certain actions because of the moral reasons he sees. This sort of necessary psychological compulsion deserves to be recognized as a form of necessity. But note how contingent and contextualized such a necessity must be, dependent as it is on upbringing and good fortune, discipline and perseverance. We might even again find reason here to understand what it is to be a morally good person in terms of the presence of such contingent connections between a person's reasons and motives. Remember claim (2), of which we have already noted the truth. We do want to be able to recognize that some people have developed themselves to be such that the recognition of a moral consideration entails being moved. What we do not find in this very weak, dare I say contingent, necessity is a foundation on which to build a stronger necessity, a purely conceptual necessity, which says that the recognition of reasons, understood in general terms, all by themselves necessitate the presence of motives. In fact, recognized reasons understood in these general terms are only contingently related to the presence of motives.

The time-gap argument can be understood by noting the conflation that is easily made between the two senses of "validity" mentioned above: "validity" as it applies to argument forms and "validity" as it applies to actual thought. The former is necessarily truth preserving and the latter is not. The KNK version of the internalist's claim must attach to the second form of validity to be descriptive of how actual people become motivated by the reasons they recognize, yet there is no necessity that can be attached to this mental process of becoming motivated. And so, there is no reason to think that recognizing a moral consideration (strongly) necessitates being motivated by it.

The point can be made in another way, for we are now certainly in a position to see how the KNK view fails. This view models the necessity of the relations between premises and motivation in practical inference on the relation between premises and conclusion in theoretical inference. The underlying assumption is that people are motivated with the same necessity with which they draw theoretical conclusions. What we find, however, is that even in theoretical inference, there is no strong or conceptual necessity when the inference is being employed; any given person is only contingently rational, and a psychological necessity is the strongest sort of necessity with which a person could draw the proper conclusion. If this is the case for theoretical inference, then, *mutatis mutandis*, by the reasoning of the KNK view, it must hold for practical inference as well. The actual connections that exist between people's reasoning and motivational structures are at least as contingent as the connections that exist between the premises and conclusion of theoretical reason. This result is devastating for the KNK view, which is precisely the view that *all* people, insofar as they rationally recognize moral considerations, are necessarily motivated by those reasons. Of course, we ought to be motivated by the reasons we recognize, and good people will be so motivated. But rationality alone cannot necessitate motivation, given the fact that being rational cannot necessarily prevent other factors from interfering with the connections that ought to exist between reasons and motives. (These other factors will be discussed in the next section.) So, the conclusion is that

Anscombe's ([1974]1995) time-gap argument ends the discussion about the plausibility of the KNK view.

In summation: given that (1) the recognition of a moral consideration, as well as the state of being motivated to do something, are both mental states, and (2) the connections between mental states are contingent, we may conclude that (3) moral agents are only contingently motivated by the moral considerations they recognize.

A Little Bit of Jimmy Carter in All of Us?

The argument against the two traditional forms of internalism can then be summarized thus: against the Humeans, our intransigent racist shows us that it is false to think that all reasons are due to the presence of an item in an agent's subjective motivational set; the obstreperous Archie Bunker–style racist has reason to change his views, though he is psychologically incapable of seeing this. Therefore, there are reasons that are "external" to whatever may succeed in motivating a person. We can read Kantians as externalists insofar as they are in agreement here. (See Frankena, 1976, and Robertson and Stocker, 1992, for the sense in which Kant is an "externalist.") But against the Kantians, we can see that these external reasons do not necessarily motivate someone who recognizes them; the time-gap argument shows that the strongest possible necessity that may be involved here is a psychological necessity, which cannot support internalism.

Where does this leave us regarding the connections between reasons and motives? We are left with a mere contingent connection, similar to the connection that obtains between recognizing what is healthy and being moved to act on it. What is surprising, perhaps, is that this may be surprising. Assuming a scientifically respectable materialism about the mental (be it reductionist or nonreductionist) and what follows from this, namely, that thinking happens in the brain, we should not expect stronger connections to exist between our reasoning and our motivational structures than there are anywhere else in the brain. And this is going to be the case unless we build in normative provisos about how the brain develops. Thus, we may say that if a brain develops as it ought to develop, then there will be psychologically necessary connections between reasoning processes and motivational states [the normative claim, claim (1).] This, however, is a claim that only applies to the very few people (if there are any at all) who always, as a matter of psychological necessity, are motivated by the reasons they recognize. It goes far beyond "normal folk," who are nowhere close to being so automatically motivated.

There are at least two different ways in which the normatively proper connections between reasoning and motivation may fail to obtain in normal folk. The first, weaker way is one in which the reasoning processes go as they ought to go, but the link in forming a motive fails for wholly different, nonrational reasons ("nonrational" as in "having nothing to do with rationality," not "irrational"). So, imagine a commuter called "J" who takes a bus home from work every day; the bus passes by an old folk's home, so J gets used to having to stand up halfway through each day, giving the seat to an old person.[3] Now, one day after having an early morning fight with a relative, and having had an equally bad day at work (troubles with the capricious boss), J is coming home, exhausted, on the bus. An old lady gets on the bus halfway through and stops in the aisle in front of our commuter. J knows, by J's own lights, to get up, as J does every day. J's reasoning faculties are in perfect working order, and they tell J it is wrong to stay seated, but J just can't get up on that day. There is nothing there motivationally; J is left cold by recognized reasons (like he or she might be by tofu). Importantly, this is no failure of rationality, nor does it even count as a proper case of *akrasia* or weakness of will. The problem is not that the wrong motive won out; it is that the proper motive did not arise in the first place and so could not be "beaten out" by another. The exhaustion of commuters does not prevent their reasoning processes from recognizing what it is that they ought to do; it is that what they ought to do sometimes fails to move them. There is nothing so terribly unusual about J's story, and the evidence that situations like this arise for all of us at one time or another (and for some of us more frequently than that) is that we can fail to be motivated to perform actions that we know we ought to perform, and we may feel guilty or shameful for our failure to even be motivated (on top of the shame for not having actually acted). If we are asked why we were not motivated to do what we knew we ought to do, the following response is completely cogent:

> Not only did I see that I had every reason to do that, but I also saw that I had no good reason not to do it; nothing more desirable or obligatory was keeping me from it, I know that—I'm not even going to say I had an excuse

---

3. This example was inspired by the writing of and conversations with Michael Stocker (1976, 1979, 1981, 1990).

(much less a good one). At that moment I just didn't care about what I knew I ought to be doing, didn't care in the least what my responsibilities were. In fact, this is the cause of my worst shame and guilt, and I hope my feeling bad about this now will make it less likely that I disregard reason again in the same fashion later.

There is no failure of rationality here, nor an *akratic* failure either. Perhaps it is a failure of discipline, but it most certainly can be a moral failure, or a failure of character. Once again, we see that "ought" does not imply "can": "I just couldn't get myself up off the couch, it just wasn't going to happen."

We are all prone to such lapses, though they are obviously not our best or proudest moments. They are moments we might not notice, or even choose to forget or at least not dwell on; perhaps they are moments to sublimate in some way and pretend that they never happened. Once again, we may become blind to such failures. If they are not too frequent, they are likely to do little harm; they are only rarely horrible mistakes with disastrous results. And after all, no human is perfect; no one is capable of always doing what ought to be done or even being so motivated. We just don't always have it in us.

The second, stronger, way for the normative connections between recognized reasons and motivation to fail is worse: an indication or sign of the state of a person's moral character. This is the possibility that (consciously or otherwise) one trains oneself (or is trained) to disregard reasons, to disregard one's conscience or to train oneself to not feel guilty or ashamed by such behavior. People can be willfully bad (similar to the way in which they can be willfully ignorant).

It is possible for us to rebel against morality, to recognize what moral reasons we have for action and to purposefully do the exact opposite. It is even possible to take pleasure in doing wrong. Nonphilosophers are shocked to learn how shocking this thought is to many philosophers. When the punks burn the cat and take evident pleasure in its pain, philosophers of the internalist stripe have to explain such an event in terms consistent with the idea that the punks were doing what reason was telling them to do, subjectively; from their point of view, the punks were behaving reasonably or perhaps out of weakness of will. The internalists cannot, however, have it that the punks knowingly and willfully (enthusiastically) do what they know they ought not to do or what is unreasonable. They could find no meaning, no sense in some (articulate) punk saying, "I knew it was wrong, and that was exactly what made me want to do it." Externalists here have common sense on their side. Common sense recognizes that some (particularly bad) people engage in behaviors because they know these behaviors are wrong. They need not take pleasure in doing what is wrong, but they might. They might do it for money or pleasure, or they may simply do it *because* it is wrong. The internalist could say that the pleasure (or money) has given the punks their reason, but the punks, who may insist that they had no good reasons to do it, need not see it that way. Here, they are in agreement with common sense, which insists that pleasure does not give anyone a reason to burn a cat; some pleasures ought not to be had. As we have seen in the discussion of the HW view, the punks' desire to burn the cat does not give them a reason to do it, regardless of the contents of their S's, and here we see that knowing that they ought not to may make it all the more desirable and thereby all the more against reason.[4]

Internalists and externalists can try to make sense of the punks in any way they want, but if one could ask the punks (without getting beaten up) if they thought they were behaving reasonably or according to reason, the punks might surely scream, "YEAH WE KNOW ITS WRONG. WE AIN'T GOT NO REASON. WE DON'T CARE. REASON HAS NOTHING TO DO WITH IT AND UP YOURS WITH YOUR REASON ANYWAY."

Happily, such language is not common in philosophical circles.[5] To an unusual degree, in this particular case, this is much to the detriment of

4. Though I have never actually met one, there are supposedly people who worship the devil. Devil worship is presumably a conceptual difficulty for internalists for it seems very hard to imagine people who wholeheartedly worship the devil and think that this is a good thing to do or that it is right or that they morally ought to. Perhaps less lofty and more in the spirit of the punks, a popular rock song, as of this is writing, is by a band called Korn, the title of which is "Make Me Bad."

5. It is difficult for academic philosophers to "keep it real." But consider this bit of commonsense moral realism from the *Montreal Mirror*, "Rant Line," 30 March 2000, where a woman called in with the following "rant": "I have something to say to people who ignore and deny the existence of or constantly bitch and complain about homeless people and street kids. You should watch one of them get the shit kicked out of them by three ignorant fucking JOCKS who run away laughing like cowards while he tries to get up and spits out blood. Then think about the fact that this is his reality and you are only perpetuating it with your ignorance. His busted up face is a direct result of your sick, twisted, dehumanizing attitude. Take that to bed with you and see how well you sleep."

philosophy. Do not think that the problem concerns how calm the punks are when we speak to them. Calm them down, put the punks in "ordinary optimal conditions," and ask the same question. One might say,

> I'm not saying I understand it all, but that's me. Yes, I can look my wrongness in the face and I'll own it. I do. Sure I knew it wasn't right, that cat never did nothing to me. I wanted to burn it anyway, I guess I don't really know why. I ain't got no excuse. But I don't care neither. I knew it was wrong, but I got no regret or shame for it. It's how I am. Might as well tell a crow to turn white.

Now, perhaps we could psychoanalyze the punk to try and make it all make sense, and in the end there will be a story and the story will make sense. There are always reasons for why the things that happen happen. But we have switched topics at this point; the sense of "reason" in the previous sentence is one that admits of a distinction between good and bad reasons. The question is not if there is some sense of "reason" that allows us to say, "The punks had a reason"; the question is "Did the punks knowingly do what they knew to be wrong?" And the answer is yes. Need they have been motivated one iota to do what they recognized as right and good? The answer is no. They very well might have seen the correct moral reasons for action: it may have run through their heads that they ought not to burn the cat, but, and this is absolutely crucial, this may only have made them more motivated to do so.

Although there is not much to be said from the moral point of view for Machiavellian realpolitik as a description of how politicians ought to behave, it may serve well as a description of how politicians actually behave. And we might say something importantly similar here about internalism. The way it is, out there in the real world, is not the way internalists describe it as being; to say the least, as a description of "realmorality" we are not all as motivationally responsive to moral reasons as we ought to be.[6] But again, we must be careful to distinguish the normative claim about what ought to motivate us [claim (1)] from the internalist's claim about what actually does motivate us (what necessarily motivates us).

What we have here are the makings for an error theory of internalism, where an error theory is (roughly) one that takes as false a claim with widespread acceptance. And as we have learned from the master of the error theory, David Hume, any cogent error theory must have two parts:

---

6. "No beast so fierce but knows some touch of pity. . . . But I know none, and therefore am no beast" (*Richard III*).

one in which the error is exposed as error and one in which an explanation is to be given of why people fell into the error in the first place. If the above discussion goes some way toward completing the task of exposing the error of internalism, there still ought to be some story for why internalism is so popular among philosophers and why they can elicit intuitions from nonphilosophers that appear to support it. We have looked a bit at the intuitions behind internalism, going back to Plato. We can begin to see how people are led to these mistaken intuitions by noting that even if we think that Hume explained the difference between "is" and "ought" incorrectly, this does not mean that we may forego being sensitive to his observations about how easily we may slip unwittingly between giving descriptions of how people actually are and how they ought to be. When one goes normative, one does not stop describing factual matters, but one does switch topics.

So, we begin to explain the popularity of internalism by agreeing with Hume that people often slip without notice from thinking about how things are to thinking about how things ought to be. Add to this the fact that most of us are at least somewhat moved to be moral, so that how we ought to be is how we hope ourselves to actually be. We tend to put ourselves in the best light, which makes us look more as we ought to look but somewhat disguises how we really are. We (and most especially we philosophers) hear Plato's story about the cave and we wish we could be the one chosen to leave the darkness of the cave and enter the light. We like to think that we would be compelled to become good if we could only see what that good really is. This is beautiful, but it is false as a picture of how human beings actually are. We all ought to be the kind of people who actually are (and are necessarily) motivated by recognized reasons. But we are not at all actually as we ought to be. The best people are (only almost) always motivated by the reasons they recognize. This is part of a description of what it is to be good, and we all ought to be good. But to think that *all* people are necessarily motivated by the reasons they recognize is to either fail to recognize actual badness or malicious evil in the world as such or to be forced into the embarrassing position of saying that this badness or evil is really something reasonable, given the bad or evil person's point of view. This is a philosophical way (in the pejorative sense of "philosophy") of describing the harsh realities of life.

So, part of why people fall into internalism is because we all tend to see ourselves as we want ourselves to be and as we ought to be, and (though sometimes we try to imagine them) we tend to block out the ugly realities and complexities of life. These are patterns of thought, habits of thought, that recall the second half of Hume's own error theory about causation: we get into the habit of thinking in a certain way and then, without realizing it, we make a "modal slip" and say that things are necessarily as we have come to think. An anecdote is told of Jimmy Carter, who is said to have said something like the following: "I just feel compelled to do what I see is the right thing. It's like I don't even have any choice in the matter: I see what needs doing and go get started." And we can all catch a blush from that moral glow.[7] Jimmy Carter is the internalist's paradigm of how we all actually are; put perhaps more weakly, internalists think that there is, necessarily, a little bit of Jimmy Carter in each of us.

This is again understandable, especially when we note that the vast majority of philosophers who actually believe in internalism most probably do have more than just a little bit of Carter in them. One can only hope that it is a fairly safe assumption that, for the most part, philosophers (externalists too) are the kind of people who actually succeed in being responsive to reason. And many of us (like many people in general) might also think that we didn't have much rational choice in becoming as we are. It is natural for people to mistake how they seem to be made for how people in general are made, and this goes for philosophers as much as for the general populace. So, another reason why many philosophers are internalists is because they tend to think that people in general are like them, that is, sensitive to reason. And there is a sense in which it is natural for philosophers to think this way. (That's why those people become philosophers.) Although it is natural, however, it does not support internalism in the least. Indeed, there is perhaps no better candidate for being a piece of "ivy-tower philosophy" than internalism.

In accusing the internalists of making the mistake of thinking that others are like them is not, of course, an argument ad hominem. Again, internalists are no different in this respect than anyone else: externalists (or those who deny internalism) are just as likely to see others as they see themselves; we think everyone is only contingently motivated to be good,

---

7. I owe this story to Fred Frohock. Certainly less genteel than Jimmy Carter is a quote from a teenager who calls himself "Free." Free is part of an activist community that organizes the sitting-in of old forest trees outside Eugene, Oregon, to keep them from being cut down. Free says, "I'm not fucking happy. I'm not sitting in fucking trees in the cold because I'm happy. Going to jail doesn't make me happy. Going to jail is a bad experience. We're out there because we know we're right." See Samuels (2000, p. 45).

just like us. The internalist's claim is natural insofar as people, in general, are committed to being good; where they go wrong is sliding from this true empirical generality about how things "are" to the modal necessity of how things "must be." If internalists are in general people who are motivationally responsive to reason (and perhaps, qua philosopher, more so than the norm), then the natural human tendency to see everyone as being similar to oneself does (at least in part) explain why internalists are internalists. There is no reason, however, to think that everyone, necessarily, has a little Jimmy Carter in them.

The thought is that when people are considering their intuitions regarding internalism, a significant amount of "modal slide" is going on. There is Plato's slide, from how we are to how we wish to be (responsive to the light of the sun). And there is the slide Hume saw between how we are and how we ought to be. There is still a final slide, between both of these and how we must be. Note that these are all very formal differences in the grammar or logic of the "intuitions" that are being considered. In fact, in (the fairly obscure) systems of "deontic" logic, the "□" is interpreted to mean "obligatory," whereas in regular modal logic it is interpreted to mean "necessity" (the idea being that what is obligatory is morally necessary). It should be no surprise that we find some conflation of the two. But when we carefully pull them apart and really think just about how people actually are, we find them to be quite different from how they ought to be or how we hope them to be. Of course, we are not different from how we must be. But we have not yet seen reason to think that we must be responsive to reason, even though we recognize from the outset that we ought to be responsive to reason. What is a fool but one who, over and over again, won't listen to reason?

We must always keep in the mind the complexity of the human condition, along with the remarkable plasticity that is exercised in our developmental processes. Humankind is manifold. Here is a parting lesson that fits well with the themes of the book but is true even if everything else here is false: although there might be a few, most folks in the world don't think like you at all, and that goes for everyone. Regarding the "internalist-externalist" debate, the application of this lesson is in explaining how it is that you are motivated by morality, how morality is practical for you. This is ultimately going to be a story about you as an individual— a story about your particular intellectual and psychological strengths and weaknesses, your talents, your needs, and your discipline; a story that includes the period of history in which you live and the family and culture to which you belong, which influenced the maturation patterns of your development and thought; and so on. Of course, some constraints are involved, for we all share in being human. But when it comes to being responsive to reason, when it comes to being motivated to do as we know we ought to do, sadly, this simply does not occur among *Homo sapiens* with the frequency to which we can and ought to aspire; it certainly does not occur necessarily. We all know we ought to love or at least be kind to our neighbor (or at least not kill him). Upon reflection, however, it is hard to agree with the thought that everyone actually is (indeed necessarily is) motivated to act toward their neighbor as they ought, even just a little. In fact, some people just don't give a damn about their neighbor at all, even if, in some ordinary, optimal, or rarefied atmosphere, they acknowledge to themselves that they ought to. Such rarefied thoughts about reasons for action very well might be 100% motivationally impotent, fly right out the window, in the face of rage or passion; they might be motivationally cold in the face of exhaustion or ennui; one might even actively rebel against such thoughts by consciously cultivating contrarian motivations. There are no necessary constraints entailing an entwinement of our rational and motivational capacities: while rationality may make normative or even ideal demands on our development or our behavior (telling us how we ought to be), our status as naturally developing, fallible mortal creatures prohibits rationality from necessitating how we are motivated by moral reality, indeed by any part of reality. And, while all our behavior can always be rationalized from some point of view, we must keep in mind that while true irrationality and insanity are fairly rare, in general, we humans are nevertheless far less sensitive to reason than we ought to be, far less rational than we care to think. Though it ought to be, morality is not actually as practical for most of us as we could wish. And we all certainly have a lot to learn.

Appendix

Entropy, Healthiness, and Goodness

This appendix is strictly for those interested in metaphysics. It may be considered a vestigial appendix for reasons discussed in chapter 1: we are committed to realism about health, independent of questions concerning its possible reduction to some more basic set of properties, and it serves well as a model for goodness, so our realism is equally independent of such questions. Nevertheless, there remains the strictly ontological question of whether or not goodness and healthiness are amenable to a reductionistic program, and if they are not, what sort of problem is this—if it is a problem at all? We could, perhaps, rely on science to tell us the status of health, but in general scientists are not interested in ontology, and for reasons that will emerge below, relying on them in this case is perhaps not the best way to get at the metaphysical truth in any case.

When I first began to look into healthiness as a potential model for goodness, I quickly found that health was generally understood in terms of proper biological function, about which there was a very large literature (as noted in chapter 1). It never seemed proper to me, however, to consider healthiness as a functional property, for "healthiness" as a predicate describes how well a function is performing, and healthiness is therefore a property of a functional property, just as malfunction or sickness is.

Health is a measure of how properly (or well) a function is performing. Still, it seemed to me then (as it does now) that understanding health requires mastering the literature on proper functions. And although I was entranced by the richness of this wonderful work in the philosophy of biology, in the end I found myself dissatisfied—in general, because there was too much emphasis on biology and not enough on metaphysics, and in particular, because much of the literature accepts an assumption that I think leads it astray ontologically: namely, that there is in·principle a distinction between the function of biological entities and the functions of artifacts (like internal combustion engines). Now, whereas it is true that different stories are to be told about where biological and artificial functions come from, this does not mean that these "different kinds" of functions need different ontologies; sight and taste have different etiological stories behind them, yet redness and sweetness are still both secondary properties. Moreover, it seemed to me that all functions are alike ontologically insofar as they all are properties of complex systems. (Thus, health will be a property of a property of a complex system.) Animals and machines are both complex systems and, as such, have much in common. So, if we are to understand the ontology of health as a property of functions, we must begin by exploring the ontology of properties of complex systems.

Another similarity among all functions is that without regular maintenance (and even with), they eventually break down or malfunction (Theseus' ship aside). Machines wear out; living things die. Health in bodies is a measure of how well or efficiently an organ or organism is operating, but organs and organisms are always on their way to wearing out and failing. Health is a measure of structural integrity. I realized at this point that I had left the study of biological systems behind and now was looking at biological systems as just a special case of physical systems. The dialectic shifts from biology to physics.[1] Even before I began my

---

1. Here is a quotation on the effects of aging on brain cells from Dr. Sherwin Nuland's (1993) excellent book *How We Die*: "Like the muscle of the heart, brain cells are unable to reproduce. They survive decade after decade because their various structural components are always being replaced as they wear out, like so many ultramicroscopic carburetors and plugs. Though cell biologists use more abstruse terminology than do mechanics (words like *organelle* and *enzyme* and *mitochondrium*), these entities nonetheless require just as efficient a replacement mechanism as do their more familiar automotive analogs. Like the body itself and

research into the foundations of thermodynamics and statistical mechanics, I knew that entropy is a measure of structural disintegration. Entropy is a property of complex systems; it is in fact what might be called a reciprocal property to healthiness or proper function: the degree to which an item is functioning properly is the degree to which it lacks entropy, and vice versa. (This thought is present in Schrodinger's (1955) wonderful little book *What Is Life?* which is unsurprisingly fine in physics but rather weak in metaphysics.) (See also pp. 45ff.)

Now, entropy is a property that has received much attention within physics and much is known about it. If entropy and health are in fact reciprocal properties, then they presumably have the same ontological status (as do positive and negative charges or black and white). It seemed to me at that point, and still seems to me today, that if we can determine the ontological status of entropy qua measure of structural disintegration, we will thereby have our ontology of health qua measure of structural integrity. Then we apply these results to goodness for the reasons adduced in the body of this book, and *voila*—we have a completed moral ontology.

Entropy brings a strong dialectical advantage into the picture. The successful reduction of goodness seems as unlikely as the reduction of healthiness or of biological functions, for these seem to presuppose ends (like survival and procreation) that are similarly resistant to reduction. It has long been recognized that biologists have not been comfortable with the question of how easily biology reduces to chemistry and physics, as mentioned in chapter 1. Aside from *functions, fitness,* and *health,* biologists have to appeal to concepts like *environment, ecology, niche,* and so on, and these do seem superficially resistant to reduction. Biologists, however, have been put off by accepting a seemingly extravagant ontology of nonreducible properties, especially since these properties did not seem to be required by the sciences of chemistry and physics. But with the introduction of entropy into the picture, biologists (and moral realists) have a perfect *tu quo que* response to the "hard-core" scientists and empiricists. We may now say, "If entropy is a property of physics and resists reduction, then biological (or moral) properties that have put up

---

like each of its organs, every cell has the equivalents of pinions and wheels and springs. When the mechanism to exchange the aging parts for new wears out, the nerve or muscle cell can longer survive the constant destruction of components that goes on with it" (p. 55).

similar resistance cannot be more of an ontological problem for us than entropy is for you."

It is not uncommon for discussions of thermodynamics to begin with a list of "Things That Don't Happen," and here are a few examples.[2]

1. One end of a spoon that is resting on a table never spontaneously gets hot while the other end cools down.
2. Once milk has been stirred into a cup of coffee, it never spontaneously collects itself in a portion of the cup.
3. Whereas a source of light emits a beam that radiates out from its source, it a spherical beam never converges inward toward a point.

These examples are all normally considered impossible reversals of so-called irreversible processes, such as the conduction of heat from something hot to something cold until a uniformity of temperature is reached or the spread of a gas to uniformly fill a container. Another example of an irreversible process is the development of an organism: oak trees never turn into acorns, and fetuses never turn into zygotes. As noted by Reichenbach (1958), biological processes are special cases of irreversible processes.[3]

These processes were studied systematically by the engineer N. L. Sadi Carnot in the first quarter of the nineteenth century, while he was investigating how engines are able to produce work. If we consider chapter 2's discussion of the epistemology of practical rationality and *phronesis*, it is worthwhile noting that Carnot was an engineer; it was his practical interest in the skill of making engines that led him to his theoretical investigations. He became interested in general laws that govern how physical systems work. Thermodynamics, as a theoretical discipline, grew out of the practical skill of building machines that produce work efficiently. It is, in a strict sense, a product of practical rationality.

2. Physics texts relied on are Fermi (1936); Gold (1962); Feynman (1963); Halliday, Resnick, and Wacker (1993); and Layzer (1975). The texts in philosophy of science that I found most useful were Reichenbach (1958), Popper (1959), Horwich (1987), and Sklar (1993).
3. All actual physical processes are irreversible. Some physically possible systems undergo "reversible processes" in which entropy neither increases nor decreases (e.g., adiabatic systems described by the Carnot cycle), but such a system has never actually been found or made and will not concern us further.

There are three laws of thermodynamics. The "zeroth" law (so called because it was originally left implicit) is that equilibrium is transitive: if system *a* is in equilibrium with system *b*, and *b* is with *c*, then *a* is with *c*. More famously, the first law of thermodynamics, that energy cannot be created or destroyed, is also known as the law of the conservation of energy. The second law, which will occupy our attention, has many different but provably equivalent formulations. Here are three definitions and then five different ways of expressing it:

Definitions:
1. "Work" is understood as a transfer of energy from one body to another by means of exerting force.
2. "Heat" is understood as a transfer of energy from one body to another by means of a difference in temperature within the bodies. (In the case of work done by friction, work is equivalent to heat.)
3. "Efficiency" is understood as the ratio of work an engine does (i.e., what you get) to the heat or energy it absorbs (i.e, what you pay for).

Equivalent formulations of the second law of thermodynamics:
4. There are no perfectly efficient engines. (Engines always use up more energy than they can convert into work.)
5. It is not possible to change heat completely into work with no other changes taking place (Lord Kelvin's formulation).
6. There are no perfectly efficient refrigerators.
7. If there are two bodies at different temperatures, the first higher than the second, then it is not possible for heat to be transferred from the second body to the first body with no other changes taking place (Clausius' formulation).
8. In any thermodynamic process that proceeds from one equilibrium state to another, the entropy of *the system + the environment* either remains unchanged or increases.

It can be shown that each of these are derivable from the others, but in particular (4) is a quick restatement of (5), as (6) is of (7). Formulations (4) and (5) say that heat cannot be extracted from one body and made to do work on a second body without externally doing some other work (expending some extra energy or heat) on the system as a whole in order to convert the extracted heat to work: more simply, heat cannot be made to do work without doing extra work to the heat. Formulations (6) and

(7) say that heat cannot be sucked out of a cooler body and put into a hotter body without other work being done on the system as a whole. The empirical result that most strongly supports (4)–(7) has been the inability to build a perpetual motion machine: we cannot build a machine that could "by cooling the surrounding bodies, transform heat, taken from its environment, into work" (Fermi, 1937, p. 29).[4]

The last formulation of the second law concerns "entropy." Entropy can be given a precise mathematical formulation, but it will suffice for our purposes to understand it as a quantity that measures how far a system is from equilibrium, homeostasis, or homogeneity. A system that is highly ordered, wherein its parts exhibit a physically differentiated structure or a heterogeneity, is one that has low entropy. If we have a container of a specific gas in a room that contains normal air and we open the container, the gas and the air will initially be separated and will come to be uniformly mixed. The initial state has a low entropy, and the final state has a high entropy. To conceptually connect (4)–(7) with (8), a particular system can undergo a decrease of entropy, only by causing an increase of entropy in its environment that is larger than the decrease within the system. In other words, the net result of all isolated physical processes or interactions between systems and their environments results in an increase of entropy in the ensemble. To conceptually connect the notion of entropy with that of an engine or refrigerator, we can note that the entropy of a system is inversely proportional to the amount of work (or heat) that can be got out of the system. Stated as plainly as possible; the second law says that systems and their environments, taken together, always move toward states of higher entropy. In expending energy to do work, there is always waste. All physical systems, taken as such, have a natural tendency to gain entropy. Entropy always increases; structure always breaks down. Order and structure always and eventually give way to disorder and homogeneity. This is the way of all things.

Now, we are in a position to see why thermodynamics, and the second law in particular, resists reduction. Thermodynamics is thought dogmatically to reduce to statistical mechanics. Statistical mechanics has, as its resources, classical mechanics and mathematical statistics. Classical mechanics, systematized by Newton, can appeal to matter, stuff, particles, and so on, as well as to forces and laws of nature such as gravity, elec-

---

4. Another kind of perpetual motion machine could produce energy *ex nihilo* and thus run forever. Such a machine, which could break the first law of thermodynamics, will not be discussed.

tromagnetic forces, and so on. The challenge for statistical mechanics is to explain the second law of thermodynamics, given its resources. The problem is that all the laws of classical mechanics are considered "symmetric" insofar as they describe interactions that could be theoretically reversed (are "reversible processes") and still be described by the very same laws. To get a handle on this, imagine watching a movie of dust floating in a sunbeam; one couldn't tell just from watching whether the movie was playing in reverse or not. Thus, this sort of Brownian motion is symmetric. The problem is that the second law of thermodynamics is asymmetric. Systems always move toward greater entropy: if one were to watch a movie of a flower's life, one would be able to discern if the movie were in reverse or not. The challenge to statistical mechanics is to explain how asymmetry can reduce to symmetry. And there are reasons to think that it cannot.

What must first be explained, if any reduction is to be satisfactory, is why it is that entropy invariably increases. At least superficially, given the resources of statistical mechanics, there is no reason that increases in entropy should be any more common than decreases. From the point of view of statistics, we should find that all physical systems develop in such a way that they can be plotted along a bell-curve distribution of entropy increases and decreases. Experience, however, shows a distribution that is far from the shape of a bell curve, for we experience only increases in entropy. To successfully reduce thermodynamics to statistical mechanics, some explanation must be given for why the distribution of actually observed systems deviates so far from the symmetrical bell curve.

Ludwig Boltzmann, a physicist in the late nineteenth century, attempted to carry out the reduction of the regularity of entropy increases in our observations by saying that it is a local phenomenon, one determined by a posited set of initial conditions of the system as a whole. Boltzmann hypothesized that we just happen to be living in a part of the universe or in a part of time in which entropy regularly increases. But there are going to be other parts of the universe (or times) that are different, such that the universe as a whole is a system in equilibrium. We just happen to be in a pocket of the universe where entropy is regularly increasing. (This is sometimes referred to as a "weak anthropic principle": it is just a coincidence that there is a place where things always develop in the manner in which we have always experienced them, but since we are there, it is hard for us to see it as mere coincidence.)

There is a variety of problems with this attempted reduction of the second law. The first is that the positing of these special initial conditions to explain our observations smacks of being ad hoc: in appealing to these sorts of conditions so that our observations may be explained, physics is availing itself of facts that transcend the subject matter of statistical mechanics. Moreover, if these initial conditions are assumed to be such that they can account for the "local" effects of entropy increase, then they appear to be both unverifiable and unfalsifiable. Similar criticisms are explored in more detail by Sklar (1993), and the interested reader can pursue them there. Here we will consider different objections to Boltzmann's reduction.

Boltzmann was empirically led to conclude that there is a certain kind of interaction between particles in which a slow-moving particle could collide with a faster particle, whereby the slower particle loses (at least some of) its speed, imparting its loss to the faster particle, which moves away at an even faster pace (Reichenbach, 1958 p. 54). Thus, Boltzmann (thought he) saw that it was possible for entropy-decreasing interactions of this kind to predominate, and what we see as irreversible processes (such as the conduction of heat) are not *in principle* irreversible but are only very, very unlikely to reverse themselves. Insofar as this particular kind of interaction is possible, entropy decreases are possible, even here, in our part of the universe; it is just very, very improbable that we find a preponderance of this kind of interaction in our place and time because of the initial conditions of the universe. It could be the case, however, that a gas, evenly distributed within a container, spontaneously compresses itself into a corner. Such a spontaneous compression is not impossible, just highly improbable. Moreover, there will be parts of the universe in which such occurrences are the norm.

So, Boltzmann is thought to have successfully reduced thermodynamics to statistical mechanics by explaining away the appearance of asymmetry within the former as just that: an appearance only. It appears to us as if there is an asymmetry in nature, insofar as our observations are of systems whose entropy always increases, but this "asymmetry" is just a local phenomenon that can be explained away by saying that it is the causal result of contingent initial conditions of the universe. But if Boltzmann's reduction is really to be successful, we must be sure that everything that we think needs explaining is explained.

Imagine being a witness to a spontaneous compression of an evenly distributed gas within a container. If we were to observe such a compression, we would (pretheoretically) normally ask for an explanation of why the gas behaved in such a manner. The scientist has two kinds of response: either (1) admit that the phenomenon existed and deny the existence of an explanation for it (an explanation that transcends appeal to the resources of statistical mechanics and the initial conditions of the universe, which deem the compression to be a mere extraordinary coincidence), or (2) deny it altogether as a phenomenon that physics is in the business of explaining. In the first response, the physicist would reply that if we want some further explanation for what seems to be more than just an incredibly improbable but evident coincidence, we are asking for something that does not exist. There simply is no further explaining to be done. The mere asking demonstrates a lack of understanding of how things are. The second response is more sophisticated and is articulated by Karl Popper (1959). He first notes that such a compression cannot be repeatable: for if a second compression occurred, it would falsify the probability distribution that is describing our observations, which find such compressions to be very, very, very improbable. (If such improbabilities repeat themselves, then we conclude that our initial assessment of their improbability was inaccurate.) And since the phenomenon is unrepeatable, Popper concludes that it would not be a "physical effect" that places it outside the realm of science (p. 203). He explains this conclusion by referring to his earlier discussion of "objectivity" (p. 46), where he says that, "any controversy over the question whether events which are in principle unrepeatable and unique ever do occur cannot be decided by science: it would be a metaphysical controversy." One wonders what to say about the Big Bang. Be that as it may, given either of these two scientific responses to singular spontaneous decreases of entropy, the conclusion we get is that the second "law" of thermodynamics is actually just a contingent statistical regularity and is not a law of nature at all—if by "law of nature" we mean a description of universal regularities within events that are due to causal necessity.[5] If Boltzmann is correct, the second law is merely a description of a statistical regularity that allows for occasional irregularities.

Before proceeding further into why this result is unsatisfactory, a very brief review of our present position in this discussion will prove helpful. The debate can be cast as one that takes place between what might be called "science" and "metaphysics." Scientists are those who are concerned with making observations and based on these, coming up with theories that allow them to make accurate predictions of the future—period (Feyn-

---

5. This can be a notion of a law of nature that can be reformulated to accommodate Hume's rejection of causal necessity. The important part is that the regularity must be universal, or exceptionless, to be a law of nature.

man, 1985). For them "metaphysics" automatically has a pejorative connotation, and they prefer to limit their attention to empirically observable and verifiable phenomena. Science can scrutinize itself, but only from a scientific point of view; so, one plausible criterion for theory acceptance within science is that a theory is acceptable to the degree that it is falsifiable by the scientific method (Popper, 1959). Since scientists are concerned only with observations and their predictions, any talk of the existence of events or causes that cannot be scientifically observed (if only because they are unrepeatable) is eschewed.

The metaphysician, of course, considers this empiricism and verification of science as itself a metaphysical stand. But the metaphysician says that this stand is incomplete; for example, the metaphysician will want to draw distinctions in reality where the scientist sees none. Of particular interest here, the metaphysician will want to insist on a difference between events that do not occur because they are improbable and those that do not occur because they are impossible. This is to insist on a difference between events that *won't* happen and events that *can't* happen. Scientists (and philosophers of science with an empirical bent, like Quine, Popper, and van Frassen) will say that since these two kinds of nonoccurrences have no observable consequences (since they are all "events that do not occur," they lack observable consequences), no problem for a theory can be adduced if it determines that something that was heretofore thought to be impossible is actually found to be merely (highly) improbable. If the number representing an improbability is small enough, science can ignore it (Popper, 1959, p. 202). Thus, any talk of the difference between an improbable event and an impossible event is mere "metaphysical speculation." The metaphysician, however, does not accept as an argument the pejorative tone that usually accompanies this phrase and wants the debate over the significance of these small numbers to press forward regardless of their strictly empirical significance. The scientist declares that the debate is already over since all the empirical data have been accounted for.

This kind of disagreement can be generally characterized as follows: by the lights of the metaphysician, the scientific method is unfalsifiable, for it refuses to accept as evidence anything that cannot be accounted for by the scientific method. By the lights of the scientist, the metaphysician is demanding that we draw distinctions in reality that make no real difference. This is quite a problem, for which a general solution may not be possible. There is a way out, however, in the particular case of the putative reduction of thermodynamics.

Let's begin with a reminder that it was the physical possibility of a particular kind of interaction between particles that allowed Boltzmann to conclude that entropy decreases are possible (however improbable). Let's also take another quote from Popper (1959) about spontaneous compression:

> I do not, for example, assert that the molecules in a small volume of gas may not, perhaps, for a short time spontaneously withdraw into a part of the volume, or that in a greater volume of gas spontaneous fluctuations of pressure will never occur. What I do assert is that such occurrences would not be physical effects, because, on account of their immense improbability, *they are not reproducible at will.* (p. 203)

So far, so good. But what must be kept at the front of our minds is that thermodynamics, and its second law, is supposed to apply to *all* physical systems and not just to gases in containers. It is supposed to explain to us why perfectly efficient machines cannot be built, why all things run down, why all biological systems develop as they do (as a result of absorbing energy from their environment), and why they all eventually die. We should be able to count on thermodynamics to explain to us why we are mortal and why we always see acorns growing into oak trees and never the opposite. Now, if we accept the reduction of thermodynamics to statistical mechanics, we find that the scientist tells us that many events we had heretofore thought of as impossible are merely improbable; such events as engines running with perfect efficiency, systems that do not wear down and out with age, and biological systems that live forever are just highly, highly improbable. The reduction of thermodynamics to statistical mechanics leaves open the physical possibility that an oak tree should "grow into" an acorn.

And now, we ask whether or not the metaphysician is making distinctions that make no difference when asking if the impossibility of immortality differs from its improbability (however high). Isn't the difference between what is impossible and what is improbable a difference in reality we should want to insist on? Isn't the possibility that an oak might turn into an acorn a possibility that it is important to recognize? Even if it won't ever occur, isn't the fact that it could occur a fact that gives us an important insight into the nature of reality or the nature of nature? If these are questions worth asking, if they even make good linguistic sense in English, then the success of the scientist's reduction must itself be questioned. And if, in fact, we think that it is impossible and not merely (however highly) improbable for oaks to turn into acorns, then we must reject the reduction as incomplete.

To see where things go wrong for the reduction, we must ask the scientist (and philosophers of science like Popper) why a spontaneous compression of gas must be short lived. Granted, such a compression may not occur again (lest we falsify our probability distribution, which deems such compressions unrepeatable), but if it does occur, the scientist can give no reason why it should not last; that it does last is just even more unlikely. The longer it endures is directly proportional to how improbable it is. But given statistical mechanics plus initial conditions, there is nothing in principle, there are no physical or causal laws of nature, that prevent it from lasting. The scientist cannot say that the compression *cannot* last. Note that such a lasting of compression would not provide falsification conditions for our probability curve; we are now only focusing our attention on a hyperattenuated portion of the tail of the distribution curve, a portion way out at the end, but which still contains some (very small, perhaps infinitesimal) measure of probability. So, contra Popper (1959), such an unusual but lasting phenomenon might be observable, even though unreplicable or unpredictable. And so it would be possible for us to sit and watch some gas (or perhaps it is milk that had been stirred into a cup of coffee) that has all spontaneously collected in the corner of the room for an hour, a day, or a year. Surely such a long-lasting event, though unrepeatable, would be an empirical event within the provenance of science, but when we ask the scientist why this is happening, the scientist must reply that there is no explanation.

The point comes through more clearly if we stop trying to imagine gases compressing "all by themselves" and attend to more concrete examples of what the scientists' position deems possible. Whereas Carnot's initial result was supposed to have shown why a machine cannot run with perfect efficiency, the reduction of thermodynamics to statistical mechanics revises this result. Now remember Fermi's (1937) words (quoted above): we cannot build a machine that could "by cooling the surrounding bodies, transform heat, taken from its environment, into work." On the contrary, the physicist Gold (1962; also cited by Horwich, 1987) explores the ramifications of using the initial conditions of the universe to explain the contingency of the direction of entropy by asking us to imagine that we have a "flashlight" that is pointed into the nighttime sky. As we turn the switch, light from the depths of the universe converges (backward) on our flashlight, making "the tungsten filament extremely hot." If this phenomenon lasted as long as the switch was on, the filament's heat could be perpetually transformed into work. It would be a perpetual motion machine. Here is Gold's conclusion:

> True . . . there are no laws of physics infringed, but all the steps that would be described are so wildly improbable that this does not merit a serious discussion.
>
> The notion of cause and effect is difficult to dismiss; yet there is no place for it in this discussion. All that could really be defined is "related events." (p. 409)

(One wonders what the quotation marks around "related events" are for.) Stable decreases in entropy might just happen, for no reason, without explanation, as a very large coincidence. So, here we are told perpetual motion machines are possible but they simply won't occur because of their high improbability. If however, *per impossible*, one should come across such a machine and insist on an explanation for how it can do what Carnot had taught us was impossible, we would be told by the scientist that we are looking for explanations when there are none to give. If we were to insist that a perpetual motion machine could not "just happen," we would have already entered the realm of metaphysical speculation. And although such a response might be fully cogent when looking at the situation from the point of view of science, it might also be taken as evidence for the narrowness of the scientific perspective. The problem, I think, becomes even worse when we look at biological systems as a subset of the physical systems describable in thermodynamic terms.

The second law of thermodynamics does not apply only to the eventual breaking down of machines and the inevitable death of biological systems. The development of an organism from its earliest developmental stages to maturity is the result of an exchange of energy between the system and its environment. When an organism is young and healthy, and it, qua engine, is "being built," its entropy levels are actually decreasing. We must remember, however, that its decrease is more than compensated for by an increase in the entropy of its environment. As it grows into its more complicated, mature form, entropy levels within the organism itself begin to increase until death occurs. What we learn from thermodynamics is that such local entropy decreases that occur in youth and adolescence are always temporary. Remember that the reduction to statistical mechanics yields the result that the directionality of all increases or decreases of entropy is contingent. That we observe these regularities within the development of biological systems is merely a statistical regularity that has no more "underlying cause" than the initial conditions of the universe. And given this, it must then be possible and not contrary to any laws of nature for an old person to spontaneously begin to grow younger and eventually turn into a baby. There would be no explanation for such an event; it is just highly (perhaps infinitesimally) improbable. Science tells us that it is possible for oaks to "grow" into acorns. If such a freak of nature did occur, however, there would be no deep explanation for this extraordinary phenomenon; it would merely be a very large coincidence.

So, let's compare a few propositions:

(9) There are no square circles.
(10) There are no effects that come before their causes.
(11) There are no humans that can fly unaided.
(12) There are no golden mountains.
(13) There are no perpetual motion machines.
(14) There are no immortal biological systems.
(15) There are no oaks that turn into acorns.

These are all ostensibly about the same kind of thing, namely, a kind of thing that does not exist. From a purely observational or empirical standpoint, none can be observed and none has any causal effects. From the point of view of metaphysics, these may differ in modal status; by this, I mean that there may be different explanations for why these various objects do not exist. Proposition (9) is true because the logical law of non-contradiction prevents objects from being both circular and square; the concepts or definitions of "square" and "circle" are contradictory. Proposition (10) is said to be a "metaphysical" or "broadly logical" truth: a truth that points out some necessary, noncontingent, but not strictly logical connection between, in this case, our concepts of causation and time. Such truths are said to have a synthetic a priori status (and are the subject matter of Kant's First Critique). Proposition (11) is true because the causal laws of nature prevent humans from unaided flight; were these contingent laws of nature to change or were they to have been different all along, it might be possible for humans to fly. The laws being what they are, however, make the inability of human flight causally necessary. Proposition (12) is merely a contingent truth; there could be a golden mountain, but there just happens to be none.

Drawing these distinctions has always proven difficult for science, if only because science sets out from the start to explain only what can be observed and to make predictions of what can be observed in the future. Philosophers with an empirical bent have spent much time trying to sort out these issues, including how it is that we can even refer to objects that do not exist, and in the end many deny empirical validity to modal distinctions. In pursuit of the nonreducibility of thermodynamics, let it be agreed by all parties that there are no useful distinctions to be drawn among (9), (10), and (11). We will call square circles, effects that precede causes, and flying humans "impossibilities." Still, even from the scientific point of view, there is some reason to want to draw a distinction between (9)–(11) and (12). Science is interested in what causal laws of nature actually do obtain, and those that do obtain do not rule out the possibility of golden mountains, as they rule out the impossibilities. Golden mountains are just unlikely to actually exist, and it was purely an empirical discovery that they do not. So, let us call golden mountains and their ilk "contingencies." The question we are then faced with concerns the status of (13)–(15). If the reduction of thermodynamics to statistical mechanics were complete, then (13)–(15) should be grouped with the contingencies and not with the impossibilities.

Now, since we have left the sphere of the observables behind, the scientist will already have balked at the course of our dialectic. We have entered the realm of metaphysics, but we should note that we are pushed there by science itself: first, because of the above-mentioned difference between (9)–(11) and (12); second, because it is surely revisionary of pretheoretical thought to think that it is only contingently true that there are no immortal biological systems, or oaks trees that turn into acorns. Here we can begin by calling on the kingpin of empiricism himself, David Hume, who in (an admittedly atypical) foray into what might be called ordinary language philosophy says, "One would appear ridiculous, who would say, that 'tis only probable that the sun will rise tomorrow, or that all men must dye" [1739] (1978, p. 124). If science is going to tell us that what we had thought were impossibilities are actually only contingencies, then it owes us an explanation for why we should accept this result. And the preservation of a reductionistic scientific theory is not an adequate explanation. Moreover, if we did empirically discover both a golden mountain and an oak that becomes an acorn, there may very well be reason to be dissatisfied with science's explanation of both of them as contingent accidents; we might be satisfied with such an explanation in the case of the golden mountain, but it would not do for the oak-acorn. I submit that were we to encounter an oak that is growing into an acorn, we would look at it, not as we would were we to discover a golden mountain, but as we would were we to witness a human flying (or perhaps even an effect preceding its cause).

Statistical mechanics went wrong by assuming that a system is no more than a collection of interactions of particles: since it is possible for single interactions between particles to be such that, if all interactions had this characteristic, decreases in entropy would occur, then (the inference goes) entropy decreases within complex systems are possible. But complex systems, such as a cyclical engine, *cannot* be such that all the particles that constitute them may interact with one another and with their environment in a way that is both frictionless and ordered; at the very least it is the cyclical nature of such an engine that makes this impossible. Even God could not build a frictionless engine that would run and remain frictionless without God's constant intervention. (Of course, if God constantly intervened, any causal laws could be broken.) The lesson is this: one cannot extrapolate what is possible for a system as a whole from what is possible for parts of it when treated as individuals.

The conclusion to draw is that physics is stuck with nonreducible properties, and so are biology and morality. Wholes (systems) are not merely the sums of their parts; they do not reduce. This is a hard ontological conclusion to grasp, but it is the conclusion. I suppose that it is possible that the preceding argument is unsound for reasons I cannot see and that one day entropy and healthiness and goodness will be successfully reduced to some lower level properties. If so, then far be it for a metaphysician to say it ain't so. But it is properly for the metaphysician to make this judgment and not for the physicist, the biologist, or the ethicist.

Bibliography

Alston, William. "Moral Attitudes and Moral Judgements." *Nous* 2.1 (1968): 1–23.

———. "Aquinas on Analogical Predication." In *Reasoned Faith*, ed. E. Stump, pp. 145–74. Ithaca, N.Y.: Cornell University Press, 1993.

Annas, Julia. *The Morality of Happiness*. New York: Oxford University Press, 1993.

———. "Virtue as a Skill." *International Journal of Philosophical Studies* 32.2 (1995): 227–43.

———. *Platonic Ethics, Old and New*. Ithaca, N.Y.: Cornell University Press, 1999.

Anscombe, G. E. M. *Intentions*. Ithaca, N.Y.: Cornell University Press, 1957.

———. "Modern Moral Philosophy." In *Virtue Ethics*, ed. R. Crisp and M. Slote, pp. 26–44. Oxford: Oxford University Press, [1958] 1997.

———. "Practical Inference." In *Virtues and Reasons: Philippa Foot and Moral Theory*, ed. R. Hursthouse, G. Lawrence, and W. Quinn, pp. 1–34. Oxford: Clarendon Press, [1974] 1995.

Arendt, Hannah. *Eichmann in Jerusalem: A Report on the Banality of Evil*. New York: Penguin, 1977.

Ariew, André. "Platonic and Aristotelian Roots of Teleological Arguments in Cosmology and Biology." In *Functions and Functional Analysis in the Philosophy of Psychology and Biology*, ed. A. Ariew, R. Cummins, and M. Perlman. Oxford: Oxford University Press, forthcoming.

Aristotle. *Nicomachean Ethics*. Trans. Terence Irwin. Indianapolis: Hackett, 1985.

Armstrong, D. M. *A Theory of Universals*, vol. II. Cambridge: Cambridge University Press, 1978.

Ashby, William R. *Design for a Brain* 2nd ed. London: Chapman & Hall, 1976.

Audi, Robert. "Intuitions, Pluralism, and the Foundations of Ethics." In *Moral Knowledge*, ed. W. Sinnott-Armstrong and M. Timmons, pp. 101–56. New York: Oxford University Press, 1996.

———. "Moral Judgement and Reasons for Action." In *Ethics and Practical Reason*, ed. G. Cullity and B. Gaut, pp. 125–58. Oxford: Clarendon Press, 1997.

Austin, J. L. *How to Do Things with Words*. Cambridge, Mass.: Harvard University Press, 1962.

Ayer, A. J. *Language, Truth, and Logic*. New York: Dover, 1952.

Ayla, Francisco. "Biology as an Autonomous Science." In *Topics in the Philosophy of Biology*, ed. M. Grene and E. Mendelsohn, pp. 312–29. Dordrect: Reidel, 1976.

Axtell, Guy. "Recent Work in Virtue Epistemology." *American Philosophical Quarterly* 34.1 (1997): 1–26.

Baier, Annette. *Moral Prejudices: Essay on Ethics*. Cambridge, Mass.: Harvard University Press, 1994.

Beatty, Paul. *Big Bank Take Little Bank*. New York: Nuyorican Poets Café, 1991.

———. *Joker, Joker, Deuce*. New York: Penguin, 1994.

———. *The White Boy Shuffle*. Boston: Houghton Mifflin, 1996.

———. *Tuff*. New York: Knopf, 2000.

Beck, Lewis White. " 'Was-Must Be' and 'Is-Ought' in Hume." *Philosophical Studies* 26 (1974): 219–28.

Beckner, Morton. *The Biological Way of Thought*. New York: Columbia University Press, 1959.

Benardete, José. "Mechanism and the Good." *Philosophical Forum* 7. 3–4 (1976): 294–315.

———. "The Deduction of Causality." In *The Philosophy of Immanuel Kant*, ed. R. Kennington, pp. 57–70. Washington, D.C.: Catholic University Press, 1985.

Bennett, Jonathan. *Linguistic Behavior*. Cambridge: Cambridge University Press, 1976.

———. "Folk-psychological Explanations." In *The Future of Folk Psychology*, ed. J. Greenwood, pp. 176–95. Cambridge: Cambridge University Press, 1991.

Bigelow, John, and Robert Pargetter. "Functions." *Journal of Philosophy* 84.4 (1987): 181–96.

Blackburn, Simon. *Essays in Quasi-realism*. New York: Oxford University Press, 1993.

———. *Ruling Passions*. Oxford: Clarendon Press, 1998.

Bloomfield, Paul. "Of *Goodness* and *Healthiness*: A Viable Moral Ontology." *Philosophical Studies* 87 (1997): 309–32.

———. "Prescriptions Are Assertions." *American Philosophical Quarterly* 35.1 (1998): 1–20.

————. "Virtue Epistemology and the Epistemology of Virtue." *Philosophy and Phenomenological Research* 50.1 (2000, January): 23–43.

Boorse, Christopher. "Wright on Functions." *Philosophical Review* 85 (1976): 70–86.

————. "Health as a Theoretical Concept." *Philosophy of Science* 44 (1977): 542–73.

Boyd, Richard. "How to Be a Moral Realist." *Essays on Moral Realism*, ed. G. Sayre-McCord, pp. 181–228. Ithaca, N.Y.: Cornell University Press, 1988.

Braithwaite, R. B. *Scientific Explanation.* Cambridge: Cambridge University Press, 1953.

Burge, Tyler. "Individualism and the Mental." In *Midwest Studies in Philosophy*, vol. IV, ed. P. A. French, T. E. Uehling, and H. K. Wettstein. Minneapolis: University of Minnesota Press, 1979.

Chalmers, David. *The Conscious Mind.* New York: Oxford University Press, 1996.

Chase, W. G. and H. A. Simon. "Perception in Chess." *Cognitive Psychology* 4 (1973): 55–81.

Chi, Michelene, Paul Feltovich, and Robert Glaser. "Categorization and Representation of Physics Problems by Experts and Novices." *Cognitive Science* 5 (1981): 121–52.

Confusius. *Analects.* Trans. D. C. Lau. London: Penguin, 1998.

Csikszentmihalyi, Mihaly. *Flow: The Psychology of Optimal Experience.* New York: Harper & Row, 1990.

Darwall, S., A. Gibbard, and P. Railton. "Toward a *Fin de Siecle* Ethics." *Philosophical Review* 101.1 (1992): 115–89.

Davies, Martin, and Lloyd Humberstone. "Two Notions of Necessity." *Philosophical Studies* 38 (1980): 1–30.

Dillard, Annie. "The Wreck of Time." *Harper's Magazine* Jan. (1998): 51–56.

Dreyfus, Hubert, and Stuart Dreyfus. *Mind over Machine: The Power of Human Intuition and Expertise in the Era of the Computer.* New York: Free Press, 1986.

Dyer, F., and J. Gould. "Honey Bee Navigation." *American Scientist* 71 (1983): 587–97.

Einstein, Albert. *Relativity: The Special and General Theory.* New York: Crown Press, 1961. [1947]

Enç, Brent, and Fred Adams. "Functions and Goal Directedness." *Philosophy of Science* 59 (1992): 635–54.

Epictetus. *Discourses.* Trans. George Long. In *Great Books of the Western World*, vol 12. Chicago: Encyclopedia Britannica, Inc. 1952.

Etienne, A., R. Maurer, and V. Seguinot. "Path Integration in Mammals and Its Interaction with Visual Landmarks." *Journal of Experimental Biology* 199 (1996): 201–9.

Falk, W. D. "Ought and Motivation." *Proceedings of the Aristotelian Society* 48 (1947–48): 111–38.

————. "Goading and Guiding." *Mind* 62 (1953): 145–71.

Fermi, Enrico. *Thermodyamics.* New York: Dover, 1937.

Feynman, Richard. *The Feynman Lectures on Physics.* Reading, Mass.: Addison Wesley, 1963.

———. *QED.* Princeton, N.J.: Princeton University Press, 1985.

Foot, Philippa. "Moral Beliefs." *Proceedings of the Aristotelian Society* 59 (1958–59): 83–104.

———. "Goodness and Choice" and "Moral Arguments." In *Virtues and Vices*, 132–47 and 96–109. Berkeley: University of California Press, 1978.

Frankena, William. "The Naturalistic Fallacy." In *Theories of Ethics*, ed. P. Foot, pp. 50–63. Oxford: Oxford University Press, [1939] 1986.

———. "Obligation and Motivation in Recent Moral Philosophy." In *Perspectives on Morality*, ed. K. Goodpaster, pp. 49–73. Notre Dame, Ind.: Notre Dame University Press, 1976.

Gallistel, C. R. *The Organization of Learning.* Cambridge, Mass.: MIT Press, 1990.

Gibbard, Allan. *Wise Choices, Apt Feelings.* Cambridge, Mass.: Harvard University Press, 1990.

Gladwell, Malcolm. "The Physical Genius." *The New Yorker*, August 2, 1999, pp. 57–65.

Godfrey-Smith, Peter. "A Modern History Theory of Functions." *Nous* 28. 3 (1984): 344–62.

Gold, T. "The Arrow of Time." *American Journal of Physics* 30. 6 (1962 June): 403–10.

Grene, Marjorie. "Aristotle and Modern Biology." In *Topics in the Philosophy of Biology*, ed. M. Grene and E. Mendelsohn, pp. 3–36. Dordrect: Reidel, 1976.

Grice, H. P. "Meaning." *Philosophical Review* 66 (1957): 377–88.

Groopman, Jerome. "Second Opinion." *The New Yorker*, January 24, 2000, pp. 40–49.

Halliday, D., R. Resnick, and J. Wacker. *Fundamentals of Physics.* New York: Wiley, 1993.

Hare, Richard. *The Language of Morals.* Oxford: Clarendon Press, 1952.

———. *Freedom and Reason.* Oxford: Oxford University Press, 1963.

———. "Relevance." In *Essays in Ethical Theory.* Oxford: Clarendon Press, [1978] 1989.

———. "Universal Prescriptivism." In *A Companion to Ethics*, ed. P. Singer, pp. 451–63. New York: Blackwell, 1991.

Harman, Gilbert. "Is There a Single True Morality?" In *Morality, Reason and Truth*, ed. D. Copp and D. Zimmerman, pp. 27–48. Totwa, N.J.: Rowman & Allenheld, 1985.

———. "Ethics and Observation." *Essays on Moral Realism*, ed. G. Sayre-McCord, pp. 119–24. Ithaca:, N.J.: Cornell University Press, 1988.

Heller, Mark. *The Ontology of Physical Objects.* Cambridge: Cambridge University Press, 1990.

Horgan, Terence. "From Supervenience to Superdupervenience: Meeting the Demands of a Material World." *Mind* 102.408 (1993 October): 555–86.

Horgan, Terry, and Mark Timmons. "New Wave Moral Realism Meets Moral Twin Earth." *Journal for Philosophical Research* 16 (1991): pp. 447–65.

———. "Troubles for New Wave Moral Semantics: The 'Open Question Argument' Revived." *Philosophical Papers* 21 (1992a): 153–75.

———. "Troubles on Moral Twin Earth: Moral Queerness Revived." *Synthese* 92 (1992b): 221–60.

———. "From Moral Realism to Moral Relativism in One Easy Step." *Critica* 28. 83 (1996a): 3–39.

———. "Troubles for Michael Smith's Metaethical Rationalism." *Philosophical Papers* 25. 3 (1996b): 203–31.

Horwich, Paul. *Asymmetries in Time.* Cambridge.:MIT Press, 1987.

Hume, David. *A Treatise of Human Nature* Ed. L. A. Selby–Bigge. Oxford: Clarendon Press, [1739] 1978.

Hursthouse, Rosalind. *On Virtue Ethics.* New York: Oxford University Press, 1999.

I Ching. The Richard Wilhelm translation. Trans. C. F. Baynes. *Bollingen Series* XIX. Princeton, N.D.: Princeton University Press, 1950.

Irwin, Terence. *Plato's Ethics.* New York: Oxford University Press, 1995.

Jackson, Frank. *From Metaphysics to Ethics.* Oxford: Clarendon Press, 1998.

Kant, Immanuel. *Foundations of the Metaphysics of Morals.* Trans. Lewis White Beck. New York: Liberal Arts Press, [1785] 1959.

Kauffman, Stuart. *The Origins of Order.* New York: Oxford University Press, 1993.

Kim, Jaegwon. *Supervenience and Mind.* Cambridge: Cambridge University Press, 1993.

Korsgaard, Christine. "Skepticism about Practical Reason." *Journal of Philosophy* 83 (1985): 5–25.

———. *The Sources of Normativity.* Cambridge: Cambridge University Press, 1996.

Kripke, Saul. *Naming and Necessity.* Cambridge, Mass.: Harvard University Press, 1972.

———. *Wittgenstein: On Rules and Private Language.* Cambridge, Mass.: Harvard University Press, 1982.

Larkin, Jill, John McDermott, Dorothea Simon, and Herbert Simon. "Expert and Novice Performance in Solving Physics Problems." *Science* 208 (1980): 1135–42.

Layzer, David. "The Arrow of Time." *Scientific American* 223 (1975): 56–69.

Lewis, David. *Convention.* Cambridge, Mass.: Harvard University Press, 1969.

———. *On the Plurality of Worlds.* Oxford: Blackwell, 1986.

Locke, Don. "The Trivializability of Universalizability." *Philosophical Review* 78 (1968): 25–44.

Locke, John. *An Essay Concerning Human Understanding.* Ed. P. Nidditch. Oxford: Oxford University Press, 1975.

Loeb, Donald. "Moral Realism and the Argument from Disagreement." *Philosophical Studies* 90. 3 (1998): 281–303.

Long, A. A. and D. N. Sedley. *The Hellenistic Philosophers*, vol. I. Cambridge: Cambridge University Press, 1987.

Lynch, Michael. *Truth in Context*. Cambridge, Mass.: MIT Press, 1998.

Mace, C. A. "Mechanical and Teleological Causation." In *Readings in Philosophical Analysis*, ed. H. Fiegl and W. Sellers, pp. 534–39. New York: Appleton, Century, Crofts, 1949.

MacIntyre, Alasdair. *After Virtue*. Notre Dame, Ind.: University of Notre Dame Press, 1984.

Mackie, John. *Ethics: Inventing Right and Wrong*. London: Penguin, 1977.

Macklin, Ruth. "Mental Health and Mental Illness." *Philosophy of Science* 39. 3 (1972, September): 341–365.

McCauley, Robert, ed. *The Curchlands and Their Critics*. Oxford: Blackwell, 1996.

McDowell, John. "Aesethetic Value, Objectivity, and the Fabric of the World." In *Pleasure, Prefrence, and Value*, ed. E. Schaper, pp. 1–16. Cambridge: Cambridge University Press, 1983.

———. "Values and Secondary Qualities." In *Morality and Objectivity*, ed. Ted Honderich, pp. 110–29. London: Routledge & Kegan Paul, 1988.

———. *Mind and World*. Cambridge, Mass.: Harvard University Press, 1994.

———. "Might There Be External Reasons." In *Mind, Value, and Reality*. Cambridge, Mass.: Harvard University Press, 1998.

McGinn, Colin. *The Subjective View*. Oxford: Clarendon Press, 1983.

———. *The Problem of Consciousness*. Oxford: Blackwell, 1990.

Martin, C. B., and M. Deutscher. "Remembering." *Philosophical Review* 75 (1966): 161–96.

Miller, William Ian. *The Anatomy of Disgust*. Cambridge, Mass.: Harvard University Press, 1997.

Millikan, Ruth. *Language, Thought, and Other Biological Categories*. Cambridge, Mass.: MIT Press, 1984.

Milo, Ronald. "Contractarian Constructivism." *Journal of Philosophy* 92. 4 (1995): 181–204.

Moore, G. E. *Principia Ethicia*. Buffalo: Prometheus Books, [1902] 1988.

Murdoch, Iris. "On 'God' and 'Good.'" In *The Sovereignty of Good*. London: Ark Paperbacks, 1970.

Nagel, Ernst. *The Structure of Science*. New York: Harcourt, Brace & World, 1961.

Nagel, Thomas. *The Possibility of Altruism*. Princeton, N.J.: Princeton University Press, 1970.

———. "Death." In *Mortal Questions*. pp. 1–10. Cambridge: Cambridge University Press, 1979.

Neander, Karen. "The Teleological Notion of 'Function.'" *Australasian Journal of Philosophy* 69. 4 (1991): 454–68.

Nuland, Sherwin. *How We Die*. New York: Vintage Books, 1993.

Olsen, Eric. *The Human Animal*. Cambridge: Cambridge University Press, 1997.

Owens, Joesph. "Teleology of Nature in Aristotle." *The Monist* 52 (1968): 159–73.

Plantinga, Alvin. *The Nature of Necessity*. Oxford: Clarendon Press, 1974.

Plato. *Apology*. In *The Last Days of Socrates*, trans. H. Tredennick and H. Tarrant, pp. 29–67. London: Penguin, 1993a.

————. *Euthyphro*. In *The Last Days of Socrates*, trans. H. Tredennick and H. Tarrant. pp. 3–27. London: Penguin, 1993b.

————. *Republic*. Trans. R. Waterfield. Oxford: Oxford University Press, 1993c.

————. *Gorgias*. Trans. R. Waterfield. Oxford: Oxford University Press, 1994a.

————. *Symposium*. Trans. R. Waterfield. Oxford: Oxford University Press, 1994b.

————. *Laches*. In *Early Socratic Dialogues*, trans. I. Lane, pp. 83–115. London: Penguin, 1987.

Popper, Karl. *The Logic of Scientific Discovery*. New York: Harper & Row, 1959.

Prichard, H. A. "Does Morality Rest on a Mistake?" *Mind* 21 (1912): 21–37.

Prior, Arthur N. *Logic and the Basis of Ethics*. Oxford: Clarendon Press, 1949.

Putnam, Hilary. "The Meaning of 'Meaning.' " In *Mind, Language, and Reality*. Cambridge: Cambridge University Press, 1975.

————. "Models and Reality." In *Realism and Reason, Philosophical Papers, Vol. 3*. Cambridge: Cambridge University Press, 1983.

Quine, W. V. "Two Dogmas of Empiricism". In *From a Logical Point of View*. Cambridge, Mass.: Harvard University Press, [1951] 1953.

————. *Word and Object*. Cambridge, Mass.: MIT Press, 1960.

————. "Natural Kinds." In *Ontological Relativity and Other Essays*, pp. 114–38. New York: Columbia University Press 1969.

Railton, Peter. "Moral Realism." *Philosophical Review* 95, 2 (1986, April): 163–207.

Rawls, John. "Symposium: Justice as Fairness." *Journal of Philosophy* 54. 22 (1957, October): 653–62.

Reichenbach, Hans. *The Philosophy of Space and Time*. New York: Dover, 1958.

Robertson, J., and M. Stocker. "Externalism and Internalism." In *The Encyclopedia of Ethics*, vol. 1, ed. L. Becker, pp. 352–54. New York: Garland, 1992.

Rosati, Connie. "Internalism and the Good for a Person." *Ethics* 106 (1996, January): 297–326.

Rosenbaum, Ron. *Explaining Hitler*. New York: Harper Perennial, 1998.

Rosenblueth, Arturo, Norbert Weiner, and Julian Bigelow. "Behavior, Purpose, and Teleology." *Philosophy of Science* 10. 1 (1943): 18–24.

Ross, David. *The Right and the Good*. Oxford: Clarendon Press, 1930.

Rozin, Paul. "Acquisition of Stable Food Preferences." *Nutrition Reviews* 48. 2 (1990, February): 106–13.

Samuels, David. "Notes from Underground: Among the Radicals of the Pacific Northwest." *Harper's Magazine*, May 2000, pp. 35–47.

Sayre-McCord, Geoffrey, ed. *Essays in Moral Realism*. Ithaca, N.Y.: Cornell University Press, 1988.

Scheffler, Israel. "Thoughts on Teleology." *British Journal of the Philosophy of Science* 9. 59 (1959): 65–284.

Schmidtz, David. *Rational Choice and Moral Agency*. Princeton, N.J.: Princeton University Press, 1995.

————. "Reasons for Reasons." American Philosophical Association Symposium Presentation, Central Division Meeting, Chicago, 1999.

Schrodinger, Erwin. *What Is Life?* Cambridge: Cambridge University Press, 1955.

Seneca. "On Anger." In *Seneca: Moral and Political Essays*, trans. J. Cooper, and J. F. Procope, pp. 1–116. Cambridge: Cambridge University Press, 1995.

Sidgwick, Henry. *The Method of Ethics*. Indianapolis: Hackett, [1907] 1981.

Sklar, Lawrence. *Physics and Chance*. Cambridge: Cambridge University Press, 1993.

Slocum, Joshua. *Sailing Alone around the World*. Hungary: Kvnemann, [1899] 1997.

Sloman, Aaron. "How to Derive 'Better' from 'Is.' " *American Philosophical Quarterly* 6. 1 (1969): 43–52.

Sommerhoff, Gerd. *Analytic Biology*. London: Oxford University Press, 1950.

Sosa, Ernest. *Knowledge in Perspective*. Cambridge: Cambridge University Press, 1991.

Stevenson, Charles. "The Emotive Meaning of Ethical Terms." *Mind* 46 (1937): 14–31.

———. "The Nature of Ethical Disagreement." In *Readings in Philosophical Analysis*, ed. H. Feigl and W. Sellars, pp. 587–93. New York: Appleton, Century, Crofts, 1949.

Stocker, Michael. "The Schizophrenia of Modern Ethical Theories." *Journal of Philosophy* 73 (1976): 453–66.

———. "Desiring the Bad: An Essay on Moral Psychology." *Journal of Philosophy* 76 (1979): 738–53.

———. "Values and Purposes: The Limits of Teleology and Ends of Friendship." *Journal of Philosophy* 78 (1981): 747–65.

———. *Plural and Conflicting Values*. Oxford: Clarendon Press, 1990.

Strawson, P. F. "Ethical Intuitionism." In *Readings in Ethical Theory*, ed. W. Sellars and J. Hospers, pp. 250–59. New York: Appleton, Century, Crofts, [1949] 1952.

Striker, Gisela. "Antipater, or the Art of Living." In *The Norms of Nature*, ed. M. Schofield, and G. Striker, pp. 185–204. Cambridge: Cambridge University Press, 1986.

Stroud, Barry. "Transcendental Arguments." *Journal of Philosophy* 65 (1968): 241–56.

Sturgeon, Nicholas. "Moral Explanations." In *Essays on Moral Realism*, ed. G. Sayre-McCord, pp. 229–55. Ithaca, N.Y.: Cornell University Press, [1985] 1988.

Taylor, Richard. *The Explanation of Behavior*. London: Routledge & Kegan Paul, 1964.

Timmons, Mark. "Irrealism and Error in Ethics." *Philosophia* 22. 3–4 (1993): 373–406.

van Fraassen, Bas. *The Scientific Image*. Oxford: Oxford University Press, 1980.

van Iwagan, Peter. *Material Beings*. Ithaca, N.Y.: Cornell University Press, 1990.

Walsh, Denis, and André Ariew. "A Taxonomy of Functions." *Canadian Journal of Philosophy* 26. 4 (1996, December): 493–514.

Wiggins, David. *Needs, Values, Truth*. Oxford: Blackwell, 1991.

Williams, Bernard. *Moral Luck*. Oxford: Oxford University Press, 1981.

Wimsatt, William. "Teleology and the Logical Stucture of Function Statements." *Studies in History and Philosophy of Science* 3 (1972): 1–80.

Wright, Crispin. *Realism, Meaning, and Truth*. Oxford: Oxford University Press, 1987.

———. "Moral Values, Projection, and Secondary Qualities." *Proceedings of the Aristotelian Society* supp. vol. 62 (1988): 1–26.

———. *Truth and Objectivity*. Oxford: Oxford University Press, 1992.

Wright, Larry. "Functions." *Philosophical Review* 82 (1973): 139–168.

———. *Teleological Explanations*. Berkeley: University of California Press, 1976

Zagzebski, Linda. *Virtues of the Mind*. Cambridge: Cambridge University Press, 1996

Index

absolutism, 35, 39, 117
Alston, W., 56n, 109
analogical predication, 109–20
Anderson, I., 5
Annas, J., 97n, 99
Anscombe, G. E. M., 21, 72–3, 166–70
anthropic principle, 185
Aquinas, T., 107, 109–10
Aristotle, 14, 17, 63, 92–102, 114n, 139, 165–6
asymmetry, 44–6, 184–5, 186
Ayer, A., 88

Beck, L., 131n
beginners. *See* experts
behavior (*b*), 136–7
Benardete, J., 15
biology, 19–20, 28, 138, 148–9
Blackburn, S., 22, 48–54, 123, 130, 133
Boltzman, L., 185–94
borrowing, 135

breathing, 4
Brownian motion, 185
Byrd, Jr., J., 23, 58, 67, 164

Carnot, S., 68, 182–3, 190–1
Carter, J., 176–8
causal theory of memory, 15
causation, 131–4
certainty, 9
ceteris paribus clause, 158–9, 168
Chalmers, D., 47n, 52n, 120n
chi, 75, 124
"come what may" attitude, 8, 91, 161, 164
commuter J, 171–2
Confucius, 77n, 115n
consequentialism, 75, 82, 85–7, 115, 117–8, 139, 142
convention, 33–5, 53–4, 71, 77, 82, 123, 125
convergence, 124–6
Cornell realists, 120–2, 124
courage, 41, 63–4, 100n

dead reckoning, 79–81, 86
denial, 12–14, 172
deontology, 75, 82–5, 115, 118–20,
    139–40, 142
devil worship, 173n
diagnosis. See phronesis
disagreement, 88–92

entropy, 45–6, 110n, 138, 179–94
environment (e), 138
Epictetus, 8
error, 21–2, 57, 125, 142
etiology, 71, 76, 80
eudaimonia, 14, 23, 97–8, 114n, 139,
    151, 166
Euthyphro, 126
exceptions, 64, 127
experts, 64–6, 94–102
externalism, 154

Falk, W., 133
fallibility, 12
Fermi, E., 184, 190
fevers, 70, 76–7
Feynman, R., 69, 187–94
fools, 5, 9, 13–4, 52, 177
Foot, P., 90
function statements, 134–43
functional equivalence, 34, 53–4, 71,
    77, 82, 123, 125, 136, 146–7
functions, 30, 32n, 108, 110, 148–50

Gallistel, R., 78, 80
Gibbard, A., 6, 130, 133
Gibbe's paradox, 36
global moral error, 125
Gold, T., 190–1
goodness
    and absolutism, 39–40
    and conventions, 40–2
    and relativism, 39
"goodness," 105, 114–20
Grice, P., 113, 118
Gyges's ring, 160

Hare, R., 31n, 48, 50, 130, 133, 136,
    146–7
Harman, G., 6, 35, 109
healthiness, 28–48, 57–8, 67–8, 74,
    103, 105–6, 108–14, 116, 122–8,
    153–6, 179–94
    and conventions, 33–5
    and functional properties, 32
    and relativism, 35–8
"healthy," 105, 108–14
Homo sapiens, 8, 12, 19, 125, 127, 162
Horgan, T., 18n, 35, 106, 107, 120–8
human condition, 13, 17, 19, 51, 92,
    193
Hume, D., 6, 159–64, 166, 174–5, 177,
    193
    and moral syntax, 129–34, 145–6,
    150–2

imperatives, 139–40
"impossibilities," 193–4
information theory, 45–6
insecurity, 13
internalism, 154–78
introspection, 3, 14, 65–7, 99–100
intuition, 58, 66, 69–70, 84
is / ought distinction, 19, 129–34, 145–
    6, 150–2
items (i), 136–7
Irwin, T., 94n

Jackson, F., 47, 52n, 108, 120n, 122,
    124

Kant, I., 40, 50, 139–40, 163–70
knack, 60–2
"Know thyself," 10
Korsgaard, C., 165–70
Kripke, S., 103, 109, 120, 128

Lewis, D., 33, 146
living
    property of being alive, 27
    and reduction, 28

Locke, D., 137n
Locke, J., 103, 128
logos, 62–4, 65, 68, 69–70, 73, 98–9
Long, R., 18n
lungfish, 138
Lynch, M., 36n

Mackie, J., 34, 35, 88, 154–5, 157
malfunction, 110, 134–5, 143–52
mechanic, automobile, 95
medicine, 41, 57, 59, 74–8, 82, 89–90,
    111, 123, 141–2
meteorology, 17
Millikan, R., 32n
mistakes, lacking appearance, 25–7
modality, 46–55, 107, 131–4, 143–52,
    168–70, 175–8, 192–3
modesty
    and realism, 14
    of transcendental argument, 15
Moore, G., 104, 108, 127–8
"the moral claim," 158, 168
Moral Twin Earth, 120–8
motivation, 24, 101, 153–78

Nagel, T., 14, 165–70
navigation, 78–81
normal forms
    function statements, 135
    prescriptions, 136
"the normative claim," 158, 162, 170
normativity, 143–52
    See also is / ought distinction; pre-
        scriptions; modality
nutrition, 19, 37, 112, 123

Ockham's razor, 69
Olsen, E., 116
"one thought too many," 10, 94, 139
ontological status, 29
open question argument, 128
ordinary language philosophy, 104,
    106
"ought implies can," 132, 163–4

parenting, 5, 8, 19, 21, 118, 143,
    151
perpetual motion, 184, 190, 194
personal identity, 54–5
phenomenological data, 6
phronesis, 68
    and diagnosis, 69–71, 82–6
    and problem solving, 71–3, 85–7
piloting, 79–81, 86
Plato, 5n, 7, 24, 51, 56, 60, 64, 94,
    119, 126, 154, 156–7, 175–7
pleasure, 12, 51, 60, 86, 97n, 112n,
    118, 172–3
Popper, K., 187–90
practical rationality. *See phronesis*
praxis/poesis, 95–8
prescriptions, 124–52
Prichard, H., 67n, 83n, 85
Prior, A., 106, 135n
problem-solving. *See phronesis*
punks, 172–4
purpose (*p*), of a function, 31, 108,
    138–40
Putnam, H., 103, 120

Quine, W. V. O., 7–8, 91, 104, 161,
    164, 188

Railton, P., 14, 105, 120
Ramsey, Carnap, Lewis method, 32n
Rant-Line, 173n
rationality, 165–70
rationalization, of ourselves, 13
realpolitik, 174
reduction, 43–7, 179–93
    and the "hard sciences," 46
    irrelevance for moral realism, 42–3,
        179
Reichenbach, H., 182, 186
relativism
    consistent with realism, 35–7
    of functions, 36
    and goodness, 39
releasing conditions, 52n, 123

riddles
  epistemic, 58, 67–8
  introduced, 24
  linguistic, 113–4
  ontological, 28, 38
  practical, 143–78
rigid designators, 109n, 122
Rosati, C., 16, 160, 162
Ross, W., 83n, 118–19

Schmidtz, D., 97n, 133
second law of thermodynamics, 46, 183
secondary qualities, 29, 122, 124
similarity, 146–7
skepticism, 20–1
skills (*techné*), 57, 60–88, 92–102
Sklar, L., 36, 186
Slocum, J., 78–9
Socrates, 56, 60, 61, 90, 119, 168–70
  See also Plato
Sorites paradox, 114n
standards of evaluation, 34
statistical mechanics, 184–94
Stevenson, C., 88, 113
Stocker, M., 41n, 83n, 139n, 171n
Stroud, B., 15
supervenience, 43–55
  and modality, 46–7
symptoms, 70–1
system (*s*), 137–8

temperance (*sophrosuné*), 13, 19, 62, 101
theory (*t*), 141–2

thermodynamics, 45–6, 110n, 138, 179–94
thick and thin concepts, 41
"Things That Don't Exist," 192
"Things That Don't Happen," 182
Thrasymachus, 7, 51, 57, 90, 143, 160–4
time-gap argument, 166–70
Timmons, M., 22n, 24n, 35, 106, 107, 120–8
tofu, 116, 153–6
transcendental arguments, 15
transparency thesis, 10
tree-sitting, 176n
truth, 140n, 141–3

ulcers, 5, 77
universalizability, 50, 136–7, 146–7
  See also functional equivalence; Hare, R.

virtue, 7, 41, 114, 129, 139, 142
  as skill, 56–7, 58n, 59, 62–4, 82, 92–102

"water," 108, 120–8
wide cosmological role, 20
Williams, B., 10, 94, 139, 159–64, 166
Wimsatt, W., 31n, 32n, 36, 134–43
wisdom, 5n, 9, 15–16, 61, 62, 87, 97
"would-be rapist," 11, 18
Wright, C., 14, 20, 90n, 114
Wright, L., 32n, 139